Perception and Reality in Kant, Husserl, and McDowell

How does perception give us access to external reality? This book critically engages with John McDowell's conceptualist answer to this question, by offering a new exploration of his views on perception and reality in relation to those of Immanuel Kant and Edmund Husserl.

In six chapters, the book examines these thinkers' respective theories of perception, lucidly describing how they fit within their larger philosophical views on mind and reality. It thereby not only reveals the continuity of a tradition that underlies today's fragmented scholarly landscape, but also yields a new critique of McDowell's conceptualist theory. In doing so, the book contributes to the ongoing bridging of traditions, by combining analytic philosophy, Kantian philosophy, and phenomenology.

Perception and Reality in Kant, Husserl, and McDowell will appeal to scholars and students working in the history of philosophy, phenomenology, Kantian philosophy, and in particular the philosophy of perception.

Corijn van Mazijk studied philosophy in Groningen and Leuven. He currently works as university lecturer and researcher at University of Groningen, Faculty of Philosophy. He recently published articles in *Continental Philosophy Review, Human Studies, Phenomenology and the Cognitive Sciences, Canadian Journal of Philosophy,* and *Southern Journal of Philosophy.*

Routledge Studies in Contemporary Philosophy

127 **Digital Hermeneutics**
Philosophical Investigations in New Media and Technologies
Alberto Romele

128 **Naturalism, Human Flourishing, and Asian Philosophy**
Owen Flanagan and Beyond
Edited by Bongrae Seok

129 **Philosophy of Logical Systems**
Jaroslav Peregrin

130 **Consequences of Reference Failure**
Michael McKinsey

131 **How Propaganda Became Public Relations**
Foucault and the Corporate Government of the Public
Cory Wimberly

132 **Philosophical Perspectives on Contemporary Ireland**
Edited by Clara Fischer and Áine Mahon

133 **Inference and Consciousness**
Edited by Anders Nes with Timothy Chan

134 **The Complex Reality of Pain**
Jennifer Corns

135 **Perception and Reality in Kant, Husserl, and McDowell**
Corijn van Mazijk

For more information about this series, please visit: https://www.routledge.com/Routledge-Studies-in-Contemporary-Philosophy/book-series/SE0720

Perception and Reality in Kant, Husserl, and McDowell

Corijn van Mazijk

LONDON AND NEW YORK

First published 2020 by Routledge

2 Park Square, Milton Park, Abingdon, Oxon OX14 4RN
605 Third Avenue, New York, NY 10017

Routledge is an imprint of the Taylor & Francis Group, an informa business

First issued in paperback 2022

Copyright © 2020 Taylor & Francis

The right of Corijn van Mazijk to be identified as author of this work has been asserted by him in accordance with sections 77 and 78 of the Copyright, Designs and Patents Act 1988.

All rights reserved. No part of this book may be reprinted or reproduced or utilised in any form or by any electronic, mechanical, or other means, now known or hereafter invented, including photocopying and recording, or in any information storage or retrieval system, without permission in writing from the publishers.

Notice:
Product or corporate names may be trademarks or registered trademarks, and are used only for identification and explanation without intent to infringe.

Publisher's Note

The publisher has gone to great lengths to ensure the quality of this reprint but points out that some imperfections in the original copies may be apparent.

Library of Congress Cataloging-in-Publication Data
A catalog record for this title has been requested

ISBN: 978-0-367-44180-7 (hbk)
ISBN: 978-1-03-233705-0 (pbk)
DOI: 10.4324/9781003010227

Typeset in Sabon
by codeMantra

For my friends Steven Willemsen, Lars Adams,
Willem de Witte, and Tycho Barnard

Contents

Sources and Abbreviations	xi
Preface	xvii
Introduction	1
1 Kant: Sensibility, Perception, Reality	12

On Sensibility 12
    Chapter Overview 12
    Introduction 12
    The Distinction between Sensibility and
        Understanding 14
    A Distinct Faculty of Sensibility 16
Idealism and the Myth of the Given 20
    Kant and the Myth of the Given 20
    On Descartes, Idealism, and Reality 22
    On the Noumenon 25
    Kant's Disjunctivism 28
    McDowell on Kant and the Subjective Ideality of
        Space and Time 31
    Concluding Remarks 33

2 Kant: Concepts, Deduction, Debates	38

The Contents of Intuition and Perception 38
    Chapter Overview 38
    Introduction 38
    General Remarks on Synthesis 41
    The Transcendental Deduction, A-Version Section 2 42
    The Transcendental Deduction, A-Version Section 3 44
    The Transcendental Deduction, Remarks on
        the B-Version 47
    The Broader Picture: What Problem Does Kant's
        Theory of Perception Address? 49

viii   *Contents*

Kant and Contemporary Debates 51
    Empirical or Category Conceptualism? 51
    Reasons to Think Intuition and Perception have
        Non-Conceptual Content 51
    The Independency Thesis 52
    The Argument from Blind Intuitions and Kant's
        Anthropology 53
    The Argument from Incongruent Counterparts 57
    Concluding Remarks 58

3   Husserl: Intentionality, Consciousness, Nature   **61**

Intentionality and Fulfillment 61
    Chapter Overview 61
    The Intentional Approach to Consciousness 61
    On Sensation Contents 64
    On Feelings and Dark Longings 66
    On Fulfillment and Justified Belief 68
    Husserl's Critique of Kant's Theory of Knowledge 72
The Space of Consciousness 74
    Accessing Consciousness 74
    On the Space of Consciousness 78
    On Drawing the Line 81
    On Descartes, Idealism, and Reality 85
    Concluding Remarks 88

4   Husserl: Perception, Judgment, Habit   **96**

Sensing, Perceiving, Judging 96
    Chapter Overview 96
    Introduction 97
    Fields of Sensations 98
    Simple Apprehension and Perceptual Explication 102
    Types of Conceptuality and Objects of Thought 104
Horizons, Habits, and Concepts in Perception 107
    Revision: What is Perception?
        On the Kinesthetic System 107
    On Habit 111
    Kinesthetic Habit and the Constitution of Spatiality 112
    Pre-Conceptual Norms and Habits in the Contents of
        Perception 115
    Conceptual Capacities in Perception 117
    Concluding Remarks 117

Contents ix

5 McDowell: Concepts, Perceptions, Debates 121

McDowell's Conceptualism 121
  Chapter Overview 121
  Introduction 121
  Conceptual Content 124
  Reflections on Concepts in Perception in McDowell,
    Kant, and Husserl 132
Arguments for Non-Conceptual Content 137
  Misinterpretations of McDowell: Psychology,
    Illusions, and Skillful Coping 137
  Concluding Remarks 141

6 McDowell: Reasons, Nature, Reality 146

Reasons and Nature 146
  Chapter Overview 146
  The Space of Reasons and the Space of Nature 146
  Remarks on Drawing the Line, Bildung, and Animal
    Consciousness 150
  Reflections on the Mental and the Transcendental 153
  Reasons and Nature: Kant, Husserl, and McDowell 157
On Reality and Idealism 163
  On Descartes, Idealism, and Reality: Kant, Husserl,
    and McDowell 163
  Further Remarks on Accessing Reality in Kant,
    Husserl, and McDowell 167
  Concluding Remarks 169

Index 173

Sources and Abbreviations

Immanuel Kant

A/B
: *Critique of Pure Reason.* Transl. P. Guyer, A. W. Wood, Cambridge, New York, Melbourne: Cambridge University Press, 1998.

Anth
: *Anthropology from a Pragmatic Point of View (1798).* Transl. R. B. Louden, in: *Anthropology, History, and Education,* G. Zöller, R. B. Louden (eds.), Cambridge: Cambridge University Press, 2007.

CG
: *Concerning the ultimate ground of the differentiation of directions in space* (1768), in: *The Cambridge Edition to the Works of Immanuel Kant: Theoretical Philosophy 1755–1770,* D. Walford, E. Meerbote (eds.), Cambridge: Cambridge University Press, 1992.

CPJ
: *Critique of the Power of Judgment.* Transl. P. Guyer, E. Mathews, Cambridge, New York, Melbourne: Cambridge University Press, 2000.

ID
: *On the Form and Principles of the Sensible and the Intelligible World [Inaugural Dissertatio] (1770),* in: *The Cambridge Edition to the Works of Immanuel Kant: Theoretical Philosophy 1755–1770,* D. Walford, E. Meerbote (eds.), Cambridge: Cambridge University Press, 1992.

NE
: *A New Elucidation of the First Principles of Metaphysical Cognition (1755),* in: *The Cambridge Edition to the Works of Immanuel Kant: Theoretical Philosophy 1755–1770,* D. Walford, E. Meerbote (eds.), Cambridge: Cambridge University Press, 1992.

OT
: 'What does it mean to orient oneself in thinking?' (1786), in: *Religion and Rational Theology.* Transl. A. Wood, Cambridge: Cambridge University Press, 1996.

Prol.
: *Prolegomena zu einer jeden künftigen Metaphysik, die als Wissenschaft wird auftreten können.* Hamburg: Felix Meiner Verlag, 2001.

xii *Sources and Abbreviations*

Edmund Husserl

APS
Analyses Concerning Passive and Active Synthesis: Lectures on Transcendental Logic. Husserliana Vol. IX, R. Bernet (ed.), Transl. A. Steinbock, Dordrecht, Boston, London: Kluwer Academic Publishers, 2001.

BW
Briefwechsel. Band VII: Wissenschaftlercorrespondenz, K. Schumann (ed.). Dordrecht: Springer Science + Business Media, B. V., 1994.

C
Späte Texte über Zeitkonstitution (1929–1934): Die C-Manuscripte. D. Lohmar (ed.), Dordrecht: Springer.

CM
Cartesian Meditations: An Introduction to Phenomenology. Transl. D. Cairns, Den Haag, Boston, London: Martinus Nijhoff, 1982.

Crisis
The Crisis of the European Sciences and Transcendental Phenomenology: An Introduction to Phenomenological Philosophy. Transl. D. Carr, Evanston: Northwestern University Press, 1970.

EE
Einleitung in die Ethik. Vorlesungen Sommersemester 1920 und 1924. H. Peucker (ed.), Dordrecht, Netherlands: Kluwer Academic Publishers, 2004.

EIP
Einleitung in die Philosophie: Vorlesungen 1922/23. Husserliana XXXV, R. Bernet, U. Melle (eds.), Dordrecht: Springer Science + Business Media, B.V., 2002.

EP I
Erste Philosophie (1923–1924): Erster Teil. Husserliana VII, H. L. Van Breda (ed.), Den Haag: Martinus Nijhoff, 1956.

EP II
Erste Philosophie (1923–1924): Zweiter Teil. Husserliana VIII, R. Boehm (ed.), Den Haag: Martinus Nijhoff, 1959.

EJ
Experience and Judgment: *Investigations in a Genealogy of Logic.* Evanston: Northwestern University Press, 1997.

GP
Grenzprobleme der Phänomenologie: Analysen des Unbewusstseins und der Instinkte. Metaphysik. Späte Ethik. Texte aus dem Nachlass (1908–1937). R. Sowa, T. Vongehr (eds.), Dordrecht: Springer.

Ideas I
Ideas Pertaining to a Pure Phenomenology and to a Phenomenological Philosophy: First Book: General Introduction to a Pure Phenomenology. Transl. F. Kersten, Den Haag, Boston, Lancaster: Martinus Nijhoff, 1983.

Ideas II
Ideas Pertaining to a Pure Phenomenology and to a Phenomenological Philosophy: Second Book: Studies

	in the Phenomenology of Constitution. Transl. R. Rojcewicz, A. Schuwer, Dordrecht, Boston, London: Kluwer Academic Publishers, 2000.
Ideas III	*Ideas Pertaining to a Pure Phenomenology and to a Phenomenological Philosophy: Third Book: Phenomenology and the Foundation of the Sciences.* Transl. T. E. Klein, W. E. Pohl. Den Haag, Boston, London: Martinus Nijhoff, 1980.
IP	*The Idea of Phenomenology.* L. Hardee (trans.), Dordrecht, Boston, London: Kluwer Academic Publishers, 1999.
KI	'Kant and the Idea of Transcendental Philosophy', *Southwestern Journal of Philosophy,* Vol. 5, No. 3, 9–56, 1974.
LI	*Logische Untersuchungen.* Band I-II, Husserliana XIX/1-XIX/2, U. Panzer (ed.), Den Haag: Martinus Nijhoff.
LW	*Die Lebenswelt: Auslegungen der Vorgegebenen Welt und Ihrer Konstitution. Texte aus dem Nachlass (1916–1937).* Husserliana XXXIX, R. Sowa (ed.), Dordrecht, Springer, 2008.
NG	*Natur und Geist: Vorlesungen Sommersemester 1927.* Husserliana XXXII. M. Weiler (ed.), Dordrecht: Kluwer Academic Publishers, 2001.
NZR	'Notizen zur Raumkonstitution', *Philosophy and Phenomenological Research,* Vol. 1, No. 1, 21–37, 1940.
PP	*Phenomenological Psychology: Lectures, Summer Semester, 1925.* Transl. J. Scanlon, Den Haag: Martinus Nijhoff, 1977.
PR	*Zur Phänomenologischen Reduktion: Texte aus dem Nachlass.* Husserliana XXXVI. S. Luft (ed.), Dordrecht: Springer Science + Business Media, B.V., 2002.
TI	Transzendentaler Idealismus: Texte aus dem Nachlass (1908–1921). Husserliana XXXVI, R. D. Rollinger (ed.), Dordrecht: Springer Science + Business Media, B.V., 2003.
Trans. Phen.	*Psychological and Transcendental Phenomenology and the Confrontation with Heidegger* (1927–1931). T. Sheehan, R. E. Palmer (eds.), Dordrecht: Springer Science + Business Media, B.V., 1997.
ZPI	Husserl, E. (1973b). *Zur Phänomenologie der Intersubjektivität: Texte aus dem Nachlass. Zweiter Teil: 1921–1928.* Husserliana XVI, I. Kern (ed.), Den Haag: Martinus Nijhoff.

xiv Sources and Abbreviations

John McDowell

CPE	'The Content of Perceptual Experience', *The Philosophical Quarterly*, Vol. 44, No. 175, 190–205, 1994.
DCE	'The Disjunctive Conception of Experience as Material for a Transcendental Argument', *Teorema: Revista Internacional de Filosofía*, Vol. 25, No. 1, 2006, 19–33.
ETW	'Experiencing the World', in: *The Engaged Intellect: Philosophical Essays*. Cambridge, Massachusetts, London: Harvard University Press, 2009.
HWV	*Having the World in View: Essays on Kant, Hegel, and Sellars*. Cambridge: Harvard University Press, 2009.
IIW	'Intentionality and Interiority in Wittgenstein', in: *Mind, Value, and Reality,* J. H. McDowell, Cambridge, Massachusetts, London: Harvard University Press, 1998.
KIR	'Knowledge of the Internal Revisited', *Philosophy and Phenomenological Research,* Vol. 64, No. 1, 97–105, 2002.
MMD	'The Myth of the Mind as Detached', In: *Mind, Reason, and Being-in-the-World: the McDowell-Dreyfus Debate.* J. K. Schear (ed.), London, New York: Routledge, 2013.
MTU	'Meaning, Truth, and Understanding', in: *Meaning, Knowledge, and Reality*, Cambridge, Massachusetts: Harvard University Press, 1998.
MW	*Mind and World.* Cambridge, Massachusetts: Harvard University Press, 1994.
NPM	'Naturalism in the Philosophy of Mind', in: *The Engaged Intellect: Philosophical Essays*. Cambridge, Massachusetts, London: Harvard University Press, 2009.
PLA	'One Strand in the Private Language Argument', in: *Mind, Value, and Reality,* J. H. McDowell, Cambridge, Massachusetts, London: Harvard University Press, 1998.
RCM	'Response to Cynthia MacDonald', in: *McDowell and his Critics*, C. MacDonald, G. MacDonald (eds.), Oxford: Blackwell Publishing, 2006.
RGM	'Response to Graham MacDonald', in: *McDowell and his Critics*, C. MacDonald, G. MacDonald (eds.), Oxford: Blackwell Publishing, 2006.
RN	*Reason and Nature: Lectures and Colloquium in Münster.* M. Willaschek (ed.), Münster: LIT – Verlag, 1999.

ST	'Singular Thought and the Extent of Inner Space', in: *Meaning, Knowledge, and Reality*, Cambridge, Massachusetts: Harvard University Press, 1998.
TBD	'Tyler Burge on disjunctivism', *Philosophical Explorations,* Vol 13, No. 3, 243–255, 2010.
TFKG	'Travis on Frege, Kant, and the Given', in: *In the Light of Experience: New Essays on Perceptions and Reasons*, J. Gersel, R. T. Jensen, M. S. Thaning, S. Overgaard (eds.), Oxford: Oxford University Press.
TSN	'Two Sorts of Naturalism', in: *Mind, Value, and Reality*, J. H. McDowell, Cambridge, Massachusetts, London: Harvard University Press, 1998.
WM	'What Myth?' *Inquiry,* Vol. 50, No. 4, 338–351, 2007.

Preface

This work compiles the results of around seven years of research, starting in 2013, when I began writing my dissertation on Edmund Husserl's philosophy of perception at KU Leuven and University of Groningen. Almost everything that lies before you was, however, written in the fall of 2018, during my research visits to UC Berkeley and Institute for Advanced Study (IAS) in Princeton. The final chapter was composed mostly in Prague, at Charles University, in 2019. For this, I would like to express my gratitude in particular to Piet Hut, Alva Noë, and Jakub Čapek for offering me the opportunity to work in such excellent company.

The present work contains three investigations that deal with the problem of our perceptual access to reality in the theoretical philosophy of Immanuel Kant, Edmund Husserl, and John McDowell, respectively. From a historiographical perspective, a study that stretches such a lapse of time is bound to run into difficulties. While I am convinced that this work is also of interest to historians of philosophy, I will make no attempt to conceal that I intend it primarily to yield new critical reflections on McDowell's theory. This means that, even though most of its contents concern figures well established in the Western-philosophical canon, it is primarily to be regarded as a work in contemporary philosophy.

I have devoted two chapters to the discussion of each of these three authors, and these appear in chronological order. However, I would advise any reader with an exclusive or very strong interest in McDowell's philosophy or contemporary philosophy of perception to read the chapter summaries at the opening of each chapter and to then proceed straightaway to the final two chapters. These include the most important results from the readings of Kant and Husserl insofar as they are relevant to the discussion of McDowell's views. The earlier chapters can then be selectively turned to afterward as they supply the more detailed investigations required to sustain these criticisms.

While I cannot list all the people that I am indebted to in the production of this work, I want to thank Detlev Pätzold and Nicolas de Warren for early support during my PhD research as well Dan Zahavi and Søren Overgaard for allowing me to visit Copenhagen University for several months in 2015 and Walter Hopp for letting me stay at Boston xviii *Preface*

University in 2016. I would further like to thank my friends and colleagues at the Faculty of Philosophy at University of Groningen. None of the academic institutions I have been fortunate enough to have visited have had such a lasting – and unmistakably positive – impact on my research as the Faculty of Philosophy in Groningen.

A special thanks goes out to those who carefully read earlier versions of this work, in particular Laura Georgescu, Victor Luinenburg, Lodi Nauta, Han-Thomas Adriaenssen, Willem de Witte, Steven Willemsen, and Jasper Geurink. I will further be forever grateful to friends and colleagues in my home country and abroad, in particular Lars Adams, Tycho Barnard, Ruud Wassink, Casper Hilbink, Patrick Elridge, Joel Hubick, Marike Masker, Catherine Robb, Kim Sauberlich, Maren Wehrle, Lennie Qiu, Maxime Doyon, Yuko Ishihara, Olaf Witkowski, Jan-Renier Moonen, Wieneke van Sonderen, as well as all of my dear friends from Bufo Dignus. Last but not least, my mother, father, brother, sister and – wisest of all, of course – my grandfather.

Introduction

If there is a single greatest mystery, it must be that there are things. The sciences describe the laws that govern these things. They can make inferences about where they go to or explain where they came from. But such inferences and explanations already presuppose that there is some real world of things which is somehow accessible to us. For that reason, there are philosophers who believe that the sciences cannot begin to address the fundamental mystery that things are accessible to us in the first place, as they first get off the ground by presupposing it.

So what about philosophy? It seems fair to say that a lot of the history of philosophy has remained within the same scientific outlook. As a result, attempts to address the presupposition that a world is accessible to us often stranded in the identification of something fundamental on which everything supposedly hinges – water, God, the Absolute, and so on. The fact that such attempts to philosophically determine the nature of reality never seemed to yield an uncontroversial outcome partially caused a dominant phase of anti-philosophy in the 20th century. Here, philosophical questions – including those pertaining to what the sciences must presuppose – were deemed unworthy of our attention altogether. Questions of reality deeper than those answerable by the sciences would simply be meaningless.

However, there is another historical trajectory of thought, one which runs from the late 18th century up until today. Here, questions about what the sciences presuppose are deemed relevant, even though unanswerable from a strictly scientific outlook. The tradition I am referring to is that of transcendental philosophy, as initiated by Immanuel Kant (1724–1804) at the end of the 18th century. Kant's key insight, which defined this new approach to the question of reality, was taken in many different directions in the centuries that followed, but arguably did not find a comparably novel and systematic application until the development of the phenomenological school of Edmund Husserl (1859–1938), just over a century later. Again in more recent years, after the prevailing silence on supposedly unspeakable matters, the same key insight has again inspired new original research, this time perhaps most noticeably in the works of John McDowell (1942).

2 Introduction

While these three thinkers, each about a hundred years apart, belong to what are today often viewed as separate traditions, they worked their way to answering the question of reality by advancing from the same key insight. The insight is roughly this: that reality is inevitably something that is given to us, and more precisely, given to us through our senses. Perhaps, therefore, in order to understand reality, we shouldn't be looking one-sidedly at things. Instead, it may prove worthwhile to reflect on that place where we and the world come together: on that gateway to the world that is our sensibility. With such a shift of attention, the question of reality changes. It is no longer: what things are most fundamental to reality? Instead, it becomes: how is it possible that our senses should give us access to reality at all?

The idea that reality is, insofar as we seem able to speak of it meaningfully, given to us via our senses may sound reassuring. However, it can also be a source of concern. For instance, it is easily seen how conceptually linking capacities of sensibility to reality can produce an image of constraint. If our grasp of reality is mediated through our senses, which are not always reliable, then how do we know that we actually have access to it? In other words, how can we assure ourselves that what we get through our senses is ever 'enough' to qualify indisputably as real?

One response to this worry is to say that what is intelligibly accessible through our senses can be broken down into elements that correspond immediately to basic facts about external reality. We could, for instance, take the operations of our faculty of sensibility to be natural operations, and then conceive of what is given to our senses as immediately reflecting at a basic level the external world as it truly is. This strategy effectively puts our senses in the closest proximity to an external reality to which they are supposed to give us direct access.

Yet it is not so clear how such a picture could bring what is thus sensibly made available within the confines of our free thinking lives. Many philosophers today would contend that facts of nature are not the sorts of things thoughts are based on. They hold that our thoughts have propositional or conceptual content; that they belong to a different explanatory space, which Sellars and McDowell call the space of reasons – a space not of giving an empirical description, as in the contrasting space of nature, but of being able to justify what one says and does – whereas our experiences of the world would, on this picture at least, be nothing but natural happenings in a causal order.

The opposite view is also on the table, however. We could think of perception or sense experience (I use these terms interchangeably in this introduction) in the closest possible proximity to thought, rather than to external reality. This can be done by claiming that perception has conceptual or propositional content. Such a view has certain advantages. For one, it answers to why our beliefs about reality can be justified by looking at the world and seeing how things are. After all, the contents of perceptions and beliefs are of the same (conceptual) kind here.

This view raises other serious concerns, however. While it earlier seemed difficult to translate the bits of nature processed in our sensibility to the realm of free conceptual thinking, it is now hard to see how perception could provide the constraint that characterizes it as opposed to the freedom of thought. Without this constraint, we lack the sense of having things *given*, rather than spontaneously generating them – which is about as bad as having no access to real things at all. Moreover, saying that we perceive a conceptually structured world could be regarded tantamount to admitting that we don't know the world at all, but only some intellectually or discursively mediated representation of it.

To some extent, the dilemma outlined above, with its two seemingly untenable extremes, reflects the way in which McDowell thinks about the problem of our access to reality. While McDowell's own position is considered to be the golden mean, it is clearly closer to the second than to the first option. This shows in the fact that McDowell defends a position called conceptualism: the view that sense experience, for us, has conceptual content, and that it is therefore fit to justify our beliefs, which also have conceptual content.

McDowell's *Mind and World* (1994), in which he first outlined his conceptualist position, has seen a lot of discussion and criticism over the past decades. It seems fair to say that most of these engagements concerned the operations of human perception and the possibility of various sorts of non-conceptual content, sometimes in attempts to challenge McDowell's claims. Only to a much lesser extent has the question of the availability of reality – McDowell's original concern and motivation for conceptualism – been made the object of a detailed study. McDowell's self-ascribed Kantianism and his connection to German philosophy in general also originate here as he believes that Kant upheld a similar conceptualist view for the very same reason: namely, to address a worry about the pre-scientific conditions for our access to reality, indeed a 'transcendental' concern (ETW 243).

Given this connection between McDowell's conceptualism and German philosophy, Kant's in particular, it is no surprise that *Mind and World* also stimulated considerable debate among Kant scholars. Here too, however, most discussions have focused just on perception's contents, leaving the question of our access to reality – originally the whole point of the conceptualist thesis – out of the picture. Whether or not Kant is to be viewed as positively disposed toward this or that account of non-conceptual content, McDowell is, to my estimation, right in affiliating himself with Kant to this extent: that Kant's theoretical philosophy can also be read as an attempt to explain how reality can be 'embraced' in thought, and that Kant too believed that this required a special focus on our sensibility.

4 *Introduction*

Historically speaking, the great 'transcendental' breakthrough of Kant's theory of perception was that it seriously attempted to construe reality as something accessible *in principle* through sense experience. That was Kant's key insight: that we must think of reality as in some sense irrevocably linked to perceptual exercises of rational beings like us. It is this insight that subsequently turned sense perception into the central topic of the first *Critique*. It is the focal point not only of the Transcendental Aesthetic, but likewise of the most important investigation of the Transcendental Analytic: the transcendental deduction. Even the Transcendental Dialectic is ultimately about the limits of possible sense experience – the negative result of the earlier Aesthetic and Analytic.

At the same time, as I show in detail in the first two chapters of this work, Kant's analysis of our capacity to access reality is not as narrowly focused on the question of perceptual content as is McDowell's. Kant sought to disclose an integrated whole of relevant conditions of possibility, which together constitute something like a universal human standpoint, from which the scientifically determinable world could first come into view to rational creatures like us. It is not just perception or its content (conceptual or otherwise) that matters here, but also, or so I argue in this work, a sense of self-identity, as well as obtaining a concrete point of view from which to orient oneself in the world.

In spite of such substantial differences, my reading in this work shows that McDowell and Kant share a similar strategy in addressing the relation between thought and perception. That is to say, they both believe, although for completely different reasons, that in order to make understandable how the world can be accessible to a thinking subject, perception must in some sense be modeled after the rational operations of the subject, that is, on thought. While this does not amount to conceptualism per se, it does involve an important claim as to which of the two constituents of the perception-thought relation ought to be taken as the standard by which to approach the other.

Moreover, I argue that their respective theories of perception are in agreement in taking all sense experience, at least insofar as it bears on our rational lives, to be open to propositional explication in thought. This amount to a thesis that I call *weak conceptualism*: the view that all intuition and perception is, for us at least, open to conceptual exercises. McDowell, however, in addition to this, claims in various writings from 1994 to 2018 that the sense experience of rational beings is also 'informed by their rationality' (WM 338), or more specifically by concepts or conceptual capacities. For McDowell, then, concepts structure sense experience, and this is in fact what first makes reality perceptually available. This is a different thesis, which I call *strong conceptualism*. On the interpretation I offer in this work, strong conceptualism was not unambiguously defended by Kant.

Introduction 5

At the same time, however, McDowell has criticized Kant for failing to account for our immediate perceptual access to reality. In short, McDowell believes that Kant failed at this because he would have made the forms of our intuitions (space and time) contingent upon a 'brute fact' (HWV 76) about our natural constitution. For this reason, the Kantian theory invokes an image of constraint, since beyond the boundary of our forms of intuition there would lie 'something we cannot know' (HWV 79).

Especially in the first chapter, I press against certain aspects of McDowell's reading of Kant. As I argue in detail, Kant's reflections on the forms of our own intuitions, on the possibility of other forms of intuitions, and on the possibility of a noumenal reality 'behind' the experienced world do not necessarily interfere with his account of our perceptual access to reality. Kant does not make our access to reality contingent upon natural facts. To the contrary, I show that Kant's interpretation of the Cartesian threat of idealism is very similar to McDowell's reading of Descartes, and that the 'dualism' (A370) Kant proposes to dissolve it is virtually identical to the disjunctive theory proposed by McDowell.

This brings me to the third author central to this work, namely Edmund Husserl (1859–1938). The fact that Husserl's theory of perception is also included here might come as a surprise to some readers. Husserl is virtually absent in mainstream theoretical debates on McDowell's philosophy. Part of the unfortunate reason for this, I suspect, has to do with Husserl's traditional (mis)placement on the 'continental side' of the infamous divide that is still often used to characterize 20th century philosophy. This has its historical causes, having to do with the smuggling of Husserl's *Nachlass* to Belgium from Nazi Germany, the delayed publication of most of his manuscripts that followed, and the correlated early exposure of his work to predominantly French-speaking communities. It could also be said to have its systematic reasons; for instance, neither the affiliation with transcendental idealism nor the baroque writing fit well contemporary Anglophone philosophy. Yet these considerations apply just as well to Kant (and even to some extent, it must be admitted, to McDowell), and therefore do not seem to provide a good reason not to engage systematically with Husserl's thought.

I hope that this work can contribute to showing that a serious study of Husserl has as much (or more) to offer to contemporary philosophers of perception as does the study of Kant. Historically speaking, Husserl and the phenomenological school he developed stand in the same tradition that flowed from Kant's key insight. As with Kant and McDowell, Husserl's oeuvre can be read as an attempt to come to terms with the fundamental question of how something like a real world can be given in sense experience. Moreover, as I discuss in detail, his realism, his reading of Descartes, and his related arguments against idealism (which he believes yields an image of constraint) are very similar to the interpretations

6   *Introduction*

found in the works of Kant and McDowell. There is thus a great deal of overlap not only in the identification of problems, but similarly in terms of their preferred solutions to them.

At the same time, as Chapter 3 outlines, Husserl proposed an alternative way of conceptualizing and investigating our perceptual access to reality. In terms of method of investigation, Husserl clearly put the most effort of these three thinkers in substantiating a theory of philosophical reflection, a theory which involved a sharp demarcation of the concerns of science and those of philosophy, of facts of nature and of consciousness respectively. It is the development of this method, or so I argue, that subsequently allowed Husserl to adopt the reverse strategy of the one employed by Kant and McDowell– namely to model thought after perception, rather than the other way around.

As I argue in detail in Chapter 3, Husserl's phenomenology can be interpreted as presenting an alternative to the division between the space of reasons and the space of nature as McDowell defends it. McDowell, in short, conceives of two autonomous spaces, namely the space of reasons and the space of nature. These spaces are divided in such a way that the space of reasons consists exclusively of conceptual content. Moreover, it alone would defy explanation in terms of natural law and can be designated in mental terms. All other contents then fall within the explanatory framework of the space of nature, and furthermore can bear no rational relation to the conceptual space of reasons.

In Husserl's alternative view, or so I argue, the relevant division is not between reasons and nature, but between (what I call) the space of consciousness and the space of nature. I argue that these two spaces do not refer to distinct tracts of reality; they are instead to be understood as comprising of the same totality of things considered from two different perspectives. This division, which constitutes the core of Husserl's thought and which he sought to ground philosophically for many years, redraws the crucial line between matters of philosophy and theory of knowledge in the widest sense – the space of consciousness – and the sorts of things belonging to the realm of scientific inquiry – the space of nature.

This division opens up new ways of thinking about our perceptual access to reality. In Chapter 4, I discuss in detail the various layers of perception Husserl distinguishes, how they bring a world into view for the subject independently of any conceptual operations, and how they make conceptual thought possible in the first place. I further discuss Husserl's understanding of the role of non-conceptual content in our mental lives, his theory about the origins of the space of reasons in the non-conceptual (what McDowell would call *Bildung*), and his views on the ways in which an external world might be brought into view for non-rational animals.

In the final two chapters, I turn to McDowell's conceptualist view and his theory of the space of nature and the space of reasons. Here I also gather results from the earlier chapters on Kant and Husserl to compare their views, and to consider whether their theories might offer better ways to think about the relations between reason, nature, perception, and reality.

Structure and Aims

The introduction so far only served to highlight some of the key themes in the discussions that follow. Before turning to a chapter by chapter overview, which surveys the contents of this work in more detail, I briefly comment on the central aims and structure here.

For the most part, the present work consists of a study of systems of ideas. It is not primarily intended as a historical study. Instead, I develop my interpretations of both Kant and Husserl in part to show that history provides us with viable alternatives to McDowell's theory of our perceptual access to reality.

Given that this work involves discussing several distinct and complex systems of ideas, I have tried to present each of the three parts in such a way as to make them accessible to anyone without any specialized background knowledge. This means that the chapters on Kant and Husserl can also be understood by anyone unfamiliar with the Kantian and phenomenological traditions.

Furthermore, I tried not to get lost in the many detailed discussions on non-conceptual content that exist today (although I survey them where needed, especially in Chapter 5), but to try instead to sketch the broader pictures within which Kant, Husserl, and McDowell come to their understanding of the relations between nature, reason, perception, and reality. I thereby hope to have retrieved something of the original question raised by McDowell's work (namely the one about accessing reality), and by connecting it to key figures of the German transcendental tradition, to contribute to uncovering a continuing tradition hidden underneath today's more specialized and fragmented philosophical landscape, as well as to develop new critical reflections on core tenets of McDowell's philosophy.

As to the structure: this work is divided into three parts, each consisting of two chapters, which deal with the theories of perception and reality of Kant, Husserl, and McDowell in chronological order. These chapters can be read independently. Moreover, any reader with a strong interest in McDowell or contemporary philosophy of perception might prefer to jump ahead to the final two chapters. These include the most important reflections gathered from the earlier discussions on Kant and Husserl. It is then possible to go back and read any of the discussions in the earlier chapters.

8 *Introduction*

Chapter by Chapter Overview

What follows now is a chapter by chapter overview, which outlines the structure and content of the present work in more detail.

The first two chapters examine how Kant constructs the relation between perception and reality, and the much discussed role concepts play in this. The complete thesis I defend here is that for Kant reality is accessible only by *spatiotemporally orienting agents with a shared capacity to determine conceptually whatever is sensibly presented to them in intuitions, and that intuitions are always already in accordance with the rules for such determination, but that they are not exhaustive of sensible representation as such.*

Chapter 1 deals primarily with the first part of this thesis, namely that embracing reality in thought presupposes spatiotemporally orienting agents. To this end, I first briefly consider Kant's early views on space in connection to Leibniz's relational doctrine, as this is where Kant first develops the idea of a distinct faculty of sensibility. This carries over into the first *Critique*, where Kant again emphasizes that sensibility must be considered as making a contribution to experience that is distinct from thought. This reveals, I argue, that Kant thought that there must be a strictly extra-conceptual element to experience.

The second part of this chapter then turns to Kant's views on our perceptual access to reality in relation to Descartes and the threat of idealism. Here I discuss Kant's critique of idealism, his concept of the noumenon, and his apparent preference for a non-disjunctive approach to perception. I argue that Kant rejects idealism, that he defends our immediate perceptual access to reality, and that he does not make forms of sensibility contingent upon natural fact, as McDowell (in *Having the World in View*) suggests in his reading of Kant. Moreover, I suggest that Kant's account of our perceptual access to reality involves the idea of a certain 'dualism' (A370) within experience, which is very similar to McDowell's disjunctive theory.

Chapter 2 turns to the role played by the understanding in determining the contents of intuition, in light of the question of our access to reality. This involves following in detail the arguments of the A and B versions of the transcendental deduction, and the sections leading up to them. I argue that the central thesis Kant sets out to defend here is that intuitions are always already at least in accordance with pure concepts, which commits Kant to weak conceptualism.

In the second part, I review the most important arguments for non-conceptual content in Kant literature and pay considerable attention to Kant's account of obscure representations in the *Anthropology*. In brief, I argue that, for Kant, whatever is sensibly represented to an agent is at least in accordance with certain conceptual rules. At the same time, Kant accepts that there are mental contents that are not conceptually explicable, in the form of obscure or blind representations, which, however, bear no relevant epistemic relation to our lives as rational subjects.

Chapter 3 turns to Husserl, who unlike Kant and the neo-Kantians of his day based his theories of perception and knowledge on a Brentanian concept of intentionality. The first part of this chapter discusses the basics of Husserl's early theory of knowledge and the new picture of belief justification it yields, which involves overthrowing key facets of Kant's philosophy, as well as a commitment to the idea that intuitive acts necessarily involve extra-conceptual content.

In the second part, I turn to Husserl's mature efforts to demarcate what I call the space of consciousness as opposed to the space of nature, arguably the central concern of Husserl's thought. By outlining the space of consciousness, Husserl sought to draw the lines between science and philosophy, cause and motivation, nature and mind. I argue that Husserl effectively endorses a double aspect theory, where the space of consciousness and the space of nature have one and the same subject matter – namely mind *and* world – approached from two different angles.

The picture this yields was, I illustrate, knowingly posited by Husserl as an alternative to attempts to draw a line 'within' consciousness, exemplified in Husserl's time in different ways by Kantian philosophy and naturalistic psychology, and with more recent parallels in the works of certain Pittsburgh philosophers including McDowell, or so I argue. I further discuss how this framework allows Husserl to sketch motivational and epistemic relations between all the contents of consciousness, whether conceptual or non-conceptual, and how it shapes his ideas about the capacity of non-rational animals to bring an external world into view.

In the final part of Chapter 3, I turn to Husserl's criticism of the Cartesian threat of idealism, a discussion which bears significant similarity to the one on Kant in the first chapter. In short, I argue that Husserl is critical of Descartes for much the same reasons as Kant was, and that he proposes a comparable solution to the problem of idealism, although there are a few technical differences.

Because of Husserl's commitment to a wider space of consciousness, he can resist the idea that non-conceptual contents fall exclusively within the explanatory framework of the space of nature. In Chapter 4, I show how this enables Husserl to explore how non-conceptual levels of perception form the foundation for conceptual thought. In the first part, I distill from Husserl's later analyses three layers of perceptual activity as well as three types of conceptuality. The first perceptual accomplishment is of so-called fields of sensations. I argue that this outlines a function of consciousness capable of operating independently of conceptual and even intentional presentation which relates to transcendent objects. These non-conceptual operations do not belong to the explanatory framework of nature, but bear a specific kind of motivational relation to the rational life of the subject.

10   *Introduction*

The second and third perceptual levels are intentional acts which make external things available to us. Both of these can operate, I argue, independently of functions of thought required to explicate the contents they make available, yet they bring the world in view for the subject. This means that concepts are not needed, on this account, to explain the perceptual availability of an external world.

In the second part of Chapter 4, I turn to Husserl's detailed work on the kinesthetic system and the role of the lived body in perception. I show that for Husserl so-called horizontal awareness is foundational for the perception of three-dimensional, external objects. Moreover, I argue that such horizontal awareness in turn relies on a pre-conceptual sense of self-movement. This means that having a sense of the capacity to move oneself belongs essentially to the nexus of the perceptual accomplishment through which an external world is given, prior to the advent of any thinking capacities. The rest of the chapter elaborates on the different ways in which acquired skill (referred to by Husserl as habit) determines perception – from learning to control one's body all the way up to cultural-linguistic upbringing.

Chapters 5 and 6 discuss McDowell's theory of our perceptual access to reality, as well as the relation between nature and reasons. In Chapter 5, I first outline McDowell's conceptualism as a response to a problem regarding our responsiveness to reasons and answerability to reality. I analyze the different ways in which McDowell has fleshed out the idea that perception would have perceptual content, over the course of 25 years of writing. This reveals a certain development of his thought, but also, or so I argue, a lingering unclarity as to what it means for perception to have conceptual content.

This unclarity mainly concerns the division between weak and strong conceptualism, which concepts would inform perceptual experience, and the question how the perceptions of non-rational animals could bring an external world in view for them, given that they lack concepts. After having highlighted these and certain other difficulties, I consider in a separate section whether the theories of Kant and Husserl might offer resources to avoid them.

In Chapter 6, I consider McDowell's distinction between the space of reasons and the space of nature, which forms the background to his conceptualism. I show that his conceptualism is tied into a broader picture of how the human mind (for McDowell captured by the space of reasons) fits into natural reality. This picture takes a certain naturalism as a default position, yet it avoids compromising the autonomy of the space of reasons.

Following Sellars, McDowell draws a line between the space of reasons and the space of nature, characterized as two ways of finding things intelligible. I argue that McDowell draws the line in such a way that the realm which resists reduction to natural explanation consists

Introduction 11

exclusively of conceptual content. In other words, only that part of our mental lives relevant to responsiveness to reasons – the conceptual part that is allegedly unique to humans – allows taking in a viewpoint toward from which it is considered outside of the realm of natural law. Non-conceptual contents, by contrast, fit unproblematically within the explanatory framework of the space of nature.

I subsequently argue that this picture faces certain difficulties. In particular, I defend the following points in Chapter 6: that (i) McDowell's conceptualism seems attractive only if his division of spaces is accepted; that (ii) his division of spaces might not be very attractive, at least not insofar as it allocates non-conceptual mental contents to the realm of nature; that (iii) the idea that the space of reasons itself ultimately consists of natural phenomena as well is not really made intelligible; that (iv) this naturalism fits uneasily with McDowell's transcendental ambitions; and that (v) the transition from the non-conceptual to the space of reasons (*Bildung*) cannot be clarified on the basis of this division of spaces. In a separate section, I illustrate how these points are dealt with differently in the Kantian and Husserlian frameworks, and discuss whether they might be able avoid some of the problems raised here.

In the final part, I turn to McDowell's realist intentions, in particular his interpretation of the Cartesian threat of idealism and his own response to this based on a disjunctive theory of perception. I argue that both the diagnosis of the problem and the solution to it are virtually identical to what was suggested by Kant in the fourth paralogism, which speaks of a 'dualism' (instead of a disjunction) in the same context. In the final sections, I briefly survey some of the differences between the largely similar solutions to the problem of idealism offered by Kant, Husserl, and McDowell.

1 Kant
Sensibility, Perception, Reality

On Sensibility

Chapter Overview

In this chapter and the next, I consider how Kant understands the relation between perception and reality, and the role concepts play in this. The main thesis I defend is that for Kant reality is accessible only by *spatiotemporally orienting agents with a shared capacity to determine conceptually whatever is sensibly presented to them in intuitions, and that intuitions are always already in accordance with the rules for such determination, but that they are not exhaustive of sensible representation as such.* This first chapter primarily deals with the first part of this thesis, namely that accessing reality presupposes spatiotemporally orienting beings. To this end, I consider Kant's early views on space as well as those in the first *Critique*. This further reveals that sensibility for Kant must be considered as making an extra-conceptual contribution to experience. In the second part, I turn to Kant's reading of Descartes and the threat of idealism. I argue that Kant rejects idealism, that he defends our immediate perceptual access to reality, and that he does not make forms of sensibility contingent upon natural fact, as McDowell (in *Having the World in View*) has suggested. Moreover, I show that Kant's account of our perceptual access to reality involves the idea of a 'dualism' (A370) within experience, which is very similar to McDowell's disjunctive theory. The exact role the understanding has in determining the contents of intuition in order to provide this kind of access to reality – thus the remainder of my main thesis – is discussed in the next chapter.

Introduction

Especially since McDowell's *Mind and World*, Kant is often viewed as the first proponent of conceptualism – the thesis that perceptual experience has conceptual content. According to McDowell, conceptualism takes away a certain worry concerning 'the very possibility of thought's being directed at the external world' (ETW 243). It is supposed to answer to a problem regarding how to 'ensure [ourselves] that we are not beset by a difficulty about the capacity of our mental activity to be about reality at all' (ETW 243). Conceptualism, then, deals with the conditions of us accessing reality. Indeed, by focusing on conditions of possibility, McDowell puts himself 'close to a Kantian way' of transcendental questioning, one that asks not for any particular 'possession of knowledge', but for a 'prior condition' (ETW 243).

McDowell's views are of no immediate concern yet. What matters is that Kant's critical efforts can at least be understood in this light: as an attempt to make understandable the necessary conditions for reality to be accessible in an immediate way, rather than through inference based on some mental representation. Understood this way, Kant's transcendental philosophy becomes the analysis of the prior conditions required for reality to be manifest to the mind at all. As such, it yields a picture of the bare essentials, so to say, of the mind-world relation.

The thesis I defend over the course of the first two chapters is that for Kant, reality is embraceable in thought only by *spatiotemporally orienting agents with a shared capacity to determine conceptually whatever is sensibly presented to them in intuitions, and that intuitions are always already in accordance with the rules for such determination, but that they are not exhaustive of sensible representation as such.* The first part of this chapter focuses on the condition of being spatiotemporally orienting, which is the topic of the Transcendental Aesthetic as well as of some pre-critical works, in which Kant aims to show that sensibility is a faculty distinct from thought. Interesting about Kant's argument is that it suggests that a specifically non-conceptual element – something irreducible to the faculty of understanding – is necessary for disclosing an external world. Perceiving the world here means to take a point of view, to orient oneself spatiotemporally in a sensibly given world. Kant's picture, therefore, or so I argue, necessarily involves the idea of a non-conceptual faculty – even though this does not imply (or point to) non-conceptual content.

In the second part of this chapter, I turn to Kant's critique of Descartes and the threat of idealism, his understanding of the noumenon, and the non-disjunctivism he appears to uphold, particularly in *Prolegomena*. I argue that Kant fuses realism and transcendental idealism in a way that, contrary to what McDowell's reading of Kant (among others) suggests, does not involve a boundary beyond which 'there is something we cannot know' (HWV 79), and which further does not make access to reality contingent upon some 'brute fact about us' (HWV 76). Moreover, I argue that Kant's account of the perceptual availability of a real world involves the idea of a 'dualism' (A370) within experience, which is similar to McDowell's own disjunctive theory. The exact role the understanding has in determining sensible intuition in a way adequate to

14 *Kant: Sensibility, Perception, Reality*

yielding this directedness at the real world – and therewith the remainder of my main thesis – is saved for the next chapter.

The Distinction between Sensibility and Understanding

One of the principal contributions Kant makes to modern philosophy is captured by his idea that knowledge must consist of the combination of intuitions and concepts. Intuitions, on this picture, are the product of the faculty of sensibility. This faculty is a receptive faculty; it allows the mind to receive representations without having to actively think about anything. Concepts, on the other hand, originate in the faculty of understanding. This faculty is said to be spontaneous; it involves the free production of concepts by exercise of thought. These capacities of producing intuitions and concepts, Kant notes, cannot be exchanged between the two faculties, for 'the understanding is not capable of intuiting anything and the senses are not capable of thinking anything' (A51/B75).

The meaning of this phrase is sometimes misunderstood. Taken precisely, Kant admits only to saying that the understanding cannot intuit, and that sensibility cannot think. He does not say that the understanding does not play any role in constituting intuitions; that intuitions would be the product exclusively of sensibility. Kant's aim here is not to drive a wedge between intuitions and concepts, but to indicate that our two faculties are mutually dependent when it comes to experiences of knowledge. The central point is that, were it not for our sensibility, no object would be given to the mind to think about, whereas without a faculty of understanding, there would be no thoughts about anything.

Kant further makes at least a fourfold distinction as to what sensibility can contain, namely sensations, appearances, perceptions, and intuitions. It is pertinent to appreciate the differences between these terms. We can start with the last one. Intuitions, for Kant, can be taken as acts of sensible representation – that through which things are sensibly presented to one.[1] If, for instance, I were to see a squirrel outside my window, I could be said to have an intuition of that squirrel. This does not require me actively determining what I intuit through an act of understanding. I might also simply gaze at the squirrel while thinking about something else, and thus have what we can call a sheer intuition. The articulation of things as being such-and-such does not therefore belong to intuition (or to any other capacity of sensibility alone).

Second, sensibility provides us with appearances. An appearance is not synonymous with an intuition. Although distinctively passive (not requiring thinking), an intuition is something I do; it is, in phenomenological parlor, an intentional act. By intuiting something, an object in turn can appear to me. This object as it is given, as long as it remains 'undetermined' (by explicit thought exercises), is called appearance (A20/B34). Thus the term 'appearance' is one way of addressing things outside us – namely as (i) receptively given (not merely thought) and as (ii) undetermined by an effort of understanding (intuited, not judged about). If an act of understanding is in place, an appearance can be put under rules of understanding and thereby cognized – but this is an additional activity which transforms the initially subjective appearance into an object of cognition.

Third, the term perception is closely linked to intuition (for instance Prol. 4: 283). Just as intuition, perception involves the representation of receptively given objects ('apprehension of the ideas of sense', Anth 7: 127). For that reason, it also involves sensation. Again like intuition, perception cannot of itself make knowledge of objects available, that is to say: perceiving isn't judging. The former lacks the active participation of the understanding which characterizes the latter. Yet Kant does consistently differentiate perception from intuition, by noting that only the former must come with conscious awareness (for instance A120). It is thus reasonable to suppose that perception for Kant is different at least from what can be called sheer intuition, which does not involve any conscious attention going out to the object perceived. This distinction will become important in Chapter 2, especially in discussing the transcendental deduction, where the role of concepts in perception and intuition respectively is discussed.

Fourth, the faculty of sensibility involves sensation. If, for instance, I see a squirrel, my faculty of sensibility receives (among others) certain color sensations. If I hear a song being played, the same faculty receives sound sensations. In both examples, the sensations received are not to be understood as appearances. I may see a black squirrel in the garden or hear Agustín Barrios play *Le Cathédrale* on guitar. But the black fur of the squirrel is an appearance I consider, and so is the melody of *Le Cathédrale*. These appearances are what we would now call intentional objects, and therefore are not themselves the sensations.

One may expect a fifth concept to be discussed in talking about sensibility, namely experience. In today's common usage, experience often connotes something like perceiving or more broadly living-through. For Kant, however, the term refers to knowledge. To experience simply means to know; to have 'knowledge of objects of sense' (Anth 7: 128). In the Kantian framework the term therefore does not belong to sensibility, nor to the understanding, but exclusively to their cooperation.

Both appearances – the things given to me sensibly – and concepts are referred to by Kant as representations. It is good to note that the German term *Vorstellung* does not have the same connotations as the English word representation. A *Vorstellung* need not be a re-presentation; it more adequately translates into 'presentation'. Kant, then, is not guilty of a representational theory of perception just for saying that perceptual appearances are representations. I continue to use the more common term 'representation' here, which should be harmless if we are aware of its original meaning.

16   *Kant: Sensibility, Perception, Reality*

By calling appearances and concepts representations, Kant does not intend to conflate the two sorts of representations. Appearances are characterized as representations 'given to us immediately' (A109), which is to say that they represent objects without the mediation of thought or judgment.[2] Sensible representations are all, as Kant claims his Transcendental Aesthetic to have shown, made possible by space and time as forms of our sensibility. Whether or not they are still representations of something else, of something perhaps altogether unavailable to our cognition, is discussed later. A concept, on the other hand, is a general and mediate representation; a 'one over many'. A concept of or a proposition about an object is therefore always a representation of a representation – whether of appearances (singular representations) or of other concepts or propositions (general representations).

Thus construed, we have two fundamental types of representation – appearance and concept – allocated to two heterogeneous sources of the mind, the combination of which alone gives us knowledge (or experience in Kant's terminology). The distinction between intuition and perception, as two ways of intending a sensible object (appearance), will become important again in Chapter 2, where the question of the contents of intuition and perception is considered in more detail.

A Distinct Faculty of Sensibility

But things soon turn out to be more complicated than this. It is nowadays not uncommon to read Kant as assigning to concepts a double role.[3] First, they would have an analytic function for us. We make use of this analytic function when we form judgments about things – for instance in judging that 'all swans are white' or that 'every event must have a cause'. In the analytic function, concepts are representations. Second, and considerably more originally, Kant would claim that concepts have a synthetic function. This means that they function as rules for the synthesis of representations – not just our conceptual representations, but also for the representations of sensibility. It is the extent and precise nature of this synthetic rule of concepts of understanding that the Kantian conceptualism debate tends to focus on.

So far, in the Transcendental Aesthetic, appearances were said to be the exclusive concern of our sensibility. After all, 'the understanding is not capable of intuiting anything and the senses are not capable of thinking anything' (A51/B75). I already made clear that this phrase does not exclude the option that the understanding plays a role in the production of intuitions. The central claim of (strong) conceptualists is, indeed, that the conclusion that it doesn't would be mistaken. For Kantian conceptualists, but also for McDowell understood on his own terms, there are no distinct contributions of sensibility. The fact that it may look as if the Transcendental Aesthetic argues for such a distinct contribution would

Kant: Sensibility, Perception, Reality   17

simply be due to the fact that, as McDowell puts it, Kant 'had to start somewhere' (HWV 83).

To understand how and to what extent Kant might be taken as speaking against the Transcendental Aesthetic later on, it is necessary to take the Transcendental Analytic into account. I do this in the following chapter. But it is interesting to explore first in more detail why Kant distinguished a distinct faculty of sensibility (from the understanding) in the first place. As it turns out, the central motive for doing so was that Kant was convinced that the constitutive functions of experience cannot be captured adequately in terms of a conceptual apparatus alone. In other words, he believed it necessary to introduce a specifically non-conceptual element to experience. It is no surprise that this is one of the main points Kantian non-conceptualists turn to.

Already in his 1755 work *New Elucidation of the First Principles of Metaphysical Cognition*, Kant takes note of the insufficiency of conceptual connections alone in order to form true judgments about the existence of things. The argument Kant develops here targets rationalist philosophers such as Descartes and Leibniz. Among other things, these rationalists sought ways of proving the existence of God. Simply put, Kant suggests that the rationalist approach to reach justified true beliefs about existing things on a basis that is exclusively conceptual is unsound. Consider the following passage:

> Form for yourself the concept of some being or other in which there is a totality of reality. It must be conceded that, given this concept, existence also has to be attributed to this being. But if all those realities are only conceived as united together, then the existence of that being is also only an existence of ideas.
>
> (NE 15)

Kant's point here is that just thinking about an object as existing cannot suffice to establish anything about the existence of that object. Hume had in point of fact developed a similar claim about two decades earlier. According to him, analytic judgments do not yield empirically justified claims. Statements are either about ideas – in which case their validity is necessary – or they are about the world – in which case their validity is not absolute. Hence a belief about the existence of god, which in the case of the rationalists is based on ideas alone, is not adequately justified.

In the 1755 text, Kant did not exploit this Humean line of thought by separating two distinct faculties, the cooperation of which alone could yield experience. In 1768, still thirteen years prior to the publication of the first *Critique*, Kant is again compelled to acknowledge an element of experience operating besides the intellect (see CG 2: 377). This time, the argument fits ongoing debates on the nature of space between Clarke's absolutist and Leibniz's relational account.[4] The argument Kant presents here is, I think, crucial to understanding Kant's Transcendental Aesthetic in the first *Critique* published thirteen years later.

In short, on the standard absolutist view of the time, the motion of objects had to be understood in relation to a background of absolute space which exists independently of objects. Against this, Leibniz's theory made space wholly dependent upon relations that obtain between objects. Space, on Leibniz view, is perhaps best understood as a property supervenient on the relations between objects, rather than existing in and of itself.

Against Leibniz, Kant wanted to show that certain properties of objects cannot be accounted for in terms of relations alone, and that therefore the relational view of space is false. His argument for this draws on so-called 'incongruent counterparts'. Kant's basic line of reasoning goes something like this. Imagine that God created a three-dimensional universe and subsequently went on to install a left and a right hand in it that are otherwise identical in every respect. Let us further imagine that there are no observers as of yet in this universe. Given these conditions, Kant asserts next, it would be impossible to determine which hand is left and which one is right. In other words, connections between points in space alone do not allow for differentiating between objects that are incongruent counterparts, that is, for objects that are incongruent but identical *qua* spatial relations. Since the relational account only considers the various (conceptual) relations between different points in space, it cannot decide which of the hands is left and which is right. To illustrate this better, consider the following drawings:

Congruent counterpart

Incongruent counterpart

In the above figure, the left two objects can be made to fit onto each other by rotation (in two-dimensional space). Although counterparts, Kant would say we can assess them exhaustively in terms of spatial relations. The two objects on the right, however, cannot be made to fit each other through rotation (in two-dimensional space), yet they are point-to-point identical. As Kant explains it in his inaugural work *The Form and Principles of the Sensible and Intelligible World* from 1770,

> there is a difference, in virtue of which it is impossible that the limits of their extension should coincide [but] in respect of everything which may be expressed by means of characteristic marks intelligible to the mind through speech, they could be substituted for one another.

(ID 2: 403)

In other words: both objects differ, but a point-to-point description fails to capture that difference.

The first conclusion of this is that incongruent counterparts cannot be completely accounted for on a relational account of space. The second conclusion is that, given that we do as a matter of fact recognize differences between incongruent counterparts, some part of our empirical cognition of objects must depend on an extra-conceptual capacity. This is the conclusion Kant drew in 1770 in his inaugural work, eleven years prior to the publication of the first *Critique*.

Kant was thus compelled from relatively early on to account for experience in a way that exceeds the exercise of conceptual capacities, first through the refutation of analytic arguments for God's existence and later through his views on space, which helped shape the Transcendental Aesthetic. It is clear that Kant deemed this an absolutely crucial discovery for an adequate account of human cognition, as is further underlined by its frequent resurfacing in later writings, among others in *Prolegomena* two years later, and again in the shorter essay *What does it mean to orient oneself in thinking?*

What exactly does the argument from incongruent counterparts show us? Several authors have attempted to use it as proof of Kantian non-conceptualism about perceptual content, for instance Hanna (2008) and Heidemann (2012).[5] Hanna's account has had considerable influence, so I focus on his here. He presents this as the *Two Hands Argument*:

> According to THA ('Two Hands Argument'), the content of perceptual states that pick out a perceivable natural object – such as a human hand – that has an actual or possible incongruent counterpart, is essentially non-conceptual. But it is clearly and distinctly conceivable, and therefore logically possible, that *any* perceivable natural object, and also *an* external part of *anyone's* body, has an actual or possible incongruent counterpart. [...] So the cognitive need for essentially non-conceptual content is ubiquitous in our world.
>
> (Hanna 2008, 57)

The arguments repeats Kant's own, but it involves an extra step and a different conclusion. The extra step is that it makes explicit that any possible object of perception has a possible incongruent counterpart. The extra conclusion is that any perceptual act must, for reasons that are not immediately apparent, involve non-conceptual content.

A response is in place here as regards the inference to non-conceptual content. I believe that, more carefully considered, the Two Hands Argument proves only that the contents of experience cannot be addressed by someone with only conceptual capacities. It does not, for that matter, prove that there are any contents that cannot be specified conceptually. Hanna's inference to non-conceptual content therefore appears to be false.

20   Kant: Sensibility, Perception, Reality

To explain this better, we can refer to, for instance, Bermúdez's definition of non-conceptual content, according to which a non-conceptual content is one that represents the world without demanding that its bearer should possess the concepts required to specify that content (even though s/he may in fact possess them) (Bermúdez 1994, 403). In line with this definition, conceptualism is the view that ascribes to concepts a determining role in structuring perceptual content without which perceptual content would be altogether unavailable. Now Hanna's argument does not, it seems, succeed in excluding such a role. While it illustrates that possession of concepts alone does not suffice to get the job done, it does not rule out that perceptual content presupposes the possession of those concepts relevant to specify that content in a judgment.

Furthermore, it appears Hanna's conclusion about content on this point does not reflect Kant's original argument. Kant's point was, as I understand it, that left and right are relative determinations that cannot be brought into view without something extra, which can be cashed out in terms of something like a definite point of view of the observer (for instance CG 2: 379, or OT 8: 135). Kant's point is better framed like this: to distinguish left from right, one needs to occupy a point in space as a basis for orientation. Put differently, perceiving the world means to take a point of view, to orient oneself spatiotemporally in a sensibly given world. While such a point of orientation is a condition for perceptual content, it is not itself a perceptual content, and there is little indication that Kant considered it that way.

Although the consequence of the case of incongruent counterparts might thus be more limited than is acknowledged by some of the non-conceptualists, I believe it is still something that a conceptualist should reckon with. McDowell, for instance, in opposing the so-called myth of the given, rejects on certain occasions any notionally distinguishable role of sensibility outside of the conceptual space of reasons. If that includes the non-conceptual capacity Kant refers to in his argument about incongruent counterparts, which it seems to, then this appears to pose a problem for McDowell's theory – granted that Kant's insight is valid.

To conclude this section: Kant had quite specific motives for introducing a non-conceptual element to his account of how we relate to the real world, but the inference to non-conceptual content some have made on its basis does not follow. To be sure, other cases for non-conceptual intuitional content can be made using Kant's writings, and I discuss these in the light of the Transcendental Analytic in the next chapter.

Idealism and the Myth of the Given

Kant and the Myth of the Given

The so-called myth of the given plays an important role in ongoing debates about the relation between perception and reason. Avoiding it

Kant: Sensibility, Perception, Reality 21

is one of the central motivations for McDowell's conceptualist theory, especially in *Mind and World*.

For some reason, debates on Kantian conceptualism tend to focus mainly on the question of the conceptual determination of perceptual content, but not so much on the problem of the myth of the given.[6] This is surprising, not only because of the importance of the myth of the given to conceptualists, but also because Kant's framework lends itself well for discussing it. In this second part, I consider some perspectives on how the problem of the myth of the given plays out from the angle of Kant's philosophy, in order to provide a fuller picture of Kant's views on the necessary conditions for having an objective world given in experience.

There are various ways in which the concept of the myth of the given can be worked out. It is important to note that the very idea that it involves a fallacy is premised upon a conceptual distinction between two spaces of meaningfully addressing things. Sellars referred to these spaces, among others, in terms of epistemic and natural facts; McDowell in terms of a space of reasons and a space of nature. The fallacy of the given would, in short, be to conflate descriptions that belong to one sphere with descriptions that belong to the other. This specifically goes in one direction: it concerns understanding facts of nature (or better: all facts that do not fall within the space of reasons) as epistemically efficacious.

One example of this fallacy is, according to McDowell, to be found in the empirical foundationalism of early modern philosophers. As McDowell discusses it in *Mind and World,* the central problem of empirical foundationalism is that it construes sensations as belonging to two images at once: to the space of nature on the one hand, as an image ruled by natural law, and to the space of reasons on the other, as a realm of human action and responsiveness to reasons (of 'freedom, exemplified in responsible acts of judging, [which] is essentially a matter of being answerable to criticism in the light of rationally relevant considerations' (HWV 6)). Invoking the idea of a given means to extend justification more widely than the space of reasons, that is, into the realm of lawful nature (MW 7). The problem McDowell has with this is that a conception of causally impinging sensations can only yield 'exculpations where we wanted justifications' (MW 8). A belief may be caused by a natural event; it is not thereby justified by it.

Having the World in View introduces the fallacy in another, but closely related, way. Here, McDowell defines empirical foundationalism as a viewpoint from which 'the grounding [of] perceptual knowledge is atomistically conceived' (HWV 6). In other words, empirical foundationalism sketches linkages between certain basic facts that are supposedly unaffected by the conceptual frameworks with which we encounter the world in thought and perception. This critique of the atomistic sense data theory reminds somewhat of Merleau-Ponty's opening of *Phenomenology of Perception*, where it is argued that the notion of sensation

22 *Kant: Sensibility, Perception, Reality*

is a theoretical construction that lacks a genuine experiential basis. An important difference is that Merleau-Ponty does not exploit the idea of a space of reasons exclusively in terms of concept-involving exercises.

For current purposes, I think it is safe to generalize this conception of the myth of the given further than the opposition between natural facts and reasons. For McDowell, any picture that accounts for responsiveness to reasons in terms of sensible operations that lie outside of the concept-involving sphere of reasons is guilty of the fallacy. This means that a positive conception of a noumenal reality (which on no viable interpretation of Kant's usage of the term is identical to nature or natural fact) would also qualify as an instance of the myth (compare, for instance, HWV 39). It is in particular this variant of the myth of the given that I shall focus on here. To examine this fully, it is necessary to consider Kant's ideas about the relation between mind and reality, and therefore also his discussion of idealism and the concept of noumenon.

On Descartes, Idealism, and Reality

There is a long and lively tradition of debate in Kant scholarship concerned with Kant's realism and the precise role of his concept of the noumenon in this. As Allais (2015) recently put it, the debate fails to show 'even a tendency toward convergence' (Allais 2015, 3). The question of realism generally construed concerns our access to reality. Allais herself takes an anti-realist stance at least insofar as Kant, on her view, bars us from access to aspects of reality: 'things (objects) of which we have empirical cognition [...] have natures or aspects that are entirely independent of us, which ground appearances' (Allais 2015, 59). In a similar vein, Guyer and Horstmann (2015) argue for Kant's 'indeterminate ontological realism', with Guyer noting earlier that this indeterminate and unknowable world is the one to which 'we ultimately intend to refer' (Guyer 1987, 335). An even more canonical example of this line of interpretation is Strawson's (1966) reading, according to which Kant thought that 'reality is supersensible and [...] we can have no knowledge of it' (Strawson 1966, 16). Other, more recent contributions within a broadly anti-realist camp include Westphal (2004) and Rockmore (2007), who both read Kant as being committed to a world beyond human cognition (Westphal 2004, 67; Rockmore 2007, 9), and Braver (2007), who holds Kant responsible for a whole wave of anti-realism in continental philosophy.

Numerous scholars resist such readings, however. An early example here is Bird (1962), who suggests that phenomenon and noumenon are two ways of looking at the same thing 'because, on Kant's view, there is only one thing at which to look, namely appearances' (Bird 1962, 29). Prauss's (1974) early discussion on the concept of the thing in itself points in the same direction, arguing that Kant's preferred locution is not 'thing in itself' (which suggests its actual existence) but 'thing considered as it is in itself' (Prauss 1974). In more recent days, Allison (2004, 50–57) and Luft (2007, 371) have provided like-minded readings, with Jansen (2014) boldly suggesting that anti-realist readings of Kant are 'symptomatic of a persisting confusion' (Jansen 2014, 83).

Idealism in its traditional signification can be considered a form of anti-realism. Kant denies being committed to it, and elaborates extensively on the difference between idealism and transcendental idealism. The most interesting discussions of this appear in the Refutation of Idealism (added in the B-edition), in Phenomena and Noumena, in crucial sections on the paralogisms (in the A-edition), and in the antinomies of pure reason.[7] It is worth briefly reconstructing Kant's main lines of argument here, as it bears directly on his views on perception's relation to reality.

In the Refutation of Idealism among other places, Kant distinguishes between two sorts of idealism (not including his own transcendental idealism): 'problematic' and 'dogmatic' idealism (B274–275). A problematic idealist – Descartes is Kant's favorite example – is defined as someone who denies that the existence of objects 'is cognized [known] through immediate perception' and who consequently holds that we 'can never [...] be fully certain of their reality' (A368–369). Problematic idealism is thus defined specifically by an epistemic restriction. It specifies that although we may have experiences and knowledge of real objects, we can never be totally sure about this.

This contrasts with dogmatic idealism, which Kant ascribes to Berkeley. A dogmatic idealist is one who 'declares things in space to be merely imaginary' (B274). Later on in the paralogisms, Kant characterizes the dogmatic idealist as 'someone who denies the existence of external objects of sense' (A368). Unlike the problematic idealist, then, the dogmatic idealist makes an ontological claim. While the problematic idealist puts a restriction on our claims to knowledge about the real world, the dogmatic idealist goes further in denying altogether the existence of external objects, claiming instead that they are nothing but imaginary entities. This leads to the sort of picture McDowell would refer to as a 'frictionless spinning in the void' (MW 11). This dogmatic view thus naturally includes the weaker epistemic restriction of problematic idealism in itself.

It is clear that Kant opposes both forms of idealism for the reason that they cannot adequately accommodate realism. He further indicates that he thinks a single conceptual error underlies both views, and that eliminating this error should remove '*every dispute* about the nature of our thinking being and its conjunction with the corporeal world' (A395 my italics). Kant's best discussion of this error is to be found in his discussions of Descartes in the fourth paralogism.

In the fourth paralogism, Kant first states his sympathy for the Cartesian starting point which seeks certainty in consciousness. He agrees

24   *Kant: Sensibility, Perception, Reality*

with Descartes that there can be no question that 'I am indeed conscious to myself of my representations; thus these exist and I myself, who has these representations' (A370). Kant, however, rejects Descartes's subsequent procedure. Interestingly, the problem is said to lie in Descartes inferential strategy: '[For Descartes] I cannot really perceive external things, but only infer their existence from my inner perception, insofar as I regard this as the effect of which something external is the proximate cause' (A368). This account, insofar as it suggests an external cause of the inner perception which is alone available to us, could be a variant of the myth of the given.

Kant believes this Cartesian fate can be avoided by rethinking the relation between object and appearance. The solution is to say instead that 'external objects [...] are mere appearances, hence also nothing other than a species of my representations [...]. Thus external things exist as well as my self, and indeed both exist on the immediate testimony of my self-consciousness' (A370–371). Kant's attempted solution here consists of eliminating the idea that perceptions *indicate* the real world, as that leads to the problem of our (inferential) access to the real based on the appearance. Instead, he claims that we simply ought to conceive of external objects as themselves a species of representations. Real objects, Kant repeatedly notes, 'are mere appearances'; 'external things, namely matter, in all its forms and alterations – are nothing but mere representations' (A371–372). This way, I have immediate perception of the real world, and 'I am no more necessitated to draw inferences' (A371).

It is tempting to interpret this is a direct relapse into dogmatic idealism. Kant, however, insists that his transcendental idealism is distinct from that. The crux of the difference lies in what we should conceive of as setting the norm for any sort of reality-ascription. On Kant's view, idealists consider objects to be merely empirically produced appearances in the mind or brain for this specific reason: they maintain that an adequate answer to the question of what qualifies as real cannot be derived from the appearances themselves. That is to say, the idealist seeks an answer to the question of reality beyond that sphere, in a world that is completely beyond experience. This is what Allison refers to as the 'implicit norm in the light of which human cognition is analyzed' which Kant maintains guides the transcendental realists (in A369, see Allison 2004, 28; 2015). Transcendental realism, then, as the tacit presupposition that underlies idealistic thought, comes down to the assumption that 'reality "is in itself" independently of how we cognize it' (Stang 2016).[8] Indeed, all idealists Kant claims to know endorsed this view, whether explicitly or tacitly (see A372).

Kant further offers something of an explanation as to why transcendental realism and the fallacy carried with it are so common among philosophers before him. This explanation bears some resemblances to Husserl's account of the relation between naturalism and the natural attitude, which I discuss in Chapter 4. Objects of experience, Kant notes, 'have in themselves this deceptive feature, that [...] they seem to cut themselves loose from the soul, as it were, and [appear to] hover outside it' (A385). It belongs to ordinary experience that it posits objects 'as objects outside us, [thereby] completely separating them from the thinking subject' (A389). It are thus the normal operations of human experience that lead to 'the common concepts of our reason in regard to the community in which our thinking subject stands to things outside us' (A389), in other words: to the transcendental realist conception of objects as enjoying radical independence from experience. However, as long as we remain in this position, 'we are dogmatic, and regard these things as objects truly subsisting independently of us' (A389).

It can now be drawn out why transcendental idealism is not a form of (dogmatic or problematic) idealism. Transcendental idealism is supposed to negate transcendental realism, as the presupposition onto which idealism rests. From the new point of view, objects are supposed to be genuinely 'outside us' (A375). This constitutes Kant's empirical realism. At least in the usual, veridical case, 'outer perception [...] therefore immediately proves something real in space [...]. To that extent, empirical realism is beyond doubt' (A375). Kant, then, thinks we have direct, non-inferential access to the real world. At the same time, however, the reality of an object here cannot indicate its radically mind-independent existence, as it does for transcendental realists. The difference is that for Kant the reality of objects is to be granted exclusively from within the space of possible experience.[9] In other words, Kant seeks to convince us that reality is always already within our grasp. Only the false idea that it somehow could not be within our grasp leads to the threat of idealism.

Kant's strategy of harboring realism within transcendental idealism – that is, within the scope of possible experience – does not sound so different, I think, from McDowell's attempt 'to embrace relatedness to the real order within the conceptual order' (HWV 63). Yet McDowell reads Kant as failing to truly commit to this view. I return to this shortly. For now it can be noted that, at the very least, Kant makes a clear effort to affirm a realist worldview. He does not do so, however, by partaking in what he deems to be the futile efforts of his predecessors, which were sustained by a transcendental realist conception of the mind-world relation. Instead, the heart of Kant's strategy can be said to lie in the attempt to re-conceptualize the norm by which we grant reality-status to an object.

On the Noumenon

The reading provided in the previous section served to establish, at the very least, Kant's serious realist intentions. I think, moreover, that this realist interpretation can be made to fit coherently within Kant's overall

26   Kant: Sensibility, Perception, Reality

critical project. In this section I extend this line of thought further by turning to the concept of noumenon, which for obvious reasons bears on Kant's realist claims.

The concept of noumenon is juxtaposed by Kant to the concept of phenomenon. In a section (deleted in the B-edition) in Phenomena and Noumena, Kant defines the latter as 'objects [...] in accordance with the unity of the categories' (A248/249), that is to say, appearances that are made to concord with objective principles of the understanding. But Kant's definition of noumena is the more striking one. There could be, Kant contends, 'things that are merely objects of the understanding and that, nevertheless, can be given as such to an intuition, although not to sensible intuition' (A249).[10] Further on, Kant aligns this concept of noumenon with that of the thing in itself: 'without this constitution of our sensibility (upon which the form of our intuition is grounded), [there] must be something [in itself], i.e., an object independent of sensibility. Now from this arises the concept of a *noumenon*' (A252).

Kant's discussion here draws on a challenging distinction between our form of intuition – which, Kant maintains, is necessarily sensible – and an intuition unlike ours. I return to this shortly. Corresponding to this is a distinction between a positive and a negative noumenon (in the second edition, but the first edition discussion is, I think, not essentially different). Subscribing to a positive noumenon would amount roughly to acknowledging that we can comprehend or have insight into the possibility (see B307; A255/B310) of 'an *object* of a *non-sensible intuition*' (B307). The emphasis on comprehension here serves to indicate that, on this conception, the affirmation of the possible reality of such an object is involved. That is to say, being able to comprehend the possibility of an object means to locate that object within the space of possible experience, and therefore in the sphere of the real (as those are one and the same for Kant).

Crucially, however, this capacity for comprehension is explicitly denied by Kant. For Kant, the very 'thing' the concept of a thing in itself denotes is not something we could possibly comprehend. It does not lie within the scope of meaningful comprehension because it (by definition) cannot possibly be experienced, given that experience must involve understanding and sensibility. By the same token, the concept has no reality to it. It is for this reason that Kant repeatedly emphasizes that the concept is 'without sense' (A240/B299), without 'significance' (A241/B300)[11], and that it 'signifies nothing at all' (B306).

Why, then, does Kant invoke the concept of noumenon at all? One way to explain this would be to say that Kant employs a 'metalanguage' (Allison 2004, 73) of things in themselves, the heuristic value of which derives from the paradigm of transcendental realism before him. Kant adds to the explanation by saying that while the concept is without sense', it is 'not at all contradictory' (A254/B310). It is for this reason, as he puts it later on in the *Critique,* that 'room remains for more and other objects; they cannot therefore be absolutely denied, but [...] they also cannot be asserted as objects' (A287–288/B344). Indeed, 'the concept of noumenon is therefore not the concept of an object, but rather the problem' (A287–B344).

I am inclined to interpret this along the following lines. Kant's talk of the noumenon does not denote any conceivably real object (that is, an object of a possible experience). Instead, he could be said to follow a distinction between real and logical possibility.[12] For Kant, a thing in itself is not a real possibility (it is without sense or meaning, because it cannot be an object of possible experience), but it is a logical possibility nonetheless, insofar as it is formally non-contradictory.[13]

The difference is crucial but easily illustrated. The proposition 'if something is blue all over then it is red all over' involves a contradiction. But it does not involve a formal contradiction. An example of a formal contradiction would be 'for any properties X and Y, if something has both X and Y then it does not have X and Y'.[14]

For Kant, all justification of meaningful propositions must come from sensible intuition, since 'thoughts without [intuitive] content are empty' (A51/B75). The concept of a world that cannot be sensibly experienced therefore becomes meaningless, even though it still stands as a valid postulation insofar as it is formally coherent. This is, in short, why Kant says that we will 'not even be able to justify' (A259/B309) accepting another kind of intuition that is non-sensible, even though we can talk coherently of the objects of such intuitions, i.e. noumena.

The very same distinction may, I think, be used to explain Kant's otherwise confusing talk of sensible and non-sensible intuitions. Kant unambiguously admits the conceivability of another kind of intuition, one which is not sensible as with us. He does so because we simply 'cannot assert of sensibility that it is the only possible kind of intuition' (A254/B310). That is to say, we cannot exclude another type of intuition on logical grounds. Kant says this much in noting that 'the possibility of a thing can never be proved merely through the non-contradictoriness of the concept of it' (A252), while continuing that he certainly also hasn't proven definitively 'that sensible intuition is the only possible intuition' (A252, see also A254/B310).

I think this line of argument is further supported by Kant's subsequent analysis of the necessity of a noumenal world (see A254/B310). To see this, it is crucial to understand this necessity as the necessity *of* the concept of the logical possibility of a noumenal world, rather than as the necessity of the reality of a noumenal world. The necessity is therefore also qualified as transcendental: the concept of noumenon is a necessary, a priori product of the transcendental structure of our experience, without thereby referring to anything real (anything intuitable). Although it sounds somewhat strange, Kant says it is produced by the mind to

28 *Kant: Sensibility, Perception, Reality*

prevent that we 'extend sensible intuition to things in themselves' (A254/B310); it is 'not only admissible, but even unavoidable, as a concept setting limits to sensibility' (A256/B311).

More precisely, the genesis of the concept of noumenon is then said to lie in the understanding. As Kant notes, the understanding 'is not limited by sensibility; on the contrary, but rather limits it by calling things in themselves noumema [through which it at the same time] immediately sets limits to itself' (A256/B312). In other words, it is the understanding which is 'not yet satisfied through the substratum of sensibility [and therefore] add[s] noumena that only the pure understanding can think to the phenomena' (A251). Likewise, in *Prolegomena,* Kant says that 'the understanding, just by the fact that it accepts appearances, also admits of the existence of things in themselves, [this] is not merely permitted but also inevitable' (Prol. 4:315). Thus understood, the restriction is clearly transcendental in origin; it comes necessarily from within experience, not from without.

To conclude: it is wrong to infer from Kant's acceptance of a negative concept of noumenon that he ascribes reality to things in themselves. That could mean committing Kant to the myth of the given, as it could lead one to think that there is a source outside of experience which supposedly gets experience going. On the reading I provided, the noumenon is better understood as replete of any significance when it comes to determining the conditions that must be satisfied for the ascription of a sense of reality to something. I return in more detail to the nature of these conditions – which partially lie in the understanding – in the next chapter, after briefly overviewing Kant's disjunctivism as well as McDowell's reading of Kant, which (contra mine here) does see Kant as regressing into some form of idealism.

Kant's Disjunctivism

Debates about disjunctivism are closely related to those concerned with how our thoughts can bear onto reality. The question of disjunctivism concerns the nature of veridical perception in comparison to non-veridical perception (hallucination). Generally speaking, for disjunctivists, a veridical perception is different from a non-veridical perception, due to the fact that veridical perception alone involves the perceived, external object as a constituent. For those sympathetic to non-disjunctivism (sometimes called conjunctivism), veridical and non-veridical perceptions are not structurally different, because the external object does not play a constitutive role in either case. Disjunctivists are generally relationalists. For them, veridical perception accomplishes a relation to an external object, whereas for instance a hallucination does not. McDowell makes it clear that he wants a relational view of perception and that he identifies himself as a disjunctivist (see for instance HWV 62).

Much of this debate should be admitted to hang on how one thinks about the term 'external object'. For McDowell, a relational conception of perception is crucial to a philosophically sound understanding of the relation between mind and world. Indeed, a core motivation for his conceptualism is that he thinks it can ensure the mind's relation to external reality. At the same time, it should be made clear that, on his account, the external object which perception is directed at is not radically external to the space of the mind's involvements. Instead, McDowell notes that 'we affirm these relations without moving outside the conceptual order' (HWV 63). For this reason, it would be a mistake to compare his relational view of perception to relational conceptions that rely on a naïve realism or empirical foundationalism (or Campbell's version of the relational view, for instance).[15]

Sellars, according to McDowell, does not fully succeed in attaining a proper relationalist conception of perception. The reason for this is well known: Sellars accepts, McDowell purports, a transcendental notion of sensation in order to assure a connection between thought and reality. For McDowell, this means 'the transcendental project [involves] a sideways-on point of view on the directedness of the conceptual at the real' (HWV 63). Properly construed it should, however, be 'executed from within the conceptual order' (HWV 63).

McDowell, then, is not interested in the sort of disjunctivism that sketches linkages between concept-laden exercises of sensibility and a reality construed as lying outside what is brought into view through such exercises. Now it seems to make sense to say that if one would, by way of contrast, be willing to take in the sideways-on point of view – the view of one committed to the myth of the given, or of the transcendental realist, as Kant would put it –, then McDowell's position could reasonably be cashed out in non-disjunctive terms instead. After all, the relation to the object outside of the order of experience plays no constitutive role for him or for Kant. The main reason McDowell considers himself a disjunctivist nonetheless is, I suspect, that he refuses to take in that very point of view.

It is interesting to note that Kant appears more willing than McDowell to emphasize a non-disjunctive approach to his theory of perception. This is not however, or so I will argue here, because they would defend substantially different theories.

In *Prolegomena*, Kant explains that 'the difference between truth and dream, however, is not decided through the quality of the representations that referred to objects, for they are the same in both, but through their connection according to the rules' (Prol. 4:290). Later on, he repeats this point differently, saying that in veridical perception there 'is contained not the least illusion or temptation toward error', because here representations 'can be connected together correctly in experience according to rules of truth' (Prol. 4:291).

30 *Kant: Sensibility, Perception, Reality*

Interestingly, this seems to be a distinctively non-disjunctive approach to the question of perception's veridicality. Kant says that a non-veridical perception is not distinguished from a veridical one for failing to establish a (causal) connection to mind-independent external objects. That would be another instance of the myth of the given. Rather, what defines veridical perception is the way in which representations are connected – its coherence – through rules of understanding. It is not the reference to mind-independent objects, but the sort of coherence veridical perceptions have that distinguishes them from non-veridical perception.

Virtually the same point is made in the Refutation of Idealism in the B-edition. Here Kant writes that whether a thing is real or illusory is to be decided 'through its coherence with the criteria of all actual experience' (B279). In other words, we have to decide upon the veridicality or non-veridicality of a perception by assessing its coherence with other experiences.

While Kant thus frames his theory of perception in a non-disjunctive manner, this does not of itself render his theory incompatible with a disjunctive view such as McDowell's. Kant is best interpreted as saying that veridical and non-veridical ought to be understood non-disjunctively to this extent: that the object considered as radically mind-independent (as noumenon) should not be regarded a necessary constituent of veridical perception. However, such an object does not, in fact, exist for Kant; the very desire to explain how perception could relate to a radically mind-independent object stems from the transcendental realist viewpoint Kant rejects. Kant's non-disjunctivism is therefore perfectly in line with the account in the fourth paralogism. Both texts suggest that we should not measure the capacity of perception to give us real things by some norm conceptualizing the real as outside of the scope of possible experience.

At the same time, the idea that the radically mind-independent object is not constitutively involved in perception does not mean that we cannot differentiate veridical from non-veridical perception. There is no need to leave the order of experience to distinguish between perception and hallucination, reality and mere appearance. This is because there is, as Kant puts it, a crucial 'dualism' (A370) to be made within the order of experience, namely between mere appearances and appearances that put us in touch with reality. That is to say: there is a legitimate distinction *within* how things seem to us; between cases in which it merely appears to one that things are thus and so and cases where one actually perceives things to be thus and so. This 'dualism' matches almost exactly, as I argue in greater detail in Chapter 6, McDowell's disjunctivism, which is likewise based on the idea that 'the notion of appearance is [itself] disjunctive' (ST 248).

For Kant, then, we decide upon the veridicality or non-veridicality of a perception by assessing its coherence with other experiences. This is not, however, a merely 'subjective' matter; considerations may include, as Williams (2017) points out, whatever relevant scientific knowledge or reports of other observers are available to one. Therefore, it is not the case that 'samenesses and differences are exhaustively determined by how things seem to the subject' (ST 249), as McDowell writes about Descartes. The reality of an experienced object does not boil down, on Kant's picture, to how things seem to the solipsistic subject.

It can be concluded that Kant accounts for our immediate perceptual access to reality not by proving that our representations correspond to things outside of the order of experience, but by allowing of a 'dualism' within experience itself. This theory is, as I discuss in more detail in Chapter 6, very similar to McDowell's disjunctive theory. The fact that Kant appears to defend non-disjunctivism nonetheless does not derive from a substantial disagreement between him and McDowell's disjunctivism, or so I have argued. Instead, it is more likely that it follows from the dialectics of Kant's work. Kant is primarily concerned with rejecting transcendental realism, which he identifies as the central dogma of philosophers before him. It is plausible that this brings him to emphasize that a radically mind-independent reality is not a constitutive component of perceptual intentionality. McDowell, on the other hand, is motivated to avoid the myth of the given, and for that reason refuses to take in that viewpoint from which his theory could be appropriated as a form of non-disjunctivism.

McDowell on Kant and the Subjective Ideality of Space and Time

In *Having the World in View,* McDowell offers an interpretation of Kant which, in contrast to what I presented, sees Kant committed to a form of the myth of the given. The problem is said to concern the faculty of sensibility. On McDowell's construal of Kant's picture, the pure forms of sensible intuition (space and time) remain in the end 'a sort of brute fact about us' (HWV 76). In short, the Kantian picture of our perceptual relation to the world is said to be contingent upon natural facts about our sensibility. Because Kant would allow sensibility to be determined by 'brute-fact externality' (HWV 85), it faces the threat of being 'indistinguishable from a subjectivistic psychologism' (HWV 76).

The reference to psychologism here is, I think, an overstatement. The point should be that linkages between the world perceptually brought into view and contingent facts about our natural constitution could lead to an image of constraint, and thereby to idealism. McDowell is certainly not the first to see a problem here. Husserl, among so many others, criticized an 'anthropological' tension in Kant's *Critique* in early lectures from 1908. Kant's philosophy, Husserl alleges, in spite of being transcendental, operates with a picture of human beings as psychophysical objects in nature. Husserl subsequently points specifically to

32 *Kant: Sensibility, Perception, Reality*

Kant's accounts of non-sensible intuition and of the thing in itself as places where this anthropological tendency leads to problems (see EP I 362–363).

For the most part, McDowell's analysis of the Kantian problem of sensibility rests on the following passage from the first *Critique*:

> The pure concepts of the understanding ... extend to objects of intuition in general, be the intuition like or unlike ours, if only it be sensible and not intellectual. But this extension of [these] concepts beyond *our* sensible intuition is of no advantage to us. For as concepts of objects they are then empty, and do not enable us to judge of their objects whether or not they are possible. They are mere forms of thought, without objective reality, since we have no intuition at hand to which the synthetic unity of apperception, which constitutes the whole content of these forms, could be applied, and in being so applied determine an object. Only *our* sensible and empirical intuition can give to them [sense and meaning].
>
> (B148–149, quoted from HWV 77)

McDowell interprets this, as I understand him, along the following lines. Kant rightly saw that objectivity and subjectivity are not radically opposed to each other. The laws that govern the object are not separate from those that govern the subject. Still, Kant risks an image of a subjective imposition of conceptual form on sensibility in a way that leads to idealism. This is because, as McDowell contends the quote above illustrates, Kant's account of the faculty of sensibility boils down to a 'mere reflection of a fact about us' (HWV 78). Consequently, Kant fails to bring the world into view after all. Our access to reality is premised on a contingent fact about our sensibility, which means that 'our capacities to know things reach only so far, and beyond that boundary there is something we cannot know: namely, whether things themselves are really spatially and temporally ordered' (HWV 79).[16]

I don't think this is a correct representation of Kant's views, because I don't agree with McDowell that 'the Aesthetic encourages us to entertain the thought that there could be differently formed sensibilities' (HWV 151), by which Kant would then introduce 'natural fact' into his transcendental theory of sensibility. This is easily shown. In the passage quoted, Kant refers to space and time as forms of our intuition. He does not, for that matter, claim that they are natural facts. To the contrary, he explicitly asserts that they have a transcendental significance that is distinct from significance of fact.

Compare, for instance, the argument from incongruent counterparts discussed in the first part of this chapter. It didn't rest on an analysis of brute facts of sensibility either. Instead, the argument was transcendental; it concerned the conditions that need to be in place for cognition

Kant: Sensibility, Perception, Reality 33

to work as it does. It is further worth noting that, although McDowell denies it, the restriction to human consciousness is in fact similarly referred to by Kant in discussing transcendental apperception and the understanding (in the second section of the B-deduction, B138–139, B145). Needless to say, these don't reduce to facts either.[17]

To sustain this further, one could point to B72, in which Kant seems to contradict McDowell's interpretation, by noting that space and time are not necessarily limited to human cognition. They may hold universally for all finite beings:

> It is also not necessary for us to limit the kind of intuition in space and time to the sensibility of human beings; it may well be that all finite thinking beings must necessarily agree with human beings in this regard (though we cannot [a priori] decide this).[18]
>
> (B72)

It is possible to take this interpretation one step further. One could also interpret those instances where Kant talks of the possibility of other forms of sensibility (or understanding) as referring to possibilities in a sense beyond the limits of what can be concretely imagined. In other words, Kant could be referring to a mere logical possibility, as I discussed earlier. One could then understand Kant as contrasting human sensibility to other forms of sensibility construed as empty (but logically non-contradictory) possibilities. This is not, in my view, an outrageous suggestion, given that Kant's entire discussion of Descartes in the fourth paralogism aims at refuting transcendental realism through this very distinction.

Kant, then, or so I have argued, is best read as not committing to the myth of the given. To the contrary, Kant actively seeks to avoid it at various places, among others in his critique of idealism and theory of the noumenon. While Kant does indeed speak of non-sensible intuition, this does not serve to put any constraints on the capacity of our sensible faculty to provide us access to reality. Instead, Kant is plausibly read as committing only to the logical possibility of such a concept.

Concluding Remarks

This chapter mainly dealt with Kant's theory of sensibility as a distinct and non-conceptual faculty, and with his discussion of Descartes and the threat of idealism. In the first part, I argued that Kant's distinction of two faculties is partially a response to a problem regarding so-called incongruent counterparts, and that his solution to that problem required understanding sensibility as a specifically non-conceptual faculty. While this did not yield a commitment to non-conceptual content, it revealed that Kant believed that taking a concrete point of view from which to

34 *Kant: Sensibility, Perception, Reality*

orient oneself is necessary for having the kind of access to reality that we do have. In the second part, I showed that Kant argues against idealism, Cartesian skepticism, and against the idea that we should think of a world beyond our experiences as the real world. Instead, a distinction between reality and mere appearance should be made within the order of experience. This leaves open the question what exactly the contents of perception have to be like in order to make reality perceptually available to us, which is what I turn to in the next chapter.

Notes

1 As Paton pointed out, there is also room to read intuition as meaning the sensible representation itself, see Paton (1936, 103). To avoid confusion I continue to use the term to refer to something we do, however, rather than to the representation that is gained through this.
2 There has been some debate about the meaning of the concept of immediacy in this context (see Hintikka 1969; Wilson 1975). For current purposes, it is sufficient to take it to point to the direct character of perceptual presentation in plain contrast to thought, which represents the world mediately through concepts.
3 See Longuenesse (1998, 48–50).
4 See also Earman (1991) and Janiak (2012) for introductions to this debate.
5 Hanna's list of arguments is longer; some of the other ones surface again in the second chapter. I also discuss Hanna's arguments in Van Mazijk (2014a, 2014b).
6 One notable exception to this is Watkins (2008). Watkins, however, focuses on another form of the myth of the given than I do here, namely on the relation between natural sensations and normative representations synthetically produced out of them. My reading here focuses on the role of noumenal reality, although I return to concerns about the natural operations of sensibility in the final section.
7 My discussion in what follows strongly focuses on the fourth paralogism and less on the Refutation of Idealism, which according to some scholars contradicts the fourth paralogism (for instance Vaihinger (1884), Kemp Smith (1918), and Bader (2012)). Guyer (1987) believes that 'exactly *what* thesis the refutation is supposed to prove is unclear' (Guyer 1987, 280). I tend to think there is no contradiction between the refutation and the fourth paralogism, and that the refutation does not bear directly on the thing in itself as some authors have assumed. I will here leave this issue to the side, however.
8 Note that Stang's definition pertains to Allison's account of transcendental realism.
9 This view should not entail that things not currently perceived by anyone do not exist. As Kant notes, 'that there could be inhabitants of the moon, even though no human being has ever perceived them, must of course be admitted' (A493/B251). In other words, we can legitimately treat the world as a place filled with real objects. It is just that this thesis can be properly maintained only within the confines of transcendental idealism, that is, from within the space of possible experience.
10 Note that Kant does not commit to this definition of the noumenon in giving it; it is explicitly phrased as a hypothesis.

11 Translated as 'meaning' in N. K. Smith's translation.
12 Note that I will not deal with Kant's practical philosophy in this section, which some scholars believe involves a stronger ontological commitment to the noumenon than is to be found in the theoretical work. At the moment I am sympathetic to Adams (1997) on this point, who concludes, after discussing the import of Kant's practical philosophy, that 'uncertain as it may be of the real possibility of noumenal causality, theoretical reason seems justified [only] in affirming the logical possibility of the concept' (Adams 1997, 821).
13 Note that the logical space of the thing in itself as here illustrated is not confined to an unknowable shadow side of appearances to which we have access, as some versions of the double aspect view have it. See also Ameriks (2003) who develops the point that 'some things in themselves could lack appearances' – at least such a thing cannot be *logically* excluded either – which means a 'one-on-one-mapping' of things in themselves (as thought entities) onto real things is impossible (see Ameriks 2003, 34–35).
14 These examples are inspired by Centrone's (2010) discussion, which deals with Husserl's views, not Kant's.
15 See Campbell (2002). MacDonald's (2006) discussion with McDowell (in his reply to MacDonald, see RCM) seems to rest on this sort of confusion. I return again to McDowell's disjunctivism in Chapter 6.
16 See also Haddock's informed discussion of McDowell's 'Hegelian' reply to Kant, which I think is largely correct – although it does not criticize McDowell's reading of Kant as I continue to do here (Haddock 2009).
17 It is worth pointing out that there might also a potential problem with McDowell's own attempt to avoid the position he believes Kant is committed to. As Haddock (2009) convincingly shows, there is a tension between McDowell's insistence that the (conceptual) space of reasons is natural – that second nature is constrained by first nature – and his insistence, against Kant on his reading, that human sensibility would be constrained by natural fact. On Haddock's interpretation, McDowell is even worse off than Kant as McDowell presents him, because on McDowell's picture this natural constraint must also be said to apply to our conceptual capacities. I return to McDowell's naturalism as well as his transcendental ambitions in more detail in Chapter 6.
18 This point is also made in Kant's annotation in his own copy of the first *Critique*, in the Transcendental Aesthetic A27/B43: 'Perhaps all created beings are bound to it [space as a priori form of sensibility], that we cannot know [with a priori certainty]'.

References

Adams, R. M. (1997). 'Things in Themselves', *Philosophy and Phenomenological Research*, Vol. 57, No. 4, 801–825.
Allais, L. (2015). *Manifest Reality: Kant's Idealism and His Realism.* Oxford: Oxford University Press.
Allison, H. E. (2004). *Kant's Transcendental Idealism: An Interpretation and Defense.* New Haven, London: Yale University Press.
Ameriks, K. (2003). *Interpreting Kant's Critiques.* Oxford: Oxford University Press.
Bader, R. M. (2012). 'The Role of Kant's Refutation of Idealism', *Archiv für Geschichte der Philosophie*, Vol. 94, No. 1, 53–73.

36 Kant: Sensibility, Perception, Reality

Bermúdez, J. L. (1994). 'Peacocke's Argument against the Autonomy of Nonconceptual Content', *Mind and Language*, Vol. 9, No. 4, 402–418.

Bird, G. (1962). *Kant's Theory of Knowledge: An Outline of One Central Argument in the Critique of Pure Reason*. London: Routledge & Kegan Paul.

Braver, L. (2007). *A Thing of This World: A History of Continental Anti-Realism*. Evanston, Illinois: Northwestern University Press.

Campbell, J. (2002). *Reference and Consciousness*. Oxford: Oxford University Press.

Centrone, S. (2010). *Logic and Philosophy of Mathematics in the Early Husserl*. Dordrecht, Heidelberg, London: Springer.

Earman, J. (1991). 'On the Other Hand...: A Reconsideration of Kant, Incongruent Counterparts, and Absolute Space', in: *The Philosophy of Right and Left: Incongruent Counterparts and the Nature of Space*. J. van Cleve, R. E. Frederick (eds.), Vol. 46 of the series *The University of Western Ontario Series in Philosophy of Science*, Dordrecht: Springer Science + Business Media, B. V.

Falkenstein, L. (1990). 'Kant's Account of Sensation', *Canadian Journal of Philosophy*, Vol. 20, No. 1, 63–88.

Guyer, P. (1987). *Kant and the Claims of Knowledge*. Cambridge: Cambridge University Press.

Guyer, P., Horstmann, R. (2015). 'Idealism', *The Stanford Encyclopedia of Philosophy* (Fall 2015 Edition), E. N. Zalta (ed.), URL = https://plato.stanford.edu/entries/idealism/.

Haddock, A. (2009). 'McDowell, Transcendental Philosophy, and Naturalism', *Philosophical Topics*, Vol. 37, No. 1, 63–75.

Hanna, R. (2008). 'Kantian Non-Conceptualism', *Philosophical Studies*, Vol. 137, No. 1, 41–64.

Heidemann, D. (2012). 'Kant and Non-Conceptual Content: The Origin of the Problem', in: *Kant and Non-Conceptual Content*. D. Heidemann (ed.), London, New York: Routledge Chapman Hall.

Hintikka, J. (1969). 'On Kant's Notion of Intuition (*Anschauung*)', in: *The First Critique: Reflections on Kant's Critique of Pure Reason*. T. Penelhum, J. J. Macintosh (eds.), Belmont: Wadsworth Publishing Company.

Janiak, A. (2012). 'Kant's Views on Space and Time', *The Stanford Encyclopedia of Philosophy* (Winter 2012 Edition), E. N. Zalta (ed.), URL = http://plato.stanford.edu/archives/win2012/entries/kant-spacetime/.

Jansen, J. (2014). 'Taking a Transcendental Stance: Anti-representationalism and Direct Realism in Kant and Husserl', in: *Husserl und die Klassische Deutsche Philosophie*. F. Fabbianelli, S. Luft (eds.), Heidelberg, New York, Dordrecht: Springer.

Kemp Smith, N. (1918). *A Commentary to Kant's Critique of Pure Reason*. London: Macmillan and Co.

Longuenesse, B. (1998). *Kant on the Capacity to Judge: Sensibility and Discursivity in the Transcendental Analytic of the Critique of Pure Reason*. Princeton, New Jersey: Princeton University Press.

Luft, S. (2007). 'From Being to Givenness and Back: Some Remarks on the Meaning of Transcendental Idealism in Kant and Husserl', *International Journal of Philosophical Studies*, Vol. 15, No. 3, 367–394.

Kant: Sensibility, Perception, Reality 37

MacDonald, C. (2006). 'Self-Knowledge and Inner Space', in: *McDowell and His Critics*. C. MacDonald, G. MacDonald (eds.), Oxford: Blackwell Publishing.

Merleau-Ponty, M. (2012). *Phenomenology of Perception*. D. A. Landes (transl.), London, New York: Routledge.

Paton, H. J. (1936). *Kant's Metaphysic of Experience: A Commentary on the First Half of the Kritik der Reinen Vernunft*. London: George Allen & Unwin Ltd.

Prauss, G. (1974). *Kant und das Problem der Dinge an sich*. Bonn: Bouvier Verlag Herbert Grundmann.

Rockmore, T. (2007). *Kant and Idealism*. New Haven, Connecticut: Yale University Press.

Stang, N. F. (2016). 'Kant's Transcendental Idealism', *The Stanford Encyclopedia of Philosophy* (Winter 2013 Edition), E. N. Zalta (ed.), URL = https://plato.stanford.edu/entries/kant-transcendental-idealism/.

Strawson, P. F. (1966). *The Bounds of Sense: An Essay on Kant's Critique of Pure Reason*. London: Routledge.

Vaihinger, H. (1884). 'Zu Kants Widerlegung des Idealismus', in: *Straßburger Abhandlungen zur Philosophie*, Akad. Verlagsbuchhandlung, 85–164.

Van Mazijk, C. (2014a). 'Kant, Husserl, McDowell: The Non-Conceptual in Experience', *Diametros*, Vol. 41, 99–114.

Van Mazijk, C. (2014b). 'Why Kant Is a Non-Conceptualist But Is Still Better Regarded a Conceptualist', *Kant Studies Online*, 170–200.

Watkins, E. (2008). 'Kant and the Myth of the Given', *Inquiry*, Vol. 51, No. 5, 512–531.

Westphal, K. R. (2004). *Kant's Transcendental Proof of Realism*. Cambridge, New York, Melbourne: Cambridge University Press.

Williams, G. (2017). 'Kant's Account of Reason', *The Stanford Encyclopedia of Philosophy* (Summer 2018 Edition), E. N. Zalta (ed.), URL = https://plato.stanford.edu/archives/sum2018/entries/kant-reason/.

Wilson, K. D. (1975). 'Kant on Intuition', *The Philosophical Quarterly*, Vol. 25, No. 100, 247–265.

2 Kant
Concepts, Deduction, Debates

The Contents of Intuition and Perception

Chapter Overview

In this chapter, I consider Kant's views on the role the understanding plays in determining the contents of intuition, in light of the question of our access to reality. This involves following in detail the arguments of the A and B versions of the transcendental deduction and the sections leading up to them. I argue that the central thesis Kant sets out to defend here is that intuitions are always already at least in accordance with pure concepts. In the second part, I review the most important arguments for non-conceptual content in Kant literature, and pay considerable attention to Kant's account of obscure representations in the *Anthropology*. In brief, I argue that, for Kant, whatever is sensibly represented to an agent is at least in accordance with certain conceptual rules, which commits him to weak conceptualism. At the same time, Kant accepts that there are mental contents that are not conceptually explicable, in the form of obscure or blind representations, which, however, should bear no relevant epistemic relation to our lives as rational subjects.

Introduction

In Chapter 1, I focused on the Transcendental Aesthetic, which mainly dealt with sensibility and the forms of space and time which Kant believes necessarily underlie any outer intuition. This revealed that our experience of the world must involve taking a concrete position from which to view things. This leaves the rest of my thesis regarding Kant standing: that being directed at reality demands *agents with a shared capacity to determine conceptually whatever is sensibly presented to them in intuitions, and that intuitions are always already in accordance with the rules for such determination, but that they are not exhaustive of sensible representation as such.* To see what this means exactly, we have to turn to the Transcendental Logic in some detail, where the role of understanding is first brought into the picture.

Kant: Concepts, Deduction, Debates   39

In 'On the Clue to the Discovery of All Pure Concepts of Understanding', Kant starts by briefly rehearsing in what respect concepts, produced by understanding, differ from intuitions. One of the defining marks of intuition was that it must rest on affection. That is to say, intuitions are the immediate result of the sensory stimulation of the faculty of sensibility. For this reason, this faculty is said to yield singular and immediate representations. Concepts, on the other hand, are general representations that relate to their object mediately. This characteristic of concepts to be able to subsume particulars under a general header is what Kant now calls the 'function' of concepts (A68/B93). When we bring concepts together in the right way, the understanding can form propositions, which are the vehicles, so to say, of all our knowledge.

To be sure, not any conceivable arrangement of concepts will yield a meaningful proposition. In other words, there is a certain base grammar, or a formal set of rules, to which our thought must comply in order to successfully express anything at all. Kant calls the study of such rules general logic. While general logic thus studies the 'absolute necessary rules of thinking' (A52/B76), this task is of no special interest to philosophers. It must therefore be kept apart from what Kant calls transcendental logic, which he does consider a strictly philosophical enterprise.

It is important to make this distinction between general and transcendental logic clear, as it eventually bears on Kant's theory of perception. The idea of a transcendental logic, on Kant's understanding of it, is linked to his introduction and defense of so-called synthetic a priori cognitions. This idea of synthetic a priori knowledge constitutes Kant's attempt to introduce a notion of absolutely certain knowledge that does not consist plainly of analytic judgments ('A=A', 'all bachelors are unmarried'). One way to understand this is as follows: Kant was so convinced of the adequacy of certain fundamental propositions in natural science (such as 'every event has a cause') that he believed we possess them (and them alone, besides pure mathematics) a priori (see B4–B5). His conviction of this was so strong that he saw no need to quarrel a lot about it. Instead, we only need to ask how it is possible that we possess them.[1]

The a priority of these propositions cannot derive exclusively from the law of non-contradiction as with analytic judgments (see A151/B191). They are, after all, fundamental laws of nature, not just logical truths. One option would be to say that we derive certain concepts (such as causality) from experience, as Hume had done. But that clearly undermines their a priority, and since we need not question that they enjoy that status, this cannot be true (cf. B6; B41; A40/B57; B128).[2] The only option left, Kant thinks, is to say that we possess certain a priori concepts that do not derive from experience, out of which these propositions are construed.

40 *Kant: Concepts, Deduction, Debates*

Kant, then, is led from a very strong belief in synthetic a priori knowledge to assert that we must possess certain pure concepts of understanding. Unlike mere logical concepts, these pure concepts actually say something about the world we experience. That every event has a cause is not an empty formal statement; the world itself abides by it. While it is tempting to say that this would be the case because we derive them from our experiences of the world, Kant thinks we are barred from that explanatory route as it would undermine the a priority of the relevant concepts.

It is this peculiar circumstance that brings Kant to conceive of an altogether new philosophical enterprise, namely that of a transcendental logic. Loosely speaking, this task consists of developing a philosophical account explaining the possibility of pure concepts and their a priori rule over the world as we experience it. To understand how exactly this in turn affects Kant's ideas about the contents of intuition and their capacity to bring the real world into view, it is necessary to explore the transcendental deduction in some detail.

The transcendental deduction is an important part of the transcendental logic, and crucial to Kant's theory of perception. Here, Kant wants to prove (deduction means proof) that the pure concepts of understanding have objective validity, even though they do not for that matter derive from experience. It is important to note that, before advancing to the actual proof, Kant admits to struggle in making the need for this proof apparent. In an attempt to illustrate this need, Kant prepares for his deduction by emphasizing that the pure concepts do not as such make intuition possible in the way space and time do. This is why an extensive proof of the objective validity of space and time was not necessary, since without them, no object can appear altogether. The pure concepts of understanding, on the other hand, are conditions of thought; they are not presupposed a priori in any appearance in the same way time and space are. It is in fact not even possible to use all 12 pure concepts simultaneously in a single intuition or experience.

Therefore, pure concepts, in Kant's view, stand at a certain distance from the world; they are not sine qua non conditions for sensible intuition in the way space and time are. As a result of this, their objective validity requires special proof, under the assumption that they are not derived from experience as Hume had argued.

This simultaneously explains why such a proof is not needed for any empirical concepts. The ordinary concepts of everyday and scientific activity are simply derived from experience. We know that the concept of 'guitar' applies to certain things and not to others because we got the concept from those things (guitars) in the first place. For pure concepts, Kant thinks this must be different, as they cannot be derived from experience. This underlines why a special deduction of pure concepts is indispensable, and why it 'must always be transcendental' (A86/B118).

It can briefly be remarked here that McDowell, in a recent contribution from 2017, appears to misread Kant on this point, which has some implications for how he construes Kant's theory of perception – namely as supportive of strong conceptualism. McDowell seems to say that Kant thinks that sensible intuition requires categories in the same manner in which it requires space and time. As he puts it: 'Kant thinks we can exploit knowledge about the forms of judgments to derive a table of corresponding forms of intuitions'. Therefore, we know that such principles hold, given that they are 'a condition for our experience of objects to be possible' (TFKG 11).

It is not clear whether McDowell uses 'experience' in the Kantian sense (as knowledge) or in his own (as sensible intuition). Either way, however, the idea that Kant derives forms of intuition from the table of judgments is wrong. The point of The Clue to the Discovery of All Pure Concepts of Understanding is, as I showed above, precisely that that claim is *not* true, and that a transcendental proof of the validity of pure concepts is needed for that very reason. In other words, it is because pure concepts are not forms of intuition that their deduction is needed.

Kant insists rather emphatically that the reader first understands this need for a deduction (of the objective validity of pure concepts) before proceeding any further (see A88/B121). To make this need even clearer, Kant even asserts a couple of times that objects could principally appear without the understanding being involved. For instance, he says that 'objects can indeed appear to us without necessarily having to be related to functions of understanding' (A89/B122); that 'appearances can certainly be given in intuition without functions of understanding' (A90/B122); and that 'intuition by no means requires the functions of thinking' (A90–91/B123).

These remarks are easily misunderstood. Kant has, at this point in the first *Critique,* already admitted (at the very beginning of The Clue to the Discovery of All Pure Concepts of Understanding) that he is going to argue later on that there is in fact something involved in intuition which essentially relies on the understanding (A79/B104–105). To show how this works is, moreover, the central aim of the transcendental deduction. We must, therefore, be careful to read these remarks in their context, namely as part of an attempt to convince the reader of the necessity of a deduction. In other words, Kant's insistence at this point that intuitions could do without the understanding serves to make the need for the following deduction apparent but not to establish definitively that intuitions have no need whatsoever of intellectual functions.

General Remarks on Synthesis

The a priori concepts of understanding constitute what Kant believes to be the universally valid foundation of natural science. This picture

42 Kant: Concepts, Deduction, Debates

requires these concepts to apply a priori to experienced reality, as otherwise they would be mere empty concepts. Kant, therefore, needs to show that pure concepts apply to our intuitions, without thereby claiming that the former are derived from the latter. In The Clue to the Discovery of All Pure Concepts of Understanding, Kant introduces a new concept which helps explain this. This is the concept of 'synthesis' (A77/B102).

Synthesis, as briefly touched upon in the previous chapter, is the counterpart of analysis. We use the analytic function of concepts when we make judgments. In this function, concepts are the kind of representations we consciously entertain in forming propositions in judgment, which we do by putting them together in various ways. The idea of synthesis plays a very different role, however. Synthesis, Kant notes, is a matter of 'putting different representations together [...] in one cognition' (A77/B103), and thereby it 'first brings forth a cognition' (A77/B103). Synthesis, therefore, is a special act of the mind of combining or gathering distinct elements, thereby somehow first giving rise to knowledge. Moreover, it is said that 'the same function which gives unity to the different representations *in a judgment* also gives unity to the mere synthesis of different representations *in an intuition*' (A79/B104–105).

This reveals that synthesis refers specifically to the combining or gathering of various sensible representations into an intuition. Moreover, it shows that Kant thinks that the unity which results from this (in the intuition) is the result of the same function which gives unity to representations in a judgment.

It is worth pointing out, however, that Kant is talking about intuition in the act of experience here, and not just about any 'sheer' intuition. By intuition in the act of experience, I mean the perceptual taking that takes place in an act of knowledge acquisition, where one makes a deliberate effort to know the object intuited. By sheer intuition, I mean the simple, passive apprehension of a sensibly given thing, regardless of any epistemic efforts.[3] As noted earlier, Kant introduces the concept of synthesis to address what is to be done with the sensible manifold 'in order for a cognition to be made out of it' (A77/B102). This orientation toward knowledge acquisition (rather than toward sheer intuition) continues throughout the first section of 'The Deduction of the Pure Concepts of Understanding', which is still largely the same in the A and B editions.

The Transcendental Deduction, A-Version Section 2

The chapter 'The Deduction of the Pure Concepts of Understanding' follows a complicated path and it is easy to get lost. It is therefore worthwhile to follow it in some detail here, at least insofar as it contributes to an understanding of Kant's views on the contents of intuition. I will follow the A-deduction first, but later return to the important sections of the B-deduction.

The A-deduction starts with a discussion of three types of synthesis, which Kant drops almost entirely in the B-version. Very generally speaking, Kant maintains that, in order for an act of knowledge to occur, a synthesis must first take place in 'apprehension'. That is to say, in order to apprehend something in sheer intuition, which is not yet a perception (which is defined as sensible representation with consciousness), a manifold of continuously changing data (say visual impressions) has to be combined; 'this manifold ... must first be run through, held together' (A99). After all, the impressions the mind receives change ongoingly as one walks around an object, or even if one stands still (due to the streaming of time). It is of course possible to distinguish various ways in which this kind of synthesis may factually occur, but Kant is only interested in the pure – that is to say, the general – form of any such combination, and this is then generically referred to as synthesis of apprehension.

The second synthesis, again insofar as we are interested in the general form of it, allows for the capacity to recollect or reproduce whatever we may have experienced on another occasion. Kant says very little about this, but what he seems to have in mind concerns the association of an ongoing apprehension with similar past apprehensions, a process which grants things presented in intuition some sort of continuity (see also A121).[4]

Third, and perhaps most importantly, these first two syntheses would be in vain 'without consciousness that that which we think is the very same as what we thought a moment before' (A103). This last act can happen only by a 'unitary consciousness'; it is something 'which only consciousness can impart to it [the content of intuition]'. Kant goes on to reserve a variety of names for this peculiar unity of consciousness – which is itself neither an intuition nor a concept (see Anth 7: 141) – but it is most commonly called (again in its general form) 'transcendental apperception' (A107). The appropriate synthesis that happens on the basis of apperception is called 'synthesis of recognition in a concept' (A103).

All things combined, we need something that '[1] combines the manifold successively intuited, and [2] thereupon also reproduced, [3] into one representation' (A103) for a unitary consciousness. To close this section, it is worth briefly making three general points explicit. First, for Kant (i) all three syntheses concern intuition. That is to say, they are about combining sensible data, the capacity to recollect what is thus combined, and finally the capacity to explicitly recognize that in a concept respectively. Second, (ii) the third synthesis is said to bring a unity into play that can only come from the unity of consciousness which Kant calls apperception. Since Kant admits both that apperception is 'the a priori ground of all concepts' (A107) and that it is a component of understanding (see A119), this unambiguously brings understanding into the discussion about the nature of (at this point at least some) intuitions. Third, (iii) this role of understanding (through apperception) in intuition must (again at this point at least) be understood in the light of knowledge. Kant is quite

44   *Kant: Concepts, Deduction, Debates*

clear about this: 'no cognition can occur in us, no connection and unity among them, without that unity of consciousness' (A107).

It follows that the three syntheses together constitute the transcendental form of knowing an object. But obviously human existence is not exhausted by knowing things. It is thus, again at least at this point in the text, only for knowing something that 'we [must] have effected synthetic unity in the manifold of intuition [namely through the unity of consciousness called apperception]' (A105). This is because without a general unity to what I sensibly apprehend, there can be no correspondence between world and mind (insofar as there's necessarily unity to the concepts in my thought). As Kant puts it, for both sides to 'agree with each other [intuition] must [at least] have that unity that constitutes the concept of an object' (A105), a unity that can only be imparted by apperception.

The Transcendental Deduction, A-Version Section 3

So far, all the way through the second section of the A-deduction, Kant ascertains only that appearances insofar as they are objects of knowledge must stand under a unity which can exclusively be provided by the unity of understanding. This general epistemological orientation is emphasized time and again: 'this unity of consciousness would be impossible if in the *cognition of the manifold* the mind could not become conscious of the identity of the function by means of which this manifold is synthetically combined into one cognition' (A108, my italics); '*in experience* they [appearances] must stand under conditions of the necessary unity of apperception' (A110, my italics); 'this identity must necessarily enter into the synthesis of all the manifold of appearances *insofar as they are to become empirical cognition*' (A113, my italics).

While this serves non-conceptualists well – to this extent that it leaves the question of the role of understanding in sheer intuition unanswered – the tables seem to turn again from A116 onward. While Kant presents section 3, starting at A115, as a kind of recap of the previous sections, it yields a markedly different picture. Kant now says he aims to show that 'intuitions are nothing for us and do not in the least concern us if they cannot be taken up into consciousness' (A116). He continues that representations 'can represent something in me only insofar as they belong with all others to one consciousness, hence they must at least be capable of being connected in it' (A116).

These remarks contain two things of interest. First, Kant again implies that one can in fact speak of intuitions in a way that does not relate them to the unity of consciousness the understanding alone can supply, even though he makes it clear he has little interest in them (they 'dot not in the least concern us'). There is some debate about the role of this idea (of blind or obscure representations) in Kant's philosophy, and I return to this in more detail in the second part of this chapter. Second, Kant now adds to his previous claims a new one: that intuitions as he wishes to speak of them must be *open* to being taken up into thought ('must at least be capable of being so connected').

This seems to entail an important shift with respect to what was said earlier. At the beginning of the deduction, Kant argued that in order to know an object right here and now, I must somehow objectify it, which involves bringing some synthetic unity to the object that I perceive or intuit. In saying this, Kant committed to virtually nothing with regard to the nature of sheer intuition. Now, however, he adds that regardless of whether I aim to know an object right here and now, the intuitions I have of things must *already* bear some relation to the unity of my understanding, a relation whereby I *could* take those intuitions to thought, if they are to mean anything to me. This second suggestion, in contrast to the first, does concern sheer intuition, insofar as it contains a claim about the relation of anything intuited (insofar as it at all concerns me) to a *possible* act of understanding.

It is worth emphasizing that this suggestion does not of itself imply an over-intellectualizion of human intuition. Kant does not say that there must always be an intellectual unity or a 'standing and lasting I' (A123) in all of consciousness. Instead, the relation intuitions bear to the understanding is itself fleshed out in terms of a potentiality. Self-consciousness or the standing I is not involved in all intuitions; there is no active, onlooking subject to whatever we do. Instead, according to Kant, appearances have to be *relatable* to a unitary consciousness, to the I, and the potential to be thus related is what appears to constitute the relevant relation.

This interpretation matches well, I think, the way Kant speaks of apperception. Kant tends to define apperception either in very weak terms, as in saying that it 'may often only be weak' (A103), or again in terms of a potentiality: the 'lasting I (of pure apperception) constitutes the correlate of all our representations, so far as it is merely possible to become conscious of them' (A123). Apperception, then, need not be understood as a permanent, onlooking I; it is rather itself the potential for the I to be awakened; a transcendental potential for becoming actively aware of what is intuited. This means that whatever is in our field of intuition, regardless of any knowledge ambitions, falls under transcendental apperception, taken as a unity of consciousness which makes it possible to become explicitly conscious, as experience (knowledge) requires.

At this point, Kant has established that one can become explicitly conscious of whatever presents itself in intuition, at least insofar as those intuitions would concern one at all. The result of this is that whatever we intuit – including sheer intuition – is open to exercises of thought, because it is relatable to apperception. This still leaves open the question of the applicability of pure concepts to all intuitions insofar as they would

46   *Kant: Concepts, Deduction, Debates*

concern me. This was, after all, the central aim of the deduction – to show that pure concepts have objective validity.

In A119, Kant for the first time clearly appreciates this difference between an involvement of apperception and of pure concepts (this can likewise be found in the B-deduction). In short, Kant seems to claim here that every intuition has a 'necessary relation' to the pure concepts of understanding. This relation guarantees the possibility of the applicability of pure concepts. The question is whether this relation concepts have to intuition is one of a constitutive involvement. Sometimes, Kant seems to suggest only that since any intuition belongs to apperception (again insofar as it concerns us at all), it is likewise possible that these intuitions come under the rule of pure concepts. Kant says this much:

> since this relation of appearances to *possible experience* is likewise necessary (since without it we could not obtain any cognition at all through them, and they would thus not concern us at all), it follows that the pure understanding, by means of the categories, is a formal and synthetic principle of all experiences.
>
> (A119)

In other words, pure concepts can be applied to intuitions in acts of knowledge acquisition (experiences), due to the relation to the I which intuitions have (insofar as they concern us at all).

If this were the full story about the objective validity of the pure concepts, then there would be no need for a necessary role of concepts in intuition. Kant could be read as claiming that because all intuitions (at least insofar as they can concern me) can be related to apperception, anything intuited can be brought under the rule of pure concepts in an experience. It is apperception, then, which guarantees that intuitions have a unity that makes them open to conceptual exercises – but the intuitions themselves do not immediately rely on concepts.

At the same time, however, the fact that sheer intuitions have the appropriate unity to be conceptualized in the first place is said to rest on synthesis of the imagination, which brings intuitions in accordance with pure concepts. Kant calls the aptitude of intuitions to be associable in a manner appropriate as to make them fit the understanding's pure concepts their affinity. This affinity is the result of synthesis, and it belongs not just to the appearance as cognized, but to sensibility itself: 'For in itself the synthesis of imagination, although exercised a priori, is nevertheless always sensible, for it combines the manifold only as it appears in intuition' (A124). Moreover, Kant appears to conclude his discussion saying that this synthesis itself, as it thus occurs in sensibility, 'is grounded' on categories (A125).

While the categories principally concern just the form of experience, therefore of knowledge and not of any sheer intuition, Kant now says that 'all formal unity in the synthesis of the imagination' – and thus also synthesis in sensibility independently of experience – is grounded on categories. This would mean that, at least with regard to intuitions that concern us, pure concepts might after all play an important role in intuition, insofar as they would supply the imagination with the forms of synthesis required to make intuitions open to conceptualization. This means that, although Kant's principal concern in the transcendental deduction clearly is to show that intuitional content is open to conceptualization (weak conceptualism), the A-deduction can be read as defending strong conceptualism as well (the thesis that the contents of intuition or perception are informed by concepts).

It can be concluded that the A-deduction provides a picture most certainly compatible with weak conceptualism, insofar as intuition is open to conceptualization on the basis of apperception and processes of synthesis. This is, I would argue, the main thesis that Kant sets out to defend in transcendental deduction, and by far most of his discussions are oriented at proving this. At the same time, a strong conceptualist reading cannot be excluded. This should suffice to explain the midpart of my main thesis, namely that *intuitions are always already at least in accordance with the rules for determining it*. It should be noted, however, that there might still be obscure or blind sensible contents, which do not concern us as agents in the relevant sense, yet which are subjectively lived through in some manner. I return to this in more detail in the second half of this chapter.

The Transcendental Deduction, Remarks on the B-Version

The second version of the transcendental deduction takes a different path from the first, although it does not seem to yield a fundamentally different picture. This section briefly overviews the relevant changes.

Already in the first paragraph (15) of section 2, Kant introduces some important innovations with respect to the first edition. First, instead of advancing a theory of three types of interrelated syntheses, Kant now introduces only one general form of synthesis. Second, this capacity for synthesis is no longer said to belong to a separate power called imagination. Instead, Kant now simplifies the matter by saying that 'all combination [...] is an action of the understanding' (B130). Third, Kant moves immediately to the unity of apperception. This is because, as he now stipulates, the unity brought to intuition cannot derive from synthesis itself. Instead, the unity that is present in the thing sensibly given to me is 'being added' (B131) to the thing intuitively represented. Kant then clarifies that this unity is not the pure concept of unity, but something 'yet higher' – which brings us straight to the unity of apperception.

As a result of this, the B-deduction succeeds better in showing that the unity of apperception is not to be understood as an active

48   *Kant: Concepts, Deduction, Debates*

self-consciousness, but rather as the unity conditional to the act of reflective self-awareness. As Kant puts it at the opening of section 16, the unity of 'the I think must *be able* to accompany all my representations', and this 'necessary relation' of 'all manifold of intuition [...] to the I think' is explicitly regarded a relation conditional to the actualization of being understandingly aware (see B132). In other words, Kant again denies that there is a strong ego-pole connected to whatever I see. The point is rather that our sensible openness to the world is of such a kind that what this openness provides one with could be actively taken up in thought, and this possibility defines the relation of all intuition to apperception. The point is not that the agent is involved, but that it can get involved.[5]

This again makes it clear that Kant believes even sheer intuition presupposes the capacity to become understandingly aware of what is thus intuited. Whether I'm consciously aware of what I intuit (as would be the case with perception) or not (as in passively gazing at things, practically dealing with them, etc.), whatever I intuit 'presupposes the possibility' (B135) of a thoughtful appreciation. This view, as pertaining to the openness of the contents of sensible intuition to understanding (weak conceptualism), is defended in the A-version as well as the B-version of the deduction. At least the general gist of this idea can also be found in both McDowell and Husserl, as I show in later chapters.

Kant has now established the role of apperception in intuition. However, as in the initial stages of the A-deduction, this leaves the question of the role of pure concepts unanswered. Indeed, the B-version has made it quite clear that the unity found in sheer intuition is not a pure concept. It is rather the unity of apperceptive consciousness, which is the condition under which alone I can become conscious of them with concepts. Kant is consistent on this matter. To be sure, apperception belongs to understanding, and for that reason the understanding is constitutively involved in all intuitions, again at least insofar as these aren't 'less than a dream' (A112) to the agent. The question to consider is whether Kant makes a similar case for the involvement of pure concepts in intuition.

As I argued in the previous section, it is not very obvious that Kant wants to make this strong conceptualist case in the A-deduction; the discussion is throughout oriented at weak conceptualism. At the same time, Kant appeared to conclude that the synthesis in sensibility 'is grounded' on categories (A125), which could point to strong conceptualism.

The B-deduction is, I think, consistent with this. Around section 20 of the B-version, Kant again emphasizes that apperception first makes possible the unity in any (sheer) intuition. Moreover, he asserts that a single 'empirical intuition' is always 'determined' by one of the pure concepts (B143). This remark, however, concerns an act of experience, not just any sheer intuition.[6] Therefore, it does not address the question whether or not a sheer intuition is already determined by concepts, prior to an act of knowledge acquisition.

Kant then goes on to introduce the concept of figurative synthesis (B151), which concerns the a priori synthesis involved in sensibility. The imagination is again responsible for this, which is said to determine the 'form of sense a priori [...] in accordance with the categories' (B152). This, again, establishes weak conceptualism.

It is only in the final sections of the B-deduction that Kant suggests that the synthesis of apprehension in intuition, depends 'on the categories', and that for that reason 'everything that can ever reach empirical consciousness [...] stands under the categories' (B164–165). The final parts of the B-deduction can therefore be taken to suggest that sensible intuition isn't just in accordance with pure concepts, but actually depends on pure concepts, and that this is why the latter have objective validity.

It can be concluded that, in both versions of the deduction, Kant's principal aim is to show that pure concepts apply unconditionally to any intuition (weak conceptualism). Furthermore, this exposition largely relies on the role of apperception in making the contents of intuition accessible to the subject. At the same time, there is, in both versions, some textual support for the view that the openness of intuitions to conceptualization (insofar as they concern us) itself rests on pure concepts.

Before closing this section, it is good to make explicit what both versions of the deduction did not address. First, neither version addressed the question of the role of empirical concepts in intuition or perception. Second, the discussions did not deal with blind plays of representations. While such blind plays of representations were affirmed, they were not deemed of any importance in the present context. I return to this in more detail in the second half of this chapter.

The Broader Picture: What Problem Does Kant's Theory of Perception Address?

The previous sections discussed Kant's views on the contents of intuition in the two versions of transcendental deduction. By and large, the results of these two versions turned out to be similar. Generalizing, Kant maintains that all intuitions – with the possible exception of blind takings, which, however, need 'not in the least concern us' (A116, I return to this in detail later) – are principally relatable to the lasting I (apperception). As a result of this, our intuitions accord, even prior to the activation of thinking capacities, with pure concepts of understanding.

In this section, I want to briefly consider Kant's background motives for endorsing his specific theory of perception. Perhaps especially for phenomenologists, who might be more accustomed to think of mind and world as mutually interacting, it could seem strange that Kant tends

50 *Kant: Concepts, Deduction, Debates*

to speak one-sidedly of the human mind forming objective reality. For instance, Husserl's theory of perception, by way of contrast, is often read as insisting equally on the world's influence on the mind. Moreover, it does not seem to single out apperception or a limited set of pure concepts in shaping the perceived world, as Kant's theory does. It is worth considering these perhaps trivial-sounding concerns here briefly, as they can help explain the shape of Kant's theory of perception.

It would probably be wrong to suggest that Kant simply failed to see the possibility of subject and object interacting in the constitution of an objective world. Kant would have no problem admitting, it seems to me, that we develop pure concepts over time, just as the objective world isn't instantly there when we're born.[7] In order for the objective world to be given in experience, all sorts of social, cultural, or historical conditions may have to be in place. Kant in fact elaborates on this to some extent in his anthropology lectures. Rather than failing to appreciate this, it is more likely that Kant simply did not ascribe any philosophical significance to such conditions.

To see why, we have to turn to Kant's understanding of science. In short, Kant operates, by today's standards, with a limited conception of knowledge, which restricts it to exact knowledge of a spatiotemporal manifold. Importantly, his explanation of how the understanding makes experience possible by determining manifolds of intuition a priori is constrained by this conception. In accepting a certain limited idea of science, Kant has no motivation to develop a theory of intuition beyond concerns about how pure concepts (forming the foundation of that idea of science) could accord with intuition. Kant's picture of science, therefore, shapes his transcendental theory of perception. This is also why, by way of comparison, Husserl's transcendental theory of perception can take a very different shape. For him, science does not exclusively evolve around physics and mathematics, but includes the social and cultural sciences.

It should further be pointed out that Kant, in his transcendental inquiry, operates with a concept of a priori that fits this understanding of knowledge. In short, Kant's discovery of the a priori forms of sensibility and understanding (in his so-called metaphysical expositions) can be said to rely on a method of formalization. To discover space and time, for instance, he suggests that we abstract from all intuitive contents, such as 'pleasure and displeasure, of desires and inclinations', and also all 'sensations of colors, sounds, and warmth' (B29, B45). This way, by abstracting from contents, we allegedly discover the necessary forms of intuition.

Kant's motivation for this strategy derives from the fact that he conceives of contents in general as empirical and a posteriori. A priori elements, on the other hand, must be formal. Kant, then, appears to models his concept of a priori on mathematics, insofar as he has a

Kant: Concepts, Deduction, Debates 51

formal understanding of a priori.[8] This, however, greatly narrows the kind of results his transcendental investigation could yield. By excludes all contents of experience, Kant's theory of perception is restricted to determining the necessary forms of perception insofar as they contribute to knowledge acquisition.

It is interesting to note that Husserl criticized Kant precisely for this mathematically inspired concept of a priori. Moreover, the great differences between their respective theories of perception can, in my view, largely be said to follow from this particular dispute. I return to this in more detail in Chapter 3.

Kant and Contemporary Debates

Empirical or Category Conceptualism?

The reading of Kant I offered so far highlighted a number of conceptualist aspects of his philosophy of perception. These all concerned either apperception or pure concepts. The majority of conceptualists in the Kant debate are, indeed, what we might call (weak or strong) category (or pure concept) conceptualists. This includes to my estimation, albeit in strongly varying ways, Longuenesse (1998, 50; 2005, 23–24, 41); Allison (2004, 193–197); Ginsborg (2008, 69), and Griffith (2010, 201–203), among many others. On the other end of the spectrum, there are Kantian non-conceptualist, to which the remainder of this chapter is devoted.

Before turning to non-conceptualism, category conceptualism can be contrasted to something we may call empirical conceptualism. Rosenberg (2005) is a proponent of empirical conceptualism: the view that all empirical concepts have a synthetic function with regard to our intuitions. This means that in, say, seeing a book, the concept of a book – for Kant an empirical concept acquired through experience – serves as the rule for synthesis (Rosenberg 2005, 129).[9]

Rosenberg might be right in extending the synthetic role of concepts in perception to empirical ones. However, it is certain that if they do play such a role, this won't have any transcendental significance for Kant, as these concepts are derived from experience. Consequently, Kant has no compelling reason to prove empirical conceptualism, which is, presumably, why he says very little about it.

Reasons to Think Intuition and Perception have Non-Conceptual Content

There is an abundance of literature on Kantian non-conceptualism, and it would be futile to try to provide an overview of all of it here. That being said, it would naturally be of interest to consider the most influential

52 *Kant: Concepts, Deduction, Debates*

cases and to judge how convincing they are. Contemporary arguments for non-conceptual content can, I think, be brought down to roughly four types. I have given these my own names here:

1 *The Independency Thesis,* according to which Kant's remarks that intuitions can present objects without the involvement of concepts serve as evidence that intuitions are or can be non-conceptual
2 *The Argument from Blind Intuitions,* according to which Kant's remarks that there are special representational contents which are 'less than a dream' (A112) and which mean 'nothing for us' (A120) supports the idea of non-conceptual content
3 *The Argument from Anthropology,* which refers to Kant's anthropological work and his remarks there on obscure representations to support non-conceptual content
4 *The Argument from Incongruent Counterparts,* according to which Kant's pre-critical work reveals his commitment to non-conceptual content.

The Independency Thesis

Some authors, including Allais (2009) and Hanna (2008, 2011a, 2011b, 2015), insist on the possibility of being presented with objects independently of functions of understanding being involved. Allais (2009), for instance, asserts that 'categories are necessary for anything to be an object for me' but not 'for me to be perceptually presented by a particular' (Allais 2009, 405). Related to this, many scholars have claimed that Kant only wants to suggest that experience (knowledge) requires concepts, whereas an act of intuition is certainly possible on its own (Hanna 2008; Grüne 2009, 2011; and De Sá Pereira 2013 among many others). This kind of claim is usually based on Kant's remarks that 'objects are therefore *given* to us by means of sensibility, and it alone affords us *intuitions*' (A19/B33); that 'objects can indeed appear to us without necessarily having to be related to the functions of the understanding' (A89/B122); and that 'appearances would nonetheless offer objects to our intuition, for intuition by no means requires the functions of thinking' (A90/B123).

It is important to appreciate the contexts within which Kant expresses sympathy for the Independency Thesis. The first quote appears right at the opening of the Transcendental Aesthetic, where Kant is briefly rehearsing his theory of two distinct sources of knowledge, in order to then venture an investigation into the a priori operations of sensibility (the Transcendental Aesthetic). It is not implausible to understand the Independency Thesis here as a way to justify the procedure of the upcoming investigation: namely to isolate the faculty of sensibility to discover its pure forms.

As to the other fragments, they are most likely part of Kant's strategy to convince the reader of the need for a special proof of the objective validity of pure concepts (the transcendental deduction). Kant insists that intuitions could do without functions of understanding because he wants the reader to understand the need for the proof he is about to offer. This means that Kant's suggestion here that intuition gives us objects without the understanding could still be compatible with the later suggestion that even the synthetic unity of intuition would be 'grounded' (A125) in pure concepts. Put differently, Kant first emphasizes the need for the deduction by saying that intuitions do not depend on concepts, while the result of the deduction actually reveals that they do depend on concepts.

Consequently, the Independency Thesis, to the extent that it is based on fragments which plausibly serve to support the need for a deduction, should not need to convince us of Kantian non-conceptualism. At the same time, a I argued previously, there is also limited textual support for strong conceptualism. In my view, it should at the very least be granted that, for Kant, the contents of intuition are all open to conceptualization. If that is a sufficient condition to call a concept conceptual, then intuition for Kant has conceptual content.[10]

The Argument from Blind Intuitions and Kant's Anthropology

While the first *Critique* may not offer conclusive textual evidence on the matter, the frequency with which Kant speaks of blind plays of representations warrants taking the idea seriously. Rather than referring to nothing at all, it seems likely that Kant maintains that it is possible for mental contents to be fragmented and unconnected in such a way that they amount to little more than a 'blind play of representations, i.e., less than a dream' (A112). This does not mean that they give us objects. To the contrary, the alleged blindness of these representations serves to indicate that no objects are being represented in them.

The first *Critique* can, in my view, be taken to suggest that there are indeed blind plays of representations. At the same time, Kant indicates that these are irrelevant at least from a transcendental viewpoint. This is, presumably, why Kant says that they are 'nothing for me' (B132), by which he then means that they are nothing for the knowing subject. Put differently, Kant seems to think that blind plays of representations could exist as conscious contents, but that such contents lack any epistemic efficacy. If this is true, as I think it is, then Kant's account of blind plays of representations may not be that far removed from McDowell's *Mind and World*, where McDowell likewise accepts blind or non-conceptual representations at a psychological level.[11]

However, and fortunately, there is more Kant says about the issue elsewhere, namely in *Anthropology from a Pragmatic Point of View*.

54   *Kant: Concepts, Deduction, Debates*

Here, Kant makes a threefold distinction between clear, distinct, and obscure representations, and correlatively between clarity, distinctness, and obscurity in intending something. Clarity is defined as 'consciousness of one's representations that suffices for the distinction of one object from another' (Anth 7: 137–138). This seems to include perception and ordinary cases of intuition, which provide us with distinguishable objects. Distinctness, on the other hand, is 'that consciousness by means of which the *composition* of representations also becomes clear' (Anth 7: 138). Distinctness, then, is reserved for acts of knowing, namely for the propositional articulation that occurs in experience – whereas intuition and perception principally cannot go beyond clarity, insofar as they cannot contain acts of propositional articulation within themselves.

So what about obscurity? Kant starts his discussion of obscure representations by noting that 'a contradiction appears to lie in the claim *to have representations and still not be conscious of them,* for how could we know that we have them if we are not conscious of them?' (Anth 7: 135). Kant goes on to straightforwardly affirm the existence of such representations, because 'even if we are not directly conscious of it', 'we can still be *indirectly* conscious of having a representation' (Anth 7: 135). Kant, in other words, asserts that there are representations of which we are not conscious in any pregnant sense, even though we can still intend them indirectly.

Kant subsequently divides the concept of obscure representations into two types: 'the field of sensuous intuitions' and 'sensations of which we are not conscious' or 'plays of sensations' (Anth 7: 135). Although it is not very explicitly drawn out in the text, it is plausible that Kant considered these as two separate types of obscure representations. Interestingly, the latter concept of 'plays of sensations' seems to match well the discussions of blind plays of representations in the first *Critique*. Although there is no mention of obscure representations there, it is possible that Kant considers them to belong to this category of obscure plays of sensations.

It is worth briefly considering the examples Kant gives of obscure representations, as they offer some valuable insight into what he means by them. One of the most striking examples Kant discusses concerns seeing a well-dressed man. In this case, Kant notes it is possible that the 'understanding still cannot prevent the impression that a well-dressed person makes of obscure representations of a certain importance' (Anth 7: 137). Kant here says that, on the basis of someone's visual appearance, we tend to instantly apperceive things like intelligence, social class, or importance. Importantly, these accomplishments are still, in phenomenological parlor, intentional: I see the other man *as* belonging to a certain social class. We should therefore understand this as an example of what Kant earlier called obscure 'sensuous intuitions' – insofar as we still have an intuition here as an intentional act, albeit an obscure one.

Kant: Concepts, Deduction, Debates   55

But Kant also gives examples of 'plays of sensations' of which we likewise are not conscious in the pregnant sense. His best example of this is what he calls 'sexual love' (Anth 7: 136). By this he appears to mean sexual intercourse insofar as it is pursued for the sake of pleasure. We should interpret Kant as saying here that in enjoying sexual love, we experience all sorts of pleasing sensations of which we aren't directly (intentionally) conscious. It is worth drawing out that this is a structurally different accomplishment of sensibility than having an obscure sensuous intuition. This is because the latter alone is an intentional accomplishment: I see the man *as* someone of a certain social standing, even when I am not consciously aware of it. In having sexual love, however, I don't see anything *as* pleasing. This is because what is enjoyable here is not some attribute of a person or other; it is the blind 'play of sensations' itself that is found pleasing. Kant affirms this explicitly in noting that in sexual love, the 'power of imagination enjoys walking in the dark' (Anth 7: 136); in other words, what we find pleasing is the blind play of sensations itself.

There is a third, more complicated example Kant gives us, which is of a musician who 'plays a fantasy on the organ with ten fingers and both feet and also speaks with someone standing next to him' (Anth 7: 136). Here we can assert first of all that, insofar as the musician is any good, an enjoyable play of representations as in the case of sexual intercourse is likely to be involved. Yet, at the same time, the activities here are of a significantly more intellectual sort. The musical performance might be skillfully and unreflectively performed by this 'freely improvising musician' (Anth 7: 136); still the whole thing stands 'in need of a special judgment as to its appropriateness, since a single stroke of the finger not in accordance with the harmony would immediately be heard as discordant sound' (Anth 7: 136).

This reminds of McDowell, who in his reply to Dreyfus's example of the skilled chess player notes that 'cultivated rationality [...] is also operative in his [the chess master's] being drawn to make his move by the forces on the board' (MMD 48). Like McDowell in the chess example, Kant acknowledges the rational component of what's going on in the musical improvisation. While the musician could never 'hope to bring off so well' (Anth 7: 136) had he thought the whole piece through beforehand, the performance is still a distinctively rational one.

We can conclude from this example that musical improvisation includes both obscure sensations as well as obscure sensuous intuitions. The more urgent question remains, however, whether these classes of obscure representations can be called non-conceptual. As regards the sensuous intuitions, these seem to be at least potentially conceptual in two relevant senses: they could be rationally informed (strong conceptualism) as well as open to being conceptually articulated (weak conceptualism). That sensuous intuitions are at least potentially rationally

56   *Kant: Concepts, Deduction, Debates*

informed is indicated by the fact that improvising music stands 'in need of a special judgment as to its appropriateness' (Anth 7: 136). In other words, improvisation requires training; it is not a dumb activity. As to the second claim, Kant seems to think that obscure sensuous intuitions are open to rationality: it is possible for the understanding to 'have the resolution afterwards to correct' (Anth 7: 137) the initial obscure intuitive representation. This means, for instance, that if I realize later that the well-dressed person is a phony, I can correct the initial representation. This kind of retroactive correction is also important to McDowell's idea of conceptual content in *Mind and World*, as it would signify that the initial representation was already within the so-called space of reasons.

So what about obscure plays of sensations? It is worth noting that while obscure sensations may also involve a kind of evaluative component (pleasing, painful, etc.), these do not seem to be open to retroactive modification in the same way. I cannot retroactively determine an orgasm to be unpleasing in the way I can retroactively determine the other person to merely pretend to belong to a certain class. This is because in the case of obscure sensations only, the evaluative component is not due to rational or intentional activity, but precisely inheres in the obscurity of the sensations itself (the imagination enjoys its very own 'walking in the dark'). This makes obscure sensations of a different kind, one which, even though perhaps containing an evaluative component, doesn't seem to be guided by rationality or open to rational scrutiny in the same way obscure sensuous intuitions are.

If this is correct, it raises the question of how to understand the epistemic status of such contents. If they are non-conceptual yet epistemically efficacious, this could commit Kant to a version of the myth of the given, at least in McDowell's understanding of it. This is because, as McDowell notes in *Mind and World*, it could mean to understand 'the contentfulness of our thoughts and conscious experiences [...] as a welling-up to the surface of some of the content that a good psychological theory would attribute to goings-on in our cognitive machinery' (MW 55). In other words, if Kant understands such contents psychologically and non-conceptually while also deeming them epistemically efficacious, he has thereby given these sensations an equal footing in two distinct realms, namely of natural fact and reason.

It is interesting to note, however, that Kant seems to explicitly rule out such an interpretation. This is what he says: 'because this field can only be perceived in his [the agent's] passive side as a play of sensations, the theory of obscure representations belongs only to physiological anthropology' (Anth 7: 136). Kant is thus far from allowing blind plays of sensations to play a role in his transcendental theory of knowledge, as was also made clear in the first *Critique*, where they were consistently acknowledged yet deemed of no importance. The *Anthropology*, then, makes it even clearer that Kant doesn't allow them a meaningful place in a philosophical theory of perception, and instead expels them to the realm of physiological fact.

Still, this seems to put blind plays of sensations in a remarkable position. On the one hand, Kant admits that we have these representations; we experience (in the sense of living through) them subjectively. But at the same time, he appears to regard them as belonging to a realm of natural explanation, and he avoids sketching linkages between such natural occurrences and our epistemic lives. Kant, therefore, seems to see no problem in dividing the subjective mental life into two halves between which there is no communication.[12]

To conclude: Kant's *Anthropology* sheds new light on his theory of blind intuitions and blind plays of representations in the first *Critique*. First, it can now be concluded that Kant affirms the existence of blind plays of representations. He in fact says that the field of obscure representations is 'immense', and even 'the largest [of all fields] in the human being' (Anth 7: 135). This effectively establishes the remainder of my main thesis: that while all sensible intake that bears a possible relation to us as agents can be conceptually explicated, *such presentation does not exhaust sensible presentation as such*. Second, we can conclude that, while acknowledging such contents, Kant makes an effort to avoid construing them as epistemically efficacious, thereby avoiding McDowell's myth of the given. While obscure sensuous intuitions can be both informed by and open to rationality (their obscure character rather derives from our peculiar indirect awareness of them), obscure plays of sensations are not – but they are regarded a concern for physiology only.

The Argument from Incongruent Counterparts

Hanna (2008) and others have argued that Kant commits to something Hanna calls 'essentially non-conceptual content'. The idea is this: since it is logically conceivable that every intuited object has an actual or possible incongruent counterpart, and since incongruent counterparts cannot be differentiated on conceptual grounds alone, every intuition must involve non-conceptual content. Therefore, as Hanna (2008), Allais (2009), and Heidemann (2012) among others claim, Kant cannot have been a conceptualist about the content of intuition.

As I showed previously, if conceptualism means either ascribing to concepts a determining role in structuring perceptual content (strong conceptualism) or regarding perceptual content open to conceptualization (weak conceptualism), then Hanna's argument seems to fall short. Kant's point in his discussion of incongruent counterparts was that the contents of experience cannot be addressed by someone with only conceptual capacities. This excludes neither that the intuition's content could be conceptualized by someone who does have both stems of knowledge nor that the intuition's content would be conceptually informed. As I showed in Chapter 1, the only thing Kant suggests is that the contents

58 Kant: Concepts, Deduction, Debates

of intuition presuppose an extra-conceptual basis; namely a concrete, spatiotemporal point of orientation.

Consequently, Kant's argument does not indicate the existence of non-conceptual content. It does, however, suffice to make claim to state non-conceptualism. The distinction between state and content non-conceptualism was first drawn by Heck (2000). On account of the state/content distinction, we can say that the contents of perception are conceptually regulated, while a perceptual state, unlike a belief state, involves a non-conceptual condition (namely a point of orientation). This distinction allows us to appreciate Kant's original contribution in terms of a non-conceptual faculty of sensibility, without thereby contradicting the main claim of the transcendental deduction (weak conceptualism).

Concluding Remarks

In Chapters 1 and 2, I analyzed Kant's views on the relations between perception, thought, and reality. Chapter 1 focused mainly on two points: why Kant believed human knowledge consists of two separate sources, and how Kant accounted for direct realism within transcendental idealism. In the second chapter, I discussed what the contents of intuition must be like to successfully accomplish a sense of being in touch with reality. The picture that resulted from this suggests that reality as we determine it in life and science is one that is never altogether remote from us as agents. An objective world can have meaning only, can exist only, as a world for self-identical consciousness. It is, I argued, an achievement which rests on *spatiotemporally orienting agents with a shared capacity to determine conceptually whatever is sensibly presented to them in intuitions, and these intuitions are always already in accordance with the rules for such determination, but they are not exhaustive of sensible representation as such.*

Notes

1 For instance: 'I need not insist upon the fact that, for instance, the concept of cause involves the character of necessity, which no experience can yield' (A112). This is taken from N. K. Smith's translation; the Cambridge version translates as 'I will not mention that', which seems less accurate.

2 Here are four examples of this: (i) 'thus convinced by the necessity with which this concept [of substance as an a priori concept] presses itself upon you, you must concede that it has its seat in your faculty of cognition a priori' (B6); (ii) locating these forms in us is 'alone makes the possibility of geometry as a synthetic a priori cognition comprehensible' (B41); (iii) 'since they [absolute realists about space and time] must dispute the validity or at least the apodictic certainty of a priori mathematical doctrines [...] they can neither offer any ground for the possibility of a priori mathematical cognitions [...] nor can they bring the propositions of experience into necessary accord with those assertions' (A40/B57); (iv) in reply to Hume's theory of

Kant: Concepts, Deduction, Debates 59

habit, Kant says that it plainly 'cannot be reconciled with the reality of the scientific cognition a priori that we possess, that namely of pure mathematics and general natural science; and is therefore refuted by fact' (B128).

3 A sheer intuition, then, as I speak of it, is not a perception, as the latter is defined by Kant as sensible representation with consciousness.

4 If this is correct, then it means there might be a significant amount of overlap between this type of synthesis and Husserl's concept of 'type', which I discuss in Chapter 4. I also touch on this in Van Mazijk (2016a, 2016b).

5 Kant says exactly this much:

> the manifold of representations that are given in a certain intuition would not altogether be *my* representations if they did not all together belong to a self-consciousness; i.e. as my representations (*even if I am not conscious of them as such*) they must yet necessarily be *in accord with the condition under which alone they can stand together* in a universal self-consciousness.
>
> (B132 my italics)

6 This is clear from Kant's emphasis that this intuition is one 'that I call mine' and that it is the 'empirical consciousness of [...] one [*einer*] intuition' (B144).

7 Longuenesse (2005) offers an illuminating reading of the pure concepts not as innate products but as 'originally acquired' concepts (in contrast to derivatively acquired empirical concepts). On this reading, the 'categories are *generated* [...] only under empirical conditions, but their content is determined independently of these empirical conditions' (Longuenesse 2005, 29 my italics).

8 This is, as I proposed elsewhere, what Husserl has in mind when, in lectures from 1923 to 1924, he refers to Kant's method of abstraction as 'peculiar' (EP I 212) or when, in *Crisis* from the 1930s, he calls Kant's conception of a priori evidence 'mythical' and 'ungraspable' (Crisis 114–118). The best illustration of the point is found in lectures from 1908, however:

> Kant confuses the knowledge which subjectivity produces out of itself by considering its own functioning – which [for Kant] is a priori just insofar as it has nothing to do with the nature of the materials which 'come from without' – with a priori knowledge in the genuine sense. [For Kant,] to refer back to the materials of sensations is to know a posteriori.
>
> (EP II 364)

I return in more detail to Husserl's criticism of Kant in the following chapter, but see also Van Mazijk (2019) for a more detailed exposition.

9 Rosenberg seems to come to this position partially on the basis of Kant's example of perceiving a house in the transcendental deduction. Rosenberg thinks that Kant claims that 'the non-perspectival concept 'house' [...] functions as a rule guiding the construction of the perspectival image' (Rosenberg 2005, 130). As an interpretation of the relevant fragment, this reading might be misleading, given that the house-example originally referred to the synthetic role of the pure concept of quantity.

10 Whether or not this should be considered a sufficient condition for calling a content conceptual is discussed in Chapter 5.

11 We should not conflate the 'respectable theoretical role non-conceptual content has in cognitive psychology [...] [with] the notion of content that belongs with the capacities exercised in active self-conscious thinking' (MW 55).

12 On this point, Husserl's transcendental theory differs from Kant's, as I show in detail in the next chapter.

References

Allais, L. (2009). 'Kant, Non-Conceptual Content and the Representation of Space', *Journal of the History of Philosophy*, Vol. 47, No. 3, 383–413.

Allison, H. E. (2004). *Kant's Transcendental Idealism: An Interpretation and Defense*. New Haven, Connecticut, London: Yale University Press.

De Sá Pereira, R. H. (2013). 'What Is Non-Conceptualism in Kant's Philosophy?' *Philosophical Studies*, Vol. 164, No. 1, 233–254.

Ginsborg, H. (2008). 'Was Kant a nonconceptualist?' *Philosophical Studies*, Vol. 137, 65–77.

Griffith, A. M. (2010). 'Perception and the Categories: A Conceptualist Reading of Kant's *Critique of Pure Reason*', *European Journal of Philosophy*, Vol. 20, No. 2, 193–222.

Grüne, S. (2009). *Blinde Anschauung: Die Rolle von Begriffen in Kants Theorie sinnlicher Synthesis*. Frankfurt am Main: Klostermann.

Grüne, S. (2011). 'Is There a Gap in Kant's B-Deduction?' *International Journal of Philosophical Studies*, Vol. 9, No. 3, 465–490.

Hanna, R. (2008). 'Kantian Non-Conceptualism', *Philosophical Studies*, Vol. 137, No. 1, 41–64.

Hanna, R. (2011a). 'Beyond the Myth of the Myth: A Kantian Theory of Non-Conceptual Content', *International Journal of Philosophical Studies*, Vol. 19, No. 3, 323–398.

Hanna, R. (2011b). 'Kant's Non-Conceptualism, Rogue Objects, and the Gap in the B-Deduction', *International Journal of Philosophical Studies*, Vol. 19, No. 3, 399–415.

Hanna, R. (2015). *Cognition, Content, and the A Priori: A Study in the Philosophy of Mind and Knowledge*. Oxford: Oxford University Press.

Heck, R. J. (2000). 'Non-Conceptual Content and the 'Space of Reasons'', *Philosophical Review*, Vol. 109, No. 4, 483–523.

Heidemann, D. (2012). 'Kant and Non-Conceptual Content: The Origin of the Problem', in: *Kant and Non-Conceptual Content*, D. Heidemann (ed.), London, New York: Routledge Chapman Hall.

Longuenesse, B. (1998). *Kant on the Capacity to Judge: Sensibility and Discursivity in the Transcendental Analytic of the Critique of Pure Reason*. Princeton, New Jersey: Princeton University Press.

Longuenesse, B. (2005). *Kant on the Human Standpoint*. Cambridge: Cambridge University Press.

Rosenberg, J. F. (2005). *Accessing Kant: A Relaxed Introduction to the Critique of Pure Reason*. Oxford: Oxford University Press.

Van Mazijk, C. (2016a). 'Kant and Husserl on the Contents of Perception', *Southern Journal of Philosophy*, Vol. 54, No. 2, 276–287.

Van Mazijk, C. (2016b). 'Kant and Husserl on Bringing Perception to Judgment', *Meta: Research in Hermeneutics, Phenomenology, and Practical Philosophy*, Vol. 8, No. 2, 419–441.

Van Mazijk, C. (2019). 'Husserl's Covert Critique of Kant in the Sixth Book of *Logical Investigations*', *Continental Philosophy Review*, Vol. 52, No. 1, 15–33.

3 Husserl
Intentionality, Consciousness, Nature

Intentionality and Fulfillment

Chapter Overviews

Unlike Kant and the neo-Kantians of the late 19th century, Husserl based his early theories of perception and knowledge in *Logical Investigations* (LI) on a Brentanian concept of intentionality. The first part of this chapter discusses the basics of these theories as well as the new picture of belief justification it yields, which involves overthrowing key facets of Kant's philosophy, as well as committing to the idea that intuitive acts necessarily involve extra-conceptual content. In the second part, I turn to Husserl's mature efforts to demarcate what I call the 'space of consciousness' as opposed to a space of nature, arguably the central concern of Husserl's thinking. I argue that these two spaces do not refer to distinct tracts of reality; they are instead to be understood as comprising of the same totality of things considered from two different perspectives. The picture this yields was, I illustrate, knowingly posited by Husserl as an alternative to attempts to draw a line 'within' consciousness, exemplified in Husserl's time in different ways by Kantian philosophy and naturalistic psychology, and with more recent parallels in the works of certain Pittsburgh philosophers including McDowell, or so I argue. In the final sections, I turn to Husserl's discussion of Descartes and his critique of idealism, a discussion which bears similarity to the one on Kant in Chapter 1, although, as I show, there are a few important differences.

The Intentional Approach to Consciousness

Husserl published his *LI* in two volumes in 1900 and 1901. The first book contains Husserl's rejection of psychologism – a then prevalent view that universal laws can be reduced to empirical-psychological facts – and it exerted considerable influence on early 20th century philosophy. This rejection of psychologism did not, however, stop Husserl from returning to the theme of consciousness in the final two books of the second volume, which are now often considered the most important.

62   *Husserl: Intentionality, Consciousness, Nature*

As stated at the opening of the penultimate (the fifth) book, meaning and objectivity, central to all scientific activity, are essentially brought about in or through intentional acts of consciousness. Moreover, Husserl believes that knowledge acquisition has to be explained on the basis of the coinciding of different types of intentional acts. But in order to understand how that works, a more general understanding of the intentionality of consciousness is needed first. That is to say, a general framework for thinking about intentionality needs to be developed. The fifth book provides some essential first steps toward this, and it is useful to follow its general outline here briefly.

Intentionality, as Husserl defines it, is an 'important class within the sphere of psychic experiences' (LI 353).[1] At least two things can be taken from this definition. First, intentionality is said to apply to 'psychic experiences', by which Husserl does not mean psychological states construed as a realm of causal facts, but rather something like our first person, consciously lived experiences (the exact demarcation of these spheres is a central concern of the mature Husserl, as I discuss later on). Second, intentionality is said to refer to an 'important class' within the totality of our consciously lived experiences. It is not, then, exhaustive of consciousness as a whole. Instead, it captures an essential part of our conscious lives, namely that through which things in the broadest sense can be said to be given to us.

Things, then, are given to us through intentional experiences (also called intentional acts; these are synonymous). This does not mean, however, that it is necessary for an intentional experience that an object is actually given in it. An act can also intend an object that does not exist (as in hallucination). It can also intend an indefinite or unspecified object (as is the case with instincts or dark longings, as I discuss further on). Intentionality does not, then, depend on the actual existence of the object; it is not defined as a real relation to an object. For Husserl, all intentional acts must at least involve *directedness toward* something. But the real object at which it is directed is not a constituent of the intentional structure. Instead, it is only the 'directedness toward' that defines intentionality (this matches what is today called an aspect view, rather than a relational view).[2]

It is typical of the Husserl of *LI* to identify phenomenological consciousness with all that is said to be 'really' (*reell*) inherent in consciousness. This concept of 'real inherence' functions differently than the English word 'real'. At no point is the empirically real structure of consciousness at stake in Husserl's phenomenology. Instead, real inherence denotes a certain way in which to speak of contents of consciousness, pointing to those contents that are 'immanent', in other words lived through, as opposed to the objects at which acts can be directed, which are (experienced as) transcendent (as opposed to immanent) to consciousness. Phenomenology, then, studies different types of intentional acts – of consciousness's comportment toward things – but it doesn't study the objects which consciousness is directed at (see LI 358, 427). Those are studied by the sciences. This is why *LI* is often read as neutral with regard to questions of realism. Put differently, to study consciousness phenomenologically should clarify the structure of knowledge and our access to reality, but not reality itself, which is left to the sciences.

In order to understand Husserl's theory of belief justification and the role of perceptual experience therein, it is useful to briefly overview the core components of Husserl's theory of intentionality first. To this end, we can observe first that there are many different ways in which we can be intentionally directed at things. The same object can be the target of different types of acts, as in judging, seeing, remembering, or wishing for the same state of affairs. In *LI*, Husserl exploits these differences in terms of act-quality. The act-quality can be characterized generally as the way of intending something. So in perceiving or wishing for a cup of coffee on one's desk, different act-qualities establish the same object-relation in different ways.[3]

In section 16 and onward, Husserl introduces another element into the intentional structure, which functions as a counterpart to the act-quality: the so-called matter. The notion of matter is important as it helps accounting for object-constancy over different act-qualities. For instance, I can desire or dislike one and the same object. That is to say, two act-qualities can have the same matter understood as object-reference.

But it is also possible, Husserl notes, that two acts relate to the same object while having different matters (see LI 497). The concept of matter is thus wider than the determination of object-reference, since one object-reference can involve different matters. Husserl makes this point to account for the fact that, for instance, the judgments 'Elvis Presley was born in Mississippi' and 'the King of Rock and Roll was born in Mississippi' have the same object-reference, yet have different contents. Something similar, we can observe, must be the case in an act of perceiving. I can have an ongoing perception of a table as I walk around it, thus having one object-reference throughout – yet the way in which the table is given changes continuously as I walk around it (it is given from different sides, in changing lights, etc.). Clearly this isn't due to act-quality, as the acts are of the same type (assertions about Elvis and perceptions of the table), and also not by object-reference, as the object remains stable. Husserl therefore distinguishes within matter the object-reference from the wider (Fregean, one could say) sense, which includes the definite ways in which the object is given, or the object in the how of its givenness (see LI 429–430, 497; Ideas I 314–316). I will reserve the term matter for the wider notion here, and refer to the other component simply as object-reference.

Together, quality, object-reference, and matter form the basic elements of Husserl's theory of intentionality. This model is very similar to

64 *Husserl: Intentionality, Consciousness, Nature*

Crane's more recently developed theory, called impure intentionalism.[4] However, while Crane considers his three-partite theory to adequately cover 'all mental phenomena' (Crane 2009, 474), Husserl goes on to specify other elements of the intentional structure as well, and furthermore develops a theory of knowledge on the basis of that. I turn to these topics in the following sections.

On Sensation Contents

Husserl's account of intentional acts in terms of quality, matter, and object-directedness can be regarded the basics of his theory of intentionality. We find the same basic divides exploited in *Ideas I* in terms of noesis and noema. The noesis here includes the act-quality among others, while the noema can refer to the object in the how of its givenness (the Fregean sense) as well as object-reference.

Yet, unlike Crane's more recent model, Husserl introduces a number of further distinctions within the intentional structure of consciousness. One of these is particularly worth surveying briefly: the sensation contents. Sensations are, Husserl maintains, 'totally different' (LI 396) from the object intended *as well as* the act's intentional directedness. We can start with how they differ from the object first. Objects, as we saw already, are given to us as transcendent to the conscious state that gives them. This likewise holds for qualities of objects, such as 'red', 'heavy', or 'loud'. To refer to the quality of red that belongs to the object as the sensation would be to conflate what Byrne more recently called sensible and sensory qualities (Byrne 2009, 272).[5] In other words, according to Husserl (and Byrne), there is a difference between the color red as perceived property of an object and the color red as an impressing datum. When Husserl speaks of sensation (compare hyle in *Ideas I*),[6] he thereby means the impressing datum which is immanent to consciousness, not the represented property of the object transcendently intended.

This apparent doubling of the term 'red' could perhaps lead to skepticism about whether it is necessary to posit special sensation (or hyletic) contents altogether. For one, in reflecting on an ongoing perception of a red apple, does one really find something other than the redness that is a property of the represented apple? Is there an additional sensation-datum which is not represented but nevertheless part of consciousness in another sense? Those today who adhere to the so-called transparency thesis – roughly the idea that introspection reveals nothing more to us than intentional contents, thus making a description of consciousness exhaustible in terms of its represented contents – would argue so.[7] Given the prominence of the transparency thesis in contemporary debates, it would seem the burden of proof is on those who believe phenomenological description does reveal something like immanent sensation data.

A number of more recent works today reflect the sorts of insights that motivated Husserl's positing of sensation or hyletic contents. Crane (1988, 1992) is not far from Husserl in his discussions of the Müller-Lyer and waterfall illusions. Crane argues that for explaining the Müller-Lyer illusion, we need to posit two levels of representation that take place simultaneously, one consciously intended to, the other not. Similarly, Dretske (1995) separates 'systemic' from 'acquired' representations. He illustrates this with an example of two dogs which are conditioned differently. Whereas one dog is trained to salivate upon hearing a clarinet play any musical note whatsoever, the other does the same thing on hearing a C-note regardless of the instrument on which it is played. Now consider a C-note is played on a clarinet, thus causing both dogs to salivate. According to Dretske, both dogs will have different 'acquired' representations: one intends a clarinet, the other a C-note. But at a non-conceptual level, they have identical representations (as they are exposed to the same sound, see Dretske [1995, 14–15]).

A third illuminating example comes from Peacocke (2002):

> Imagine you are in a room looking at a corner formed by two of its walls. The walls are covered with paper of a uniform hue, brightness and saturation. But one wall is more brightly illuminated than the other. In these circumstances, your experience can represent both walls as being the same colour: it does not look to you as if one of the walls is painted with brighter paint than the other. Yet it is equally an aspect of your visual experience itself that the region of the visual field in which one wall is presented is brighter than that in which the other is presented.
>
> (Peacocke 2002, 274)

Just like Crane and Dretske, Peacocke claims that perceptual intentionality is not exhausted by what is intended. While we intend the walls as (say) uniformly white, there is also a sense in which our visual system represents other colors. The examples of Peacocke, Dretske, and Crane all support a concept of sensation content also defended by Husserl. Whereas these contemporary authors prefer to exploit the relevant difference by introducing a notion of non-conceptual or non-representational content, Husserl calls the former immanent and the latter transcendent.

This discussion on sensations should suffice to make clear Husserl's motivation for distinguishing sensation contents from the sensible qualities of objects intentionally experienced. Second, Husserl maintains that sensations are also different from the intentional acts. This is because acts, as we saw earlier, are essentially directed at something. Sensations, however, are not. To be sure, they can certainly be taken up into intentional acts. An act of perception, for instance, involves the givenness of objects as well as sensations – but the sensations are not *themselves*

66   *Husserl: Intentionality, Consciousness, Nature*

object-directed. Indeed, Husserl deems this obvious: 'no one would think of referring to the sensations themselves as [intentional] experiences' (LI 406).[8]

I think this has to be understood in the following way. Throughout Husserl's writing from *LI* onward, sensation contents are not accounted for intentionally. This means that, at least taken for themselves, sensations cannot be adequately analyzed in terms of the intentional structure laid out so far. This is because sensations are neither directed at anything transcendent in the sense in which intentional acts are nor are they reducible to objective properties of represented (transcendent) objects. At the same time, Husserl thinks sensations do have *some* structure – they aren't the sort of unstructured data which Sellars (from an epistemological viewpoint) and (among others) Dennett (from a philosophy of mind viewpoint, as qualia) criticize.[9] Therefore, another model is needed to account for them. While Husserl in earlier work mostly leaves the problem of accounting for sensations in non-intentional terms open, the later writings do address it more substantially, and I return to this in Chapter 4.[10]

This point about the non-intentional structure of sensation contents is worth insisting upon for two reasons. First, it shows that Husserl displays consistency on his account of sensations, insofar as his later work clearly commits to a non-intentional account of sensory awareness, as I discuss in the next chapter.[11] Second, it is an important part of Husserl's philosophy that the whole sphere of so-called pure consciousness – which the phenomenological reduction is to bring into our purview – has a kind of epistemic efficacy.[12] Sensations, for Husserl, as experiences (from the German *Erlebnis,* not the Kantian *Erfahrung*) we live through, are not merely of a physiological order; they are epistemically relevant processes, even when they cannot be addressed intentionally. In this respect, or so I argue, he parts ways both with Kant and McDowell. On Kant's account, discussed in Chapter 2, but also for McDowell (see Chapter 6), contents that don't bear the right kind of relation to (for Kant) the subject or (for McDowell) the space of reasons are banned to the realm of natural fact. This is not the case for Husserl. Clarifying this important point further requires looking at how Husserl draws the lines between nature and consciousness, or natural fact and reason – which I do in the second half of this chapter.

On Feelings and Dark Longings

So far, I exploited Husserl's theory of intentionality by means of four relatively simple concepts, namely act-quality, matter, object-reference, and sensation contents. In everyday life, however, acts usually cannot be separated that simply. This is due to the fact that acts are frequently complexly founded. It is therefore worth briefly reviewing Husserl's idea of complex founded acts, which he largely adopts from Brentano.

Consider the acts of feeling joy over a melody, agitation over a shrill whistle, or sorrow over someone lost. On Husserl's account, these feeling acts must be understood as founded upon simpler presenting acts. The basic thought is this: an act of presenting (say) a melody can occur without (say) joy, but not vice versa. Therefore, presenting acts (of melodies, whistles, or losing someone) are founding, while the feelings (of joy, agitation, or sorrow) are founded acts. Rather than simply stapling onto each other, however, these acts then combine to form one new act, as in listening with enjoyment (see LI 443, 466).

One could try to insist that, in the given examples, the feelings are not themselves intentional. The act of presenting (say the melody) is intentional, but the feeling only latches onto that, without itself being directed at anything. But Husserl rejects this view. At least in most cases, feelings don't just latch onto presenting acts; we feel joyful *about* a melody, agitated *about* a shrill tone, or sad *about* someone's passing. For Husserl, then, feeling themselves are intentional acts, albeit ones that are in their very nature founded – which is generally speaking also Brentano's view.[13]

Experiencing pleasure in a song is an example of a founded act. But are all feelings truly founded on simpler intentional acts? Are there not also, to use a Kantian phrase, more 'obscure' feelings? Indeed, the early Husserl acknowledges certain 'dark longings and urges' and also a 'broader sphere of natural instincts' (LI 409–410). Much as with Kant's obscure sensuous intuitions (and in contrast to his obscure plays of sensations, which were not properly intentional), these obscure feelings are also considered intentional. For instance, one can be in love with someone without have noticed it oneself, with the loved person nonetheless appearing 'in a rosy gleam' (LI 408). Likewise, feelings of hunger or sexual desire are still intentionally directed at something, even though here only vaguely, at an 'undetermined "something"' (LI 410, see also GP 93–94).

With regard to undetermined feelings and dark longings, then, Husserl does not seem far removed from Kant's theory of obscure sensuous intuitions in the *Anthropology*. Moreover, as Husserl states in the first paragraphs of the sixth book of *LI*, these feeling acts – and all intentional act generally – can principally be brought to conceptual expression (a point also emphasized in later works). This means that, insofar as feelings have the aboutness-structure characteristic of intentionality, they are open to conceptualization and in that sense within (what McDowell calls) the space of reasons.

With sensations, as discussed previously, things stand differently. For the fact that sensations (and likewise processes of so-called association and motivation) are non-intentional implies that they are also non-conceptual. The fact that Husserl nonetheless can take sensations up into a theory of knowledge is, or so I will argue later on in this chapter,

68   *Husserl: Intentionality, Consciousness, Nature*

due to his unique construal of spaces, where the ideas of a conceptual and of an intentional space is accommodated within a more fundamental distinction between a space of consciousness and a space of nature.

On Fulfillment and Justified Belief

So far, the fifth book paved the way for Husserl's theory of knowledge in the sixth book by introducing a basic repertoire of distinctions pertaining to intentional consciousness. The most important of these were the act-quality and the matter – which together constituting the 'intentional essence' (that which any act has) – and the intentional object, which itself is not a part of the act but rather that which the act aims at. While these concepts should allow us to understand the fundamental ways in which consciousness can relate to objects, Husserl does not think they suffice to clarify the phenomenological operations of acquiring and justifying knowledge. This process, central to the sixth book, is captured with the term 'fulfillment' (*Erfühlung*). This theory of fulfillment best displays the full extent of Husserl's departure from and critique of Kant's theory of knowledge, which I survey briefly in a separate section after this one.

To account for the acquisition and justification of knowledge – a task clearly beyond the scope of Brentano's psychological analyses of intentionality – the sixth book introduces another crucial distinction within the class of intentional acts. This is referred to as the 'interpretative form' of acts (LI 624), of which Husserl distinguishes two kinds: signitive and intuitive ones. This means that acts can now be classified as either signitive or intuitive (or a mix between both), while all of them in turn have a quality and a matter. This new distinction between signitive and intuitive acts is of great importance, as all knowledge is said to concern the relation between them (see LI 736) – rather than a relation between understanding and sensibility, as Kant's theory had it.

It is crucial that to observe first that, in Husserl's view, signitive acts alone can be defined as meaning (*Bedeutung*) acts. That is to say, signitive acts are intentional acts which express or give voice to meaning. In the first sections of the sixth book, Husserl puts considerable effort in showing that the meaning of an expressing act is always contained in these special signitive acts – which are 'founded' acts – and never, for instance, in a simple 'founding' act of seeing. To sustain this, he offers elaborate discussions of what we today would call demonstrative reference, where the 'place' of the expressed meaning is arguably most difficult to decide. In a demonstrative reference, as in seeing and then expressing '*this* is a table', we have a judgment act tied directly to a perceptual content at which it is directed. In short, Husserl accepts that the perceptual act can present all sorts of things to me, but he denies that it contains the act of meaning (LI 554). As Husserl illustrates, 'when I say *this*, I do not plainly perceive; instead, on the basis of seeing a *new act* builds itself, which directs itself to it and [...] which is dependent upon it, namely the act of meaning-this' (LI 554 my italics). Although this new meaning act is, in the case of demonstrative reference, built onto the perception, it could principally be separated from it, which would show that the expressed meaning is not in the perceptual act itself.

Husserl thus separates the pure act of meaning or expressing something from (in this example) the concrete act of seeing. The latter here provides all the richness of content, and is therefore called an intuition; the former is only the act of expression. For this reason, Husserl can refer to the act of meaning as principally a completely *empty* act (see LI 607). In order now to have an empty belief justified – to provide warrant for it – the empty act must come to some kind of coincidence with an appropriately fulfilling act. For instance, one can emptily entertain the thought that there is a blackbird in the garden. If one then were to turn around and see that this is actually the case, the act of seeing would, Husserl maintains, come into a sort of coincidence or overlap with my empty intention, thereby providing fullness to the empty intention. This process Husserl calls a *synthesis of fulfillment.* In its most general structure, this process of fulfillment serves to capture how beliefs are justified.

This is already an unorthodox idea by today's standards, but the theory of fulfillment gets more extraordinary still. It is still relatively easy, one could say, to see how acts of perception could provide fullness to empty intentions. For Husserl, however, perception is not the only intuition that can provide fullness. We also have it, for instance, in memory. An act of remembering, on Husserl's view, likewise involves an intention which grasps something in degrees of fullness. For instance, if I try to remember the town I grew up in, I grasp it imaginatively; I 'see' buildings from this or that side; I imaginatively wander the streets, and so on. I could further ask myself what color this or that building used to be, and subsequently grasp that color with, Husserl would say, intuitive evidence. To be sure, the evidence sustained by the fullness of the act of remembering does not measure up to that of perceptual intentionality. Only the latter has the character of giving the real thing; it peculiarly claims to stand in need of no further fulfillment (see LI 589).[14] Yet non-sensible acts are capable of providing fullness to a corresponding meaning act, or so Husserl insists (see LI 646–647). Because of this capacity to provide fullness to meaning acts, Husserl thinks memory can legitimately be called a type of intuition.

Closer scrutiny reveals that memory and perception together cannot provide fullness to all types of meaning acts that we know can be fulfilled. One can also, for instance, have an empty meaning intention of a mathematical formula, without really grasping its meaning. One can express, say, the Pythagorean Theorem without having an intuition in the sense of an act which gives the sense expressed. To be sure, I can sensibly intuit one triangle drawn in the sand, and I can see written signs

70 *Husserl: Intentionality, Consciousness, Nature*

symbolically representing the general rule. But grasping the universal (a priori) rule expressed in those signs isn't done by the senses, or so Husserl claims. Therefore, according to Husserl, we must invoke something like intellectual intuitions: acts which give us ideal objectivities that provide fullness to empty intellectual meaning acts.[15]

Something similar is said to hold for the intuition of states of affairs. According to Husserl, simple perception does not give us states of affairs; it only gives us objects – a view he consistently maintained and elaborated in later works. If we think of the state of affairs 'A is B', or 'either A or B', what shows in simple perception is 'A' and 'B' in each case. However, their relation – the 'is' and 'or' – cannot be intuited in simply perception, since the 'is' or 'or' isn't something sensibly seen. Therefore, Husserl claims, simple perception is incapable of providing fullness to categorial meaning intentions, since the relevant categorial relations cannot be simply seen. That is to say, while things certainly appear perceptually as standing in relations to each other, explicating those relations categorially – such as 'being' or 'conjunction' – require an additional mental act.

On the one hand, this theory is not so different from Kant's. For Kant, on a strong conceptualist reading at least, the contents of perception involve categorial relations (pure concepts), albeit only synthetically. To subsequently bring out those relations is to activate the understanding by forming a judgment, which is no longer just a perception. Husserl makes a similar distinction between perception, in which categorial relations are somehow pre-figured, and judgments proper, which first bring out those relations. On the other hand, the crucial difference, of course, is that Husserl believes that the very fact that we have justified beliefs about empirical states of affairs (as in 'this pen is larger than that one') and universals (as in the Pythagorean Theorem) makes it necessary to introduce objects that could fulfill these beliefs, which have to be objects of a strictly 'super-sensuous' kind (LI 673). No such idea is to be found in Kant. For him, all (human) intuition is sensible.

Perceptual, categorial, and universal intuition are the most important classes of intuition for Husserl. In all three cases, the justification of a belief is experienced, Husserl claims, as a kind of coincidence between full and empty acts, by which the former 'fulfills' the empty meaning act – hence the term synthesis of fulfillment.[16] Three things are further worth observing about this process. First, while beliefs find epistemic warrant through a synthesis of fulfillment, it should be noted that what comes up for fulfillment is not the complete intuitive act as such. What directly matters for fulfillment is only that part of the intuitive act that comprises what is intended through it. For instance, if I emptily entertain the thought that there is a blackbird in the garden, then a perceptual act subsequently presenting a blackbird would fulfill this act insofar as 'a blackbird in the garden' is given in it. The overlap does not concern, at least not immediately, the whole perceptual act, with all its sensation contents, matter, object-reference, and act-quality. Most of the contents of consciousness, then, can never come up for propositional articulation. In other words: my belief finds direct warrant *only* in *what* I intend, and that is just a moment of the complete act-structure.

This same point resurfaces in *Ideas I* and *Ideas II*. Here Husserl writes that 'there is inherent in each noema a pure object-something as a point of unity', also called the 'determinable X' (Ideas I 314–315), and this content is as a rule 'expressible by means of significations' (Ideas I 295). Indeed, *any* act that is not itself objectifying 'allows objectivities to be drawn from itself' by a 'change of attitude' (Ideas II 18). In other words: *all and only* intentional contents come up for fulfillment and allow of propositional articulation. Husserl, then, clearly defends a version of weak conceptualism.

A second point worth drawing out concerns sensations. As I noted earlier, Husserl sees sensations and other non-intentional contents not merely as natural facts. They are still experienced (lived-through) by us, and therefore they belong to phenomenology and the space of consciousness it studies. Yet we now see that sensations do not for that matter have the appropriate structure to figure directly as reasons for a belief. A belief must have a certain *articulated* (propositional) structure, and whatever fulfills it must have an *articulable* structure ('expressible by means of significations'). This reminds of McDowell, according to whom we 'cannot really understand the relations in virtue of which a judgment is warranted except as relations within the space of concepts' (MW 7). The reference to concepts here falls short, however, of adequate phenomenological description, insofar as it suggests perceptual warrant is a matter of concepts. Husserl, by contrast, seems to accept only that intuitive acts must intentionally present something articulable in order to function as belief warrant, a task which sensations cannot live up to.

Third, and perhaps most importantly, it is worth noting that the articulable content of the fulfilling act (say, a perceptual content) can play its fulfilling part only by virtue of the fact that it is *not just* a conceptual content.[17] That is to say, a conceptual, expressive act (a thought) is empty; the fact that a perception can provide warrant for it is due precisely to the fact that the latter provides something new to it – hence something extra-conceptual. Put differently, the fact that perception provides a kind of warrant – something the empty proposition cannot possess out of itself – means that it makes an extra-conceptual contribution. This is why we have to look in order to check our beliefs.

In a contribution published in 2009, McDowell notes that a perceptual 'experience [...] itself already has content that is *just as firmly conceptual* as the content of a judgment' (ETW 250, my italics). But if that is accepted, then there is no space to explain the fact that perception makes a contribution which is extraneous to the propositional content emptily intended. It seems to me that Husserl has a good point in characterizing perceptual contents (and the contents of intuitive acts generally)

72 Husserl: Intentionality, Consciousness, Nature

as articul*able* contents, instead of calling them conceptual. This way, we can better accommodate the extra-conceptual contribution intuition makes relative to our empty beliefs.

In summary, Husserl holds, in my view, that not all the contents of consciousness are propositionally articulable. However, that which is intended through intentional acts is by a general rule explicable, even when it's a non-theoretical act, such as a sheer intuition. At the same time, Husserl identifies a good reason not to call contents propositional or conceptual contents just for the fact that they can be so articulated (weak conceptualism). This is because, as I showed, the fact that intuitive acts (perception, memory, categorial intuition, universal intuition) can fulfill empty meaning acts must be due to something extra-conceptual. It is this peculiar character of fullness which, in Husserl's view, distinguishes perception (as an intuitive act) from thinking (as an empty act) – instead of, say, a real causal relation to an object.

Husserl's Critique of Kant's Theory of Knowledge

Husserl was aware, already around the time of *LI*, to what extent his theory of epistemic justification opposed the prevailing Kantian trends.[18] Before turning to the second part on the line drawn between consciousness and nature, it is worth overviewing Husserl's opposition to Kant briefly, in order to gain a better understanding of how the intentional analysis of consciousness differs from the Kantian study of how perception gives us access to reality.

Kant, as Chapter 1 showed, has no other positive concept of intuition than the one provided by sensibility. This limitation was essential to the critical function of his work, as it created a framework to critique the rationalist quest for knowledge based on concept analysis alone. However, in thus restricting intuition to sensibility, or so Husserl claims, Kant overlooked the essential phenomenological kinship of sensible, categorial, and universal intuition, to the extent that the latter two are not recognized at all. This is why Husserl says in *LI* that Kant failed to 'reach out to the fundamental widening of the concepts of intuition and appearance to the categorial [and eidetic] realm' (LI 732).

The insistence on two separate faculties is thus, from Husserl's viewpoint, a big problem in the Kantian theory of knowledge (and likewise his practical philosophy[19]). However, in the second edition of *LI* from around the time of *Ideas I,* Husserl indicates an even more fundamental mistake in the Kantian outlook:

> All principle obscurities of the Kantian critique of knowledge have to do with the fact that Kant has not made clear the unique nature (*das Eigentümliche*) of pure 'ideation', [...] that he thus failed to see the phenomenologically true concept of *a priori*.
>
> (LI 733)

Husserl here alleges, in his own admittedly esoteric terms, that all problems of Kant's philosophy can be brought back to a wrong concept of a priori. Earlier, in lectures from 1908, we find some clues as to what this means:

> Kant confuses the knowledge which subjectivity produces out of itself by considering its own functioning – which [for Kant] is a priori just insofar as it has nothing to do with the nature of the materials which 'come from without' – with a priori knowledge in the genuine sense. [For Kant,] to refer back to the materials of sensations is to know a posteriori.
>
> (Husserl 1956, 364)

It is worth briefly considering these two fragments here, as they summarize, in somewhat cryptic terms, how Husserl's phenomenology differs from Kantian philosophy. As was also touched upon in Chapter 2, Kant uses a method of formalization to discover pure forms of experience. To discover space and time, for instance, we abstract from all intuitive contents, such as 'feelings', 'sight, hearing, touch, [...] sensations of colors, sounds, and heat' (B29, B44). This is because, as Husserl points out above, for Kant a priori must have 'nothing to do with the nature of the materials that 'come from without''. In other words, Kant draws (from Husserl's viewpoint at least) a line within the sphere of subjective experience between the necessary (a priori) and the contingent (a posteriori), where the latter refers to sensible materials, and the former exclusively to content-emptied form.

Husserl's rejection of this view defines, I would argue, his opposition to Kantianism. In short, Husserl believes Kant's formal concept of a priori is biased by a mathematical ideal and should be abandoned for that reason.[20] The only thing a priori means is absolute certainty, which in turn depends on two capacities: one for the 'free variation' of possible worlds in our imagination, and another for intuiting through that very process that something (as far as the imagination stretches) could not possibly be otherwise. These capacities, Husserl claims in later work, are 'everywhere the same' (EJ 354), and therefore 'from every concrete actuality, and every individual trait actually experienced in it or capable of being experienced, a path stands open to the realm of [...] a priori thinking' (EJ 353–354). This clearly contradicts Kant's view, where certain conscious contents are deemed inherently a posteriori, as a result of which they are ignored in Kant's transcendental investigations into the operations of the mind.

While this may seem like a needlessly abstract and complex point, it helps to better understand (i) the analyses of intentionality dealt with so far and likewise (ii) Husserl's theory of sensations and other non-intentional contents. To start with the first: the concepts of act, matter, fullness, fulfillment, and even intentionality are a priori distinctions for

74 *Husserl: Intentionality, Consciousness, Nature*

Husserl. Relative to Kant's philosophy of the mind, Husserl seems to have an endless field of mental phenomena to be studied in an a priori fashion. This is precisely due to the fact that an a priori statement for Husserl is simply one that holds in all imaginable cases, whatever the domain to which it pertains. So one can have a priori propositions about all of consciousness as such, intentionality as such, perception as such, perception without subjective attention as such, sensation as such, and so forth. Husserl's framework thus allows for investigating perceptual intentionality transcendentally in much greater detail than the Kantian framework does. There, the transcendental analysis of perception and intuition more or less terminated with pointing to space and time, and showing what intuition must be like in order to sustain the objective validity of certain pure concepts.

Second, and related to the first, Husserl's feud with the Kantian concept of a priori is an important step in his attempt to draw the lines between spaces of nature and reasons, and between causal and justificatory explanations, differently than the Kantians did. Husserl insisted strongly that the Kantian concept of a priori is simply false. This is allegedly due to the fact that it is, as mentioned, biased by the ideal of mathematics – by the link between apodictic certainty and formalization which the modern mathematical worldview tacitly suggests. By correcting what it actually means to hold something in certainty, Husserl wanted to reveal something of the root of the fallacy that he believed to be involved in attempts to draw a line within subjective consciousness, by regarding certain subjective sensation contents as empirical and physiological, as Kant for instance did. In the second part, which I now turn to, I aim to show why Husserl believed this carving up of the space of consciousness into matters of fact and reason is indeed fallacious.

The Space of Consciousness

Accessing Consciousness

So far I addressed the key features of Husserl's theory of knowledge as well as the nature of its departure from Kant's theory. While Husserl's thought continuously develops, the transcendental turn that defines the final 30 years of his life does not suddenly make the earlier work obsolete; it rather involves a 'radical change of meaning' (Trans. Phen. 235) of it.[21] This change of meaning results primarily from Husserl's increasing efforts to demarcate the field of phenomenological study, which in turn yields a significant reconfiguration of the relations between consciousness, nature, and reality. In what follows, I first overview the relations between consciousness and nature, reasons and facts, and afterward

Husserl: Intentionality, Consciousness, Nature   75

turn to the question of our access to reality and the problem of idealism in a separate discussion.

It is no overstatement that the attempt to demarcate a space of consciousness constitutes the core of Husserl's thinking. This space of consciousness is supposed to be a well-marked sphere, distinct from the space of nature through a unique sort of epistemic access, from which alone questions of reason, justification, knowledge, and reality can be asked and clarified. By bringing this space properly into view and justifying its unique status in a purportedly entirely a priori fashion, it would subsequently also be possible to identify errors in our existing conceptions of the relations between mind and world, perception and thought, fact and reason. Before getting to those criticisms, however, some of which I postpone to the final chapters on McDowell, the space of consciousness must be brought into view. I do this by considering, first, what brought Husserl to his sharp demarcation of a space of consciousness from the natural world and, second, how he came to ascribe a special transcendental or philosophical significance to it.

Regarding the first, it is useful to note that Husserl had the traditional custom to designate regions to various sciences, so that 'to each science there corresponds an object-province' (Ideas I 7). Traditional physics, for instance, studies laws of matter and motion, biology the structures of living systems, and sociology the structures of human society. Most of these regional divides are not hard, and it is in part up to practicing scientists to determine them. What fascinated Husserl above all, however, is that all these sciences are sciences of nature in the broadest sense. That is to say, they are all in one way or another about the world understood as something natural, real, objective, or at least as something transcendent to our own experience. Sciences study things given in experience – not the lived, subjective experiences through which alone these things are, in the end, given. This goes even for most forms of psychology (which studies the human mind as object, brain as object, etc.). In this respect, all the sciences can be said to share a similar vantage point, such that to science in general there corresponds a certain perspective on the totality of being. This perspective Husserl calls the natural attitude.

The natural attitude is not, however, exclusively a scientific let alone naturalistic attitude. For Husserl, it likewise captures our naturally default mode of practical experiencing. It is an attitude that is ingrained in the very structure of our dealings with the world. That is to say, in experiencing the world, we don't usually notice our own experience at all. We precisely experience *things*, while our experiences remain, so to say, transparent. Indeed, so skillfully does our experience erase its own traces in opening up an existing world for us that we tend to take the givenness of that world for granted. The sciences are, Husserl believes, ultimately erected upon this attitude which takes the world for granted

76 Husserl: Intentionality, Consciousness, Nature

(in the sense that the subjective sources which first enable the givenness of the world are not a focal point here).

Importantly, there is, according to Husserl, nothing wrong with this attitude. It is utterly practical, generally unavoidable, and completely legitimate in the pursuit of knowledge. At the same time, it does not and could not possibly give us the full story about the world, ourselves, or their relation. To see why, a complicated and certainly unorthodox line of argument must briefly be exposed.

In overviewing Husserl' earlier theory of knowledge, it already became apparent that Husserl posits objective regions wherever we are capable of entertaining and fulfilling empty meaning intentions. For example, I can entertain a proposition in thought that there is an orange chair in the corner of my room. If I now turn around and see that orange chair, I have an intuition which fulfills the empty thought intention entertained before and which provides it with epistemic warrant. If we generalize this particular perception to sensible intuition as such, we can say that to sensible intuition there corresponds a distinct ontological region of objects of the senses, in other words, a region of material things. The class of material things thus constitutes an ontological region because it can fulfill (provide intuitive evidence for) certain empty intentions.

Generalizing this point, Husserl believes ontological regions are demarcated through phenomenological analyses of fundamental types of objects that can fulfill empty intentions. Husserlian ontology, then, does not presume on the basis of common sense or some plausible scientific argument that certain things really exist and others don't. Husserl would never adopt Alexander's Dictum that to be is to have causal powers (as a reductionist like J. Kim (1998) does). Instead, he attempts to ground ontology exclusively in the analysis of the fundamental types of objects that can be intuited, that is, can provide warrant for empty intentions (see Ideas III 25–26). As we saw earlier, it is this type of reasoning that brought Husserl to believe there is an ontology of ideal objects. Our beliefs about mathematical propositions are not fulfilled by sense experience; yet they can find fulfillment, and therefore an ontology of ideal (non-material and non-spatial) objects corresponds to them.

Husserl's extensive efforts to outline various levels of ontologies on the basis of this kind of inquiry are not directly relevant here. What does matter is that Husserl thinks there is a sense in which all the regions of the various sciences can be grouped together: they all study transcendent objects. That is to say, all possible beliefs we entertain in these domains are fulfilled by considering various sorts of intentional objects, in other words, things outside of us (though not necessarily in real space).[22] There is only one domain, Husserl maintains, for which this isn't the case: namely for our own consciousness.

Husserl, then, maintains that there is a unique epistemic gap between the kind of access and knowledge of one's own consciousness and access

Husserl: Intentionality, Consciousness, Nature   77

and knowledge of external (transcendent) things. That is to say, I access my own mind in a fundamentally different way than I access anything outside me, including other minds. Correlatively, my beliefs about my own mind can also only be fulfilled in an entirely unique way.

This can be illustrated with an example. For Husserl, the belief *that I see an orange chair* is correctly speaking about *my seeing of an orange chair*. This is a subjective, mental act; something I subjectively experience and live through. As such, it can be adequately verified only by the evidence provided by a (non-sensible) intuition of my own consciousness, through which I grasp *that I see an orange chair*. It is (a priori) inconceivable, Husserl maintains, that this type of evidence would be translated into the sort of evidences transcendent intuitions provide. A neuroscientist might, for instance, also be able to show *that I see an orange chair*. Yet the neuroscientist's evidence is secondary; it is not, so to say, first-hand. Without me having the accompanying phenomenological evidence, the belief *that I see an orange chair* is not originally fulfilled, no matter how advanced the neuroscientist may be. This is plainly because my belief *that I see an orange chair* is about *my seeing of an orange chair*, which is a subjective, conscious state. It is the sort of belief only one particular sort of intuition can fulfil.[23]

With consciousness we have thus stumbled upon a unique space of being, one which doesn't consist of transcendent things that anybody can access. The point, indeed, is somewhat Searlean: with consciousness 'there are no appearances of, but rather [only] experience of it itself, experience' (Ideas III 68).[24] This unique sort of being, which can hardly be called an object (as it isn't transcendent), warrants, Husserl believes, speaking of a space of consciousness as a distinct region or space of being.

This gives some first insight into the space of consciousness. To provide a fuller picture, two matters still require clarification: first, (i) the status of the evidence of the intuition of one's own mental life; second, (ii) a more precise delineation of its scope, that is, an outline of the complete space of consciousness. Regarding the first, Husserl held that our evidences of transcendent, natural reality are never quite perfect. This is because it is always (a priori) conceivable that things turn out different than one thought. For instance, new facts, insights, or measurements disprove older theories, whether in physics, biology, or sociology. Whereas Kant tried to make some beliefs about reality a priori – regarding causality, space, and time, for instance – Husserl denies this.[25] Wherever we study the real world, however certain we may be, our results are a posteriori.

Our knowledge of consciousness, on the other hand, has a different type of certainty; it is supposedly non-negatable. This is due to the fact, Husserl argues, that consciousness doesn't claim to exist. It isn't itself a transcendent, real object, but rather that through which transcendent

78 Husserl: Intentionality, Consciousness, Nature

objects are given. Because it doesn't make this transcendence claim, it would lack the kind of possibility of a future negation characteristic of natural knowledge. Consider, by way of example, the perception I have of the orange chair in the corner of my room. The chair, Husserl would argue, conceivably does not exist. Although unlikely, it could be an extra-terrestrial creature pretending to be an orange chair. Since this can never be ruled out, knowledge of the chair is a posteriori. On the other hand, the insight or intuition *that I have a perception of an orange chair*, which claims in turn to present a real, orange chair, is something I allegedly cannot doubt. The pure, conscious act of perceiving doesn't exist as a transcendent object; therefore it doesn't make the corresponding 'uncertain' claim to existence. Put more simply, while I can doubt 'that the chair is real', I cannot doubt 'that I have the experience that the chair is real'. Husserl refers to this type of being of pure consciousness as immanent, as opposed to the transcendent being of objects.

This point about the certainty of the evidence of one's own consciousness was certainly of great importance to Husserl, even though many have found it hard to swallow. I think it can be helpful to note that Husserl does not seek to suggest that we are completely infallible when it comes to our own consciousness. As a field of study, consciousness is still something about which we, as investigators, can be mistaken. To produce results, we need contemplation, deliberation, and discussion. The point, then, is less about a supposedly infallible access to inner emotions or feelings, something Schwitzgebel (2008) targets in his critique of naïve introspection. Instead, it speaks more to the unique kind of being of consciousness; namely not as a thing, which inherently claims to be something it may not really be, but as the sort of medium through which things are given to us.

The critique by Schwitzgebel alluded to, which focuses on 'inner' states like emotions and feelings, bridges nicely to the second point: getting the right grip on the scope of the space of consciousness. This is ultimately, or so I would submit, the central concern in Husserl's philosophy. Revealing the full space of consciousness would show the inevitable need for philosophy (phenomenology), that is, a study not of transcendent objects, but of immanent consciousness. But this task proves far more difficult than it looks. It requires a way of looking at the world that we are not attuned to, and new ways of capturing in language what is thus explored. The result: a complicated but certainly original picture of where the lines are to be drawn between nature and consciousness, fact and reason, cause and motivation, science and philosophy.

On the Space of Consciousness

As noted earlier, the space of consciousness does not consist simply of transcendent objects as in any other sphere. For Husserl, this means neither laws of causality nor the exactitude of mathematics can apply to it. It is a space which can only be described, a process often necessitating new terminology, in order to avoid misconstruing this space in causal or natural terms. We saw this already with notions such as intentionality, matter, and quality, which for Husserl do not refer to physical-causal structures, but to consciousness as found immediately in phenomenological reflection.

While the previous section gave an idea of how Husserl warrants the idea of a distinct space of consciousness, its scope hasn't been accurately delineated yet. This delineation is crucial as it shows, Husserl thinks, where scientific explanation ends and philosophical exploration begins. Moreover, this divide between nature and consciousness, with its corresponding natural and phenomenological attitude, was knowingly posited by Husserl as an alternative to the sorts of nature-reason divides that prevailed in Husserl's time, and which has its parallels in some more recent Pittsburgh philosophers like McDowell, Sellars, and Haugeland. The main step toward a proper demarcation of these spheres is called phenomenological reduction.[26]

Normally, in the natural attitude, we comport ourselves smoothly toward things. We are not aware that the objects we experience are objects *we experience*. The phenomenological reduction is the attempt to become aware of this. Instead of just looking at the orange chair for whatever practical or theoretical purpose, I now shift attention to this entire subjective process of the chair being given to me. Crucially, this isn't something other than what I had in the natural attitude. After all, nothing more was really given to me than the subjective experience of the chair in the first place. The difference lies only in my attitude. While in the natural attitude, I simply took the chair to be transcendent and real, something my experience skillfully accomplished, the reduction shifts focus to the whole subjective process of the chair as appearance (noema) for me (noesis).

This shows already that speaking of a reduction can be misleading. The shift toward the phenomenological attitude does not involve losing anything. Instead, it only aims to bring about a different perspective on the totality of what was already going on:

On the left, in the natural attitude, I am intentionally directed at things (as indicated by the arrow). Although I might not be actively theorizing about the reality of things, Husserl would say I at least tacitly take the

80   *Husserl: Intentionality, Consciousness, Nature*

world to be real and independent of me. The subject itself, insofar as it comes into the picture at all here, is likewise implicitly apprehended as part of the natural world. One could say that, in this attitude, the world is everything that is the case. It is the totality of transcendent being, where the subject itself is taken as a part of that reality.

On the right, then, we perform the phenomenological reduction. Here I keep everything just as it was before (see CM 59–60, 69, 71–75, 116–117), as illustrated by the brackets. This is strictly necessary since it is ordinary world-appearance that we want to study. However, at the same time, I now consider all of that as the immanent unfolding of consciousness-of-the-world – which is again just what I had before, but there unwittingly, as I there dwelled naturally in the intentional accomplishments of my experience. While I thus keep my ordinary experience of the natural attitude, including the belief in the world that accompanies it, I now simultaneously add a second perspective to the first (CM 71–75), as illustrated by the arrows above. The result: I make thematic, from the added perspective, the very same concrete world under a different aspect, namely as it is given (noema) to my streaming consciousness (noesis).

The importance of keeping everything as it was in outlining the space of consciousness cannot be overstated. There is a constant tendency, Husserl believes, to misunderstand the space of consciousness, because of the natural temptations set by our object-oriented acting and thinking. We tend to think of consciousness as something inner as opposed to outer, as here rather than there (as with Schwitzgebel's focus on the 'inner' emotions and feelings). But the space of consciousness doesn't match the subject over against the object. Consciousness isn't cut loose from the transcendent, as if one sphere is here and the other out there. To the contrary, the transcendent is included as a moment in intentional consciousness, as just that very world I was already directed at.[27] It is only the relevant *aspect* under which the sciences study the transcendent, which is put on hold to let the new, added perspective prevail (this is illustrated by the arrows above, which indicate that phenomenological reflection does not target just the subject but the whole subject-object correlation).

Husserl, then, I would argue, favors a unique sort of double aspect theory; not regarding the subjective mind, but the universe (or the All of Being) itself. Rather than pointing to a realm of separate entities, to something one could ostensibly point out as being over here, next to, or alongside other things, the space of consciousness encompasses me together with just this very world as I always had and understood it: 'the always presumed world, as and how it is presumed, the always known and knowable world, precisely as it is known and knowable' (KI 43); 'we make the world as such our theme together with every natural consideration of the world' (PP 170); 'phenomenology shows [...] that the whole world and therewith the universe of all positive being is comprehensible' (EP II 361). The space of consciousness isn't here nor there, but encompasses everything that was there before within itself: 'every imaginable sense, every imaginable being [...] falls within the domain of transcendental subjectivity' (CM 84).

All these fragments purport to convey, or so I would argue, that the discovery of the space of consciousness does not involve the introduction of any new entities; it rests exclusively on a change of perspective. Rather than dividing the world into two separate entities, Husserl thus endorses a double aspect view, which allows for just one world and two ways of looking at it – as real and transcendent on the one hand, and as a manifestation in my streaming conscious life on the other.[28]

While this division allows there to be one world, studied both in science and phenomenology (philosophy), it simultaneously renders the respective fields of nature and consciousness distinct, as a result of the separate attitudes and correspondingly sui generis intuitive evidences. On the one hand, this picture allows sciences of nature to study both mind *and* world under a natural aspect – even though, strictly speaking, they will never address consciousness directly. On the other hand, phenomenology can study both mind *and* world – even though it says nothing about either mind or world in terms of natural entities in causal nature.

The legitimacy of philosophy is, Husserl thinks, hereby forever secured. Philosophy can never succumb to naturalism. While it encompasses the whole mind-world relation, it is restricted in scope; it can never answer questions that belong, if only partially, to the realm of nature. Likewise, naturalism cannot enter into philosophy. The divide between these spheres, then, is hard; while there can be correlations, there can be no genuine bridges.

On Drawing the Line

The question of how to draw the line has effectively already been answered – but it is useful to try and spell it out a bit more carefully, by comparing Husserl's position to what it is opposed to.

Kant, as we saw earlier, restricted the study of the mind to a limited formal investigation. This method certainly didn't reduce to naïve introspection in Schwitzgebel's sense; laws of consciousness (causality, space, time) were as much 'inner' laws as they were laws of the natural world. Kant's formal angle, however, did force all the concrete contents of experience to the domain of a posteriori, empirical science. This means, for instance, that Kant regards color contents or sound sensations as a matter of fact, not of consciousness. There is, for him, not much philosophically interesting to say about those contents, even though, strangely enough, they too are subjectively experienced and thus have their legitimate immanent being. To this picture, Husserl would reply that it wrongly carves up the space of consciousness into two halves. It divides what is one legitimate sphere of inquiry into one half of supposedly empirical

82 *Husserl: Intentionality, Consciousness, Nature*

contents belonging to the realm of fact and another half of a priori forms which alone would belong to the study of mind.

I discuss McDowell's views in detail in Chapters 5 and 6, but for the sake of comparison, it is worth noting that, from Husserl's viewpoint, at least, McDowell likewise carves up consciousness into two halves. For McDowell, only concepts figure in the space of reasons, and this is for him where the line should be drawn between the spaces of reasons and natural fact. As a result, all lower-level mental processes are transposed to the realm of natural-scientific explanation. This means that the consciousnesses of non-rational animals, which don't partake in the space of reasons, can be considered exclusively from within the realm of natural fact. 'Dumb animals', McDowell writes, 'are natural being[s] and no more'; they are 'entirely contained within nature'; their 'sensory interactions with their environment are natural goings-on' (MW 70). Elsewhere, he notes that the 'merely biological [...] clearly includes the second-natural dispositions and performances of trained dogs' (RGM 236). Or again: 'Apart from how it [a dog's act of rolling over after it has been conditioned to do so] originates, the second nature of dogs is just like their first nature' (RN 98).

I don't necessarily want to make a point about McDowell's views on animal consciousness. What matters is that McDowell sees lower-level accomplishments of consciousness as encompassed entirely within the sphere of intelligibility belonging to natural science. The lives of animals are governed by 'immediate biological imperatives' (MW 115), which can be accounted for sufficiently by sciences of nature, whereas there are only 'some second-natural phenomena that [...] natural science cannot accommodate, on the ground that their intelligibility is of the special [conceptual] space-of-reasons kind' (RGM 236).

From Husserl's viewpoint, this way of drawing the line betrays the inability to see the unity of conscious life throughout its lower level accomplishments and its higher level intentional and rational ones. Husserl, in fact, criticizes naturalistic psychology for a picture very similar to the one McDowell here commits to. As Husserl notes, naturalistic psychology is 'blinded by the naturalistic example set by the successful natural sciences and [searches] to transpose that method to the mental life' (EE 333). Its subsequent mistake is 'that it posits the passivity of association and of the whole psychic life unfolding without the activity of the I at the same level with the passivity of the physical natural process'. 'However', Husserl continues, "passive motivation is [...] a sphere of understandability standing under pure essential laws and, therefore, having a completely different meaning than natural causality and natural lawfulness' (EE 333). In other words, all subjective processes and contents that belong to the space of consciousness, including non-intentional sensations, associations, etc., are here wrongly located in the space of nature.

Interestingly, this point can be transposed to animal consciousness as well. Animals, as Husserl claims in some remarkable manuscripts, aren't mechanical objects. To reduce a dog's behavior to natural causality fails to capture the dog's experiential life and furthermore contradicts how we all understand its behavior. The zoologist, Husserl notes, or anyone observing animals for that matter, doesn't just study physical-organic interactions in studying any of the higher animals. To the contrary,

> [t]he experiencing zoologist [studies and relies on] the animal being [*tierische Dasein*] in its subjective surroundings, that of which it [the animal] is conscious, the instinctual life of the animal in its inner development [...] and its subject-intentional development in connection with the development of its subjective surroundings.
>
> (GP 98)

Put differently, we observe animals and interact with them as animate beings with subjective experiences, thus apprehending them, in part, under the aspect of consciousness, rather than factual nature.

Moreover, Husserl insists throughout that higher animals have full-fledged intentionality, even when they don't actively form propositional judgments. McDowell tends to equate intentionality and conceptuality,[29] but Husserl maintained that intentional consciousness is separable from the capacity for reason and judgment. Animals, for instance, are perceptually directed at objects; they have a 'steady perceptual field, comparable to ours, with changing perceptions in which objects [...] enter and go' (C211); they have 'one world' intentionally given with 'familiar and unfamiliar things' (C 213). They also have instinctual longings with unspecified intentional targets, as well as patterns of expectations that can be fulfilled or negated (see GP 99). Furthermore, as Husserl elaborates, they have a sense of self over against the not-self, they stand in an inter-subjective world with group members, with primitive relations between males, females, and infants, and they sometimes even have an indirect apprehension of personal mortality.

What is the motivation for trying to construe the experiential lives of animals as mere natural fact, as McDowell does? Part of the answer is, I believe, that McDowell, in *Mind and World* and elsewhere, appears convinced that only the conceptual cannot be accommodated by natural science, and that for that reason it alone belongs to a special space of reasons. This could be a case of drawing a line from out of the 'factum' of science; it departs from a reading of what science can and cannot accommodate, and from there demarcates a space of reasons as opposed to one of fact. The original evidences pertaining to consciousness are then traded for a transcendently informed picture that happens at this moment to be scientifically attractive.

84　*Husserl: Intentionality, Consciousness, Nature*

Moreover, it is worth pointing out – although I return to these matters extensively in Chapter 6 – that McDowell draws the line in such a way that to acknowledge animal intentional consciousness would effectively force him to ascribe conceptual spontaneity and rational deliberation to them. This is because, in his view, ascribing to animals capacities that are not intelligible from the perspective of natural fact implies ascribing conceptuality and rational deliberation to them, since here only the conceptual space of reasons allows of an explanatory framework that is irreducible to the explanatory framework of nature.

Such an implication is, it seems to me, undesirable, but it is perhaps also quite unnecessary. Husserl's picture, by contrast, allows for the acknowledgment of the intentional lives of animals without ascribing spontaneous deliberation to them. For Husserl, animals have intentionality, but since that nor conceptuality exhausts the space of consciousness, there is room to appreciate how they are different from us. For instance, Husserl remarks that animals can recognize familiar objects transposed to new surroundings, even though they do not recognize things in the way we do (see C 211). An animal such as a dog, he continues, 'has no questions and therewith no answers' (C 211); 'the theme of truth, method of verification, etc., it doesn't have' (C 212); '[t]he animal doesn't have a world with the sense of knowledge and sense of purpose of humans, one world that is on its own [an sich], true reality as to be [...] won through knowledge activities' (C 210).

As said, the lives of animals need be of no special concern here. But there is a point to be taken from it, namely that, for Husserl at least, the structure of that space which cannot be made understandable in terms of the kind of intelligibility that belongs to the realm of nature is not marked exclusively by conceptual or higher level cognitive activity. From this viewpoint, the very distinction between supposed natural contents of consciousness and higher level contents of the space-of-reasons kind appears artificial. In fact, the so-called space of reasons itself, as the holistic conceptual sphere McDowell theorizes (See ETW 254), no longer needs to be self-enclosed in that manner. While rationality is still a special achievement for Husserl, it is only a part of the bigger space of consciousness, and therefore need not be isolated from the rest of that space. Indeed, most of Husserl's later work is devoted to showing that 'passive motivation is the mother soil of rationality' (EE 332); that 'all intentional experiences [...] are interweavings of passive motivation' (EE 333). In other words, intentionality and conceptuality cannot be understood without reference to the broader life of subjective consciousness, as they grow within that sphere:

> upon the first world of recognized things given in perception there builds itself out of a new accomplishment – that of 'thinking' – the

apperception of all worldly things determinable according to true reality and as distinguishable in terms of truth and appearance.

(C212)

Precisely this 'genesis' of reason out of a passive consciousness will be the theme of the next chapter.

To conclude: for Husserl, the world, including ourselves and our subjective minds, can be considered under two aspects. This means that, rather than drawing a line within consciousness or handing over all of it to an all-consuming naturalism, Husserl sketches a picture where there is no line to be drawn within the mind-world relation. It is the unity of mind and world that can be approached legitimately as natural fact and as my streaming conscious life. All lines between fact and reason, nature and conceptuality, cause and motivation, science and philosophy, have to be drawn accordingly.

On Descartes, Idealism, and Reality

Like Kant, Husserl claimed to endorse a form of transcendental idealism. At the same time, he suggests that 'there can be no stronger realism' (Crisis 191), and that 'no ordinary realist has ever been so realistic and concrete' as he has been (BW 16). As I purport to show in this section, Husserl's mature views on the mind's relation to reality are to a large extent similar to Kant's. Among others, Husserl criticizes Descartes's representationalism for the same reasons Kant did, and similarly ascribes (only) logical possibility to the idea of a noumenal world. Nevertheless, there are also some important differences – improvements perhaps – which could make Husserl's account less vulnerable to the sort of objections that were raised against Kant by McDowell – and likewise by Husserl himself. I will discuss Husserl's treatment of Descartes here as it compares nicely to Kant's discussion of him earlier as well as to McDowell's, which I discuss in Chapter 6.

In *Cartesian Meditations,* Husserl praises Descartes for being someone who 'seriously intends to become a philosopher' (CM 44). Descartes, Husserl thinks, understood that radical philosophy demands beginning anew within oneself, because of the recognition that absolute certainty can never take its departure from the naive acceptance of the existing world or the opinions and theories of others. The philosopher must, at least at first, withdraw from that world, into the immediacy of something more certain, namely immanent consciousness.

Husserl continues to grant Descartes initial success in finding a correct starting point for philosophy, just as Kant did before him. Descartes's 'famous and very remarkable method of doubt' successfully reveals that the world's existence is not given absolutely, and Descartes correctly follows up on that intuition by claiming that 'the being of the world must

86   *Husserl: Intentionality, Consciousness, Nature*

remain unaccepted at this initial stage' (CM 45). Descartes thus 'keeps only himself, qua pure ego of his *cogitationes*, as having an absolutely indubitable existence, as something that cannot be done away with' (CM 45, also IP 38).

It is only in appropriating the significance of this discovery of certainty that Descartes allegedly goes amiss. Descartes 'stands on the threshold of the greatest of all discoveries [but] he does not grasp its proper sense' (CM 64). In spite of the attempted radicalism, Husserl maintains that certain 'prejudices were at work' (CM 63), by which he refers specifically to the 'ideal of science' (CM 48) of the modern period, namely geometrical-axiomatic deduction. This assumed ideal led Descartes to conceive of the ego cogito as 'the axiom of the ego's absolute certainty of himself' (CM 49), thus transforming the ego into 'a little *tag-end of the world*', after which 'the problem is to infer the rest of the world by rightly conducted arguments' (CM 63). In other words, Descartes erred in assuming that philosophy should be modeled on mathematics, an assumption which subsequently perverts the problem of the mind's relation to the world as one of inference.

So far, Husserl's critique mirrors Kant's. As discussed in Chapter 1, Kant, too, applauded Descartes's proof of the fact that 'these representations and I myself [...] exist' (A370). Moreover, Kant's appraisal likewise terminated with Descartes questioning our 'position to *perceive* external things' (A368) and the resort to inference that follows from it. In Kant's view, Descartes simply wanted too much: he was implicitly guided by the impossible ideal of knowledge of radically mind-independent objects (transcendental realism). But the whole idea of inferring from the appearances could to an outside reality is false; reality must be embraced from within experience (see my discussion in Chapter 1).

The question to consider is whether Husserl also constructs his solution to the problem of realism in the same way as Kant did, namely by embracing realism from within the space of possible experience, rather than viewing it as something radically mind-independent.

Husserl scholars have discussed this issue for decades, a debate which has become known as the noema-debate between East and West Coast interpreters.[30] On the one hand, there are those who, eager to avoid subscribing idealism to Husserl, maintain a rigid distinction between the experience and the being of an object.[31] These scholars emphasize that the noema or the object as experienced is a separate entity (for instance, Smith and McIntyre 1989, 162). This is to ensure that Husserl's intentional analyses only reveal how consciousness lets a world appear to a subject, without suggesting that it somehow creates the world *ex nihilo*.

This strategy successfully eliminates the threat of idealism. However, it risks doubling the intentional object, as East Coast readers have keenly pointed out.[32] In doing so, West Coast interpreters undesirably make Husserl susceptible to the kind of Cartesian representationalism he argued against. Moreover, the two entities theory fits uncomfortably with Husserl's frequent denial of it. For instance, Husserl argues that reality does not contain two beings which 'dwell peaceably side by side' (Ideas I 111), and that the 'true being of nature is not a second one next to mere intentional being' (EIP 276).

The only right solution to this debate is, or so I would argue, the double aspect view I outlined earlier. That is to say, there is only one world, one totality of being (mind *and* world), which can be viewed either under the aspect of nature or that of consciousness. This means, first, that a 'physical thing [is] a priori, like any object at all, referable to a subjectivity, as experienceable and knowable by it' (PP 89). In other words, reality must be experienceable by a consciousness (otherwise it is a noumenal object). At the same time, Husserl continues, 'in its sense as an object, a thing includes nothing of a subjectivity related to it'. That is to say, while reality is to be embraced from within the space of possible intentional experience, according to its very sense it is independent of the mind.[33] The suggestion advanced by some readers to cash out the legitimate distinction between noema and transcendent object in terms of separate entities is therefore wrong – a distinction in perspectives on the same object suffices.

The comparison to Kant can be taken one step further, namely to the concept of noumenon. Although Husserl is often read as rejecting the noumenon (and Kant as accepting it), he explicitly accepts the logical possibility of it in *Ideas I*. A noumenal world, that is, a reality which principally cannot be experienced, is said to be logically possible, insofar as it is formally coherent.[34] That this is so is deemed evident by Husserl: 'something real outside this world is, of course, "logically" possible; obviously it involves no formal contradiction' (*Ideas I* 108). Yet the idea is, in Husserl's terminology, a material countersense. That is to say, while the idea is not a nonsense, as it at least conforms to formal rules of thought, it lacks meaningful content. As soon as 'we ask about the essential conditions on which its validity would depend', we 'recognize that something transcendent necessarily must be experienceable' (Ideas I 108). This is just what Kant had claimed before, namely that the idea of a noumenal world is to be regarded as formally coherent, yet without meaning (see Chapter 1). It turns out, then, that their views on the noumenon are much more alike than is standardly acknowledged.

Nevertheless, it is worth noting that Husserl, much like McDowell, takes Kant's philosophical efforts to succumb to anthropological or psychological tendencies (see especially EP 357–364, 377–381). Moreover, like McDowell, Husserl points specifically to the problem of another possible type of non-sensible intuition in Kant's thinking – the problem that Kant would leave open the option that 'something belongs to [objects that] we cannot know anything about. God knows better' (EP 363).

88 *Husserl: Intentionality, Consciousness, Nature*

Whether one accepts this reading of Kant or not (I have argued against it in Chapter 1), Husserl has two crucial tools to avoid being interpreted as vulnerable to the same criticism. The first is the sharp demarcation of the space of consciousness from that of nature. On Husserl's picture, speaking about the mind-world relation under the aspect of consciousness means not to speak about natural facts (and vice versa). The space of consciousness is therefore distinct from the empirical realm: it is a space 'into which nothing can penetrate and out of which nothing can slip' (Ideas I 112). As a result, there is virtually no way to read Husserl as vulnerable to any form of the myth of the given. Any scientific or speculative claims about transcendent entities or natural facts have no holding in the space of consciousness.

The second tool is Husserl's 'updated' concept of a priori. As discussed earlier, Husserl believed that Kant's concept of a priori was tainted by the modern mathematical view on certainty. The right concept of a priori simply means the unimaginability of a proposition's negation. So, for instance, the expression a 'physical thing [is] a priori, like any object at all, referable to a subjectivity' (PP 89) is a priori because it is unimaginable that a physical thing is not referable to a possible consciousness (not meeting this criterion means referring to an empty noumenal idea). This law does not hold just for physical things, but for any 'thing' no matter what: 'every thinkable world in general is only thinkable as relative, relative to the reality of consciousness' (NG 78); 'the world is only thinkable as idea in the coherence of transcendental subjectivity' (PR 26).

Husserl, then, by having reconsidered what it means to hold something in absolute certainty, claims to know a priori that the world stands within the space of consciousness. We must (a priori) have access to reality, for the idea of an inaccessible reality is a countersense – even though the idea may be formally coherent. By thus changing what it means to hold something in absolute certainty, Husserl can avoid some of the problems he (and McDowell) saw in the Kantian approach, insofar as it might be interpreted as making transcendental claims contingent upon natural facts about human cognition. I return again to the Cartesian threat of idealism in the context of McDowell's writing in Chapter 6, where I also compare their respective views in more detail.

Concluding Remarks

This chapter overviewed three of the most important facets of Husserl's philosophy: (i) his theory of belief justification, (ii) his understanding of the relations between nature and consciousness, and (iii) his realist intentions. Regarding the first, I showed that Husserl's theory of intentionality yields an understanding of how beliefs are justified that doesn't rely on two faculties, but instead broadens the concept of intuition to include any kind of fulfilling act. One important result of this was that intuitive

Husserl: Intentionality, Consciousness, Nature 89

acts must be regarded as having extra-conceptual content. Second, I discussed Husserl's arguments for drawing a line between nature and consciousness in such a way that scientific and philosophical explanations enjoy mutual independence, while simultaneously addressing the same world. This picture effectively yielded a critique of the different ways in which both Kant and McDowell draw a line within consciousness, by locating certain conscious contents – those lacking the right relation to apperception or those outside of the space of reasons – within the space of nature. Third, reality for Husserl requires (a priori) the possibility of its intentional givenness, which amounts to an embracing of reality from within the order of possible experience. I have argued that this is more similar to Kant's account than is standardly acknowledged.

In the next chapter, I will show how this framework enabled Husserl to develop a far more detailed theory of perception than is found in works of either Kant or McDowell. While Husserl acknowledges that all and only intentional contents possess the characteristic of being exploitable in propositional terms, this does not make intentionality depend on conceptual activity in any way. Instead, Husserl's work suggests that the simplest conscious activities of movement and sensation already accomplish rich contents independently of operations of thinking, and indeed make the latter possible.

Notes

1 Note that I use my own translations for *Logical Investigations* and some other works of Husserl, based on the German *Husserliana* editions. In these cases, page numbers refer to the original German pagination.
2 See Locatelli and Wilson (2017) for an introduction to the relational view.
3 There are competing ways of interpreting the notion of act-quality, which I bypass here. See also Smith (1977), Smith (1989), Hopp (2008a), or Siewert (2016).
4 Crane speaks of content, mode, and object instead. See Crane (2009) or my discussion of him in Van Mazijk (2017, 2019a).
5 See also Lycan (2015) for more on this ambiguity, which also prevails in discussions on the concept of phenomenal content.
6 In *Ideas I*, Husserl introduces noesis and hyle separately as distinct notions, even though in a footnote dating from 1923 it is noted that the hyle is a component of the noesis (Ideas I 213). I will focus primarily on *LI* here, and therefore I will not go into such details any further.
7 Harman (1990) and Loar (1990) contributed to this idea. It is now often taken to support intentionalism, as defended by Byrne (2001, 2009), Marcus (2006), and Stoljar (2007), among others, and representationalism, as defended by Dretske (1995), Tye (1995), Shoemaker (1998, 2000), Bain (2003), Lycan (2001, 2015), Schellenberg (2011), and Bourget (2015), among others.
8 This point resurfaces in *Ideas I*, where Husserl remarks that 'we cannot say of each experience that it has intentionality' (Ideas I 199), and that sensation (now called *hyle*) for itself has '*nothing pertaining to intentionality*' (Ideas I 203). Husserl also notes in *Ideas I* that the issue of non-intentionally structured sensations is 'not to be decided here' (Ideas I 204).

90 Husserl: Intentionality, Consciousness, Nature

9 Sellars (1963), Dennett (1988).

10 What I thus call 'non-intentional' is not fundamentally different from what other scholars have called 'preintentional'. Other interpretations of Husserl that go beyond an exclusive concern with intentionality include Zahavi (1998a, 1998b, 208–209), Costello (2012, 84–85), Bower and Gallagher (2013, 114), Pokropski (2015, 165), and Kozyreva (2016, 4–5), among others.

11 In phenomenological literature, Sokolowski (1964) popularized the view that the early Husserl sees sensations as unstructured data that await the 'animation' of intentional acts, with the later Husserl changing his mind about this. I prefer to view Husserl as consistent on this matter, however. As I have shown, already in *LI* Husserl says that 'no one would think of referring to the sensations *themselves* as [intentional] experiences' (LI 406 italics added). Again in *Ideas I*, he says that 'we cannot say of each experience that it has intentionality' (Ideas I 199), and that hyle for itself has '*nothing pertaining to intentionality*' (Ideas I 203). For an overview of or introduction to this debate, see also see McKenna (1984), Gurwitsch (2010), or Marcelle (2011).

12 Hopp made the case that certain structural features of acts, such as sensations and horizons, do not contribute to an explanation of the epistemic purport of acts, but only to their ontological structure. Such ontological features may contribute to an act being a (true) belief, but they don't contribute to it being true. Although I can see where Hopp comes from, Hopp's view appears to make sensations 'patently contingent premises about my own psychological condition' (Hopp 2008a, 201). On this point I must part ways with him.

13 In his classic work *Psychology from an Empirical Standpoint*, see Brentano (1995).

14 An exception should be made for perceptions of images, maps, statues, and the like (LI 605–606). Such intentions involve perceptual fullness, but they lack the claim of giving the real thing as in an ordinary perception.

15 See (LI 690–691). This view was not well received by neo-Kantians, who thought Husserl's theory of ideal objects led to intuitionism and to an ontologizing of what are really operations of thought. I will not go into this matter here, but see for instance Zocher (1932) for an early critique, and Fink (1933) for a reply to this (that was approved by Husserl).

16 Note that this synthesis of fulfillment is not itself consciously experienced. Instead, it is the object to which the attention goes out; it is identified and recognized as being there (intuited with fullness) just as it is (emptily) meant. Regarding the question what coincides exactly, Husserl notes it principally concerns not both acts as such but rather the matter (see LI 596). Interpretations of this vary in the literature, however. See for instance Bernet's (1985) reading, and Hopp's (2008a, 225–226) for an overview of some of the ways to interpret the concept of fulfillment.

17 This is also a point Hopp elaborated substantially on in his book, see Hopp (2011).

18 As Kern (1964, 5–22) shows, Husserl lectured on Kantian philosophy in 1897–1898, and continued to renew his studies of Kant throughout virtually all important phases of his intellectual development. See also Van Mazijk (2019b), where I discuss Husserl's critique of Kant in *Logical Investigations*.

19 As Husserl notes elsewhere, the problems of Kant's faculty distinction likewise affect his practical philosophy. In his lectures on ethics, Husserl notes the following:

> the whole contrast between sensibility and reason, in which on the side of sensibility stands the sensuousness of sensation as well as that of feelings

Husserl: Intentionality, Consciousness, Nature   91

and instincts, and on the side of reason the non-sensuous categories which first shape sensibility, is fundamentally wrong.

(EE 220)

See also Dodd (2009) for Husserl's work on ethics in relation to Kant's practical philosophy, and Melle (1991) for a general assessment of the development of Husserl's ethics.

20 Consider, for instance, the following, much later remark: "there is not the slightest reason to consider the methodological structure of *a priori* thinking [...] as an exclusive property of the [formal] mathematical sphere" (EJ 353).

21 Husserl's commitment to transcendental idealism was first publicly announced in *Ideas I* from 1913, but it dates back to the winter lectures from 1906 to 1907. See also Melle (2010).

22 While mathematical objects may not seem outside of us at first sight, Husserl claims that their validities are independent of our own minds. Intending "2 + 2 = 4" is not intending my own mental state; it is a universal object that anyone could potentially access. To speak of transcendent objects thus does not imply speaking of real (material) objects.

23 This is what Husserl seeks to convey in *Ideas III*, when he says that "*natural-scientific description* [an external observer's perspective such as the neuroscientist's] determines only the appearance [as a transcendent thing], not, however, *that itself* [the experience, consciousness] which is supposed to be determined" (Ideas III 68). Earlier on, Husserl also acknowledges the possibility of a reductionist viewpoint: one can choose to "maintain dead silence about the psyche, one can scornfully designate it as a façon de parler" (Ideas III 17). But this, Husserl claims, amounts to denying "the dominant thing in the apprehension". In other words, free of prejudice, we allegedly see that the mind is inevitably given in its own way, which resists reduction to transcendent being and thereby warrants regional demarcation.

24 Cf. Searle: "where appearance is concerned we cannot make the appearance-reality distinction because the appearance is the reality" (Searle 1992, 112).

25 Husserl's phenomenology, in fact, does not justify or secure the validity of any body of knowledge. The foundationalism involved in Husserl's project is principally clarificatory: it doesn't seek to prove the legitimacy of certain scientific enterprises, in the way Kant's philosophy arguably does.

26 The overview that follows is a systematic and simplified reconstruction of the phenomenological reduction mostly based on Husserl's best known demonstrations such as in *Ideas I*. See also Kern (1977) for three ways to do the phenomenological reduction.

27 For instance in *Ideas I*, consciousness is determined as the "All of absolute being" (Ideas I 116), which "contains within itself [...] all worldly transcendencies" (Ideas I 113). In *Cartesian Meditations*, it is said that the "transcendence [of the empirically real object] is part of the intrinsic *sense* of anything worldly, *despite* the fact that [it] necessarily acquires *all the sense determining it, along with its existential status*, exclusively from my experiencing" (CM 26 my italics). In other words, transcendence is a sense accomplishment of consciousness, and thus belongs to the space of consciousness. It is only the transcendent *as* transcendent, that is, the transcendent under the aspect of its transcendent being as determined in the natural attitude, that is left out in the alternative phenomenological attitude.

92 Husserl: Intentionality, Consciousness, Nature

28 One might think I am unduly downplaying Husserl's ontological commitment to consciousness as a so-called region of being here. But I am not; as I illustrated earlier already, within Husserl's framework, a change of perspective (a sui generis way of givenness) can suffice to warrant speaking of a new ontological region.

29 See HWV 8; note that the discussion here pertains to Sellars.

30 An early variation on this debate is the one between Ameriks's (1977), Solomon (1972), and Ingarden (1973), among others, which concerns the term "constitution" in Husserl's work. This discussion ultimately boils down, it seems to me, to the same thing at stake in the noema-debate.

31 Here I gather West Coast readers Føllesdal (1969), Dreyfus and Hall (1982), Smith and McIntyre (1982, 1989), McIntyre (1986), Smith (2007, 2012, 2013), among others.

32 This includes Drummond (1992, 2009) and Zahavi (2004, 2008, 2010, 2017), among many others.

33 The same point is emphasized in *Ideas III*: The issue we need to understand is "how *'the same thing'* functions as to concepts and propositions in ontological [scientific] and phenomenological [transcendental] research [respectively]" (Ideas III 80 my italics).

34 See also Leichtle (2002) and Centrone (2010) for more elaborate discussions of Husserl's view on formal and material countersense.

References

Ameriks, K. (1977). 'Husserl's Realism', *The Philosophical Quarterly*, Vol. 86, No. 4, 498–519.

Bain, D. (2003). 'Intentionalism and Pain', *The Philosophical Quarterly*, Vol. 53, No. 213, 502–523.

Bernet, R. (1985). 'Perception, Categorial Intuition, and Truth in Husserl's Sixth Logical Investigation', in: *The Collegium Phaenomenologicum, the First Ten Years*. J. C. Sallis, G. Moneta, J. Taminiaux (eds.), Den Haag: Kluwer Academic Publishers, 33–45.

Bourget, D. (2015). 'Representationalism, Perceptual Distortion and the Limits of Phenomenal Concepts', *Canadian Journal of Philosophy*, Vol. 45, No. 1, 16–36.

Bower, M., Gallagher, S. (2013). 'Bodily Affects as Prenoetic Elements in Enactive Perception', *Phenomenology and Mind*, Vol. 4, No. 1, 108–131.

Brentano, F. (1995). *Psychology from an Empirical Standpoint*. T. Crane, J. Wolff (eds.), London, New York: Routledge.

Byrne, A. (2001). 'Intentionalism Defended', *The Philosophical Review*, Vol. 110, No. 2, 199–240.

Byrne, A. (2009). 'Sensory Qualities, Sensible Qualities', in: *Oxford Handbook of Philosophy of Mind*. A. Beckermann, B. P. McLaughlin, S. Walter (eds.), Oxford: Oxford University Press.

Centrone, S. (2010). *Logic and Philosophy of Mathematics in the Early Husserl*. Dordrecht, Heidelberg, London: Springer.

Costello, P. R. (2012). *Layers in Husserl's Phenomenology: On Meaning and Intersubjectivity*. Toronto: University of Toronto Press.

Crane, T. (1988). 'The Waterfall Illusion', *Analysis*, Vol. 48, No. 3, 142–147.

Crane, T. (1992). 'The Nonconceptual Content of Experience', in: *The Contents of Experience*. T. Crane (ed.), Cambridge: Cambridge University Press.

Crane, T. (2009). 'Intentionalism', in: *Oxford Handbook to the Philosophy of Mind*. A. Beckermann, B. McLaughlin (eds.), Oxford: Oxford University Press.

Dennett, D. C. (1988). 'Quining Qualia', in: *Consciousness in Modern Science*. A. Marcel, E. Bisiach (eds.), Oxford: Oxford University Press.

Dodd, J. (2009). 'Husserl and Kant on *Persönlichkeit*', *Santalka Filosofija*, Vol. 17, 29–38.

Dretske, F. (1995). *Naturalizing the Mind*. Cambridge, Massachusetts: The MIT Press.

Dreyfus, H. L., Hall, H. (1982). *Husserl, Intentionality, and Cognitive Science*. Cambridge, Massachusetts: MIT Press.

Drummond, J. (1992). 'An Abstract Consideration: De-Ontologizing the Noema', in: *The Phenomenology of the Noema*. J. Drummond, L. Embree (eds.), Dordrecht: Springer Science + Business Media, B. V.

Drummond, J. (2009). 'Phénoménologie et ontologie', transl. G. Fréchette, *Philosophiques*, Vol. 36, 593–607.

Fink, E. (1933). 'Die Phänomenologische Philosophie Edmund Husserls in der Gegenwärtigen Kritik', *Kant Studien*, Vol. 38, No. 1–2, 319–383.

Føllesdal, D. (1969). 'Husserl's Notion of Noema', *Journal of Philosophy*, Vol. 66, No. 20, 680–687.

Gurwitsch, A. (2010). 'The Field of Consciousness: Theme, Thematic Field, and Margin', in: *The Collected Works of Aron Gurwitsch (1901–1973)*, vol. III. Dordrecht: Springer.

Harman, G. (1990). 'The Intrinsic Quality of Experience', *Philosophical Perspectives*, Vol. 4, 31–52.

Hopp, W. (2008a). 'Husserl on Sensation, Perception, and Interpretation', *Canadian Journal of Philosophy*, Vol. 38, No. 2, 219–246.

Hopp, W. (2011). *Perception and Knowledge: A Phenomenological Account*. Cambridge: Cambridge University Press.

Ingarden, R. (1973). 'About the Motives Which Led Husserl to Transcendental Idealism', in: *Phenomenology and Natural Existence: Essays in Honor of Marvin Faber*. D. Riepe (ed.), Albany, New York: State University of New York Press.

Kern, I. (1964). *Husserl und Kant: eine Untersuchung über Husserls Verhältnis zu Kant und zum Neukantianismus*. Den Haag: Martinus Nijhoff.

Kern, I. (1977). 'The Three Ways to the Transcendental Phenomenological Reduction', in: *Husserl: Expositions and Appraisals*. F. Elliston, P. McCormick (eds.), South Bend: University of Notre Dame Press.

Kim, J. (1998). *Supervenience and Mind*. Cambridge, Massachusetts: MIT Press.

Kozyreva, A. (2016). 'Non-Representational Approaches to the Unconscious in the Phenomenology of Husserl and Merleau-Ponty', *Phenomenology and the Cognitive Sciences*, doi:10.1007/s11097-016-9492-9.

Leichtle, S. (2002). '*The Idea of Phenomenology*: Husserl's Program', in: *The New Yearbook for Phenomenology and Phenomenological Philosophy*. B. Hopkins, S. Crowell (eds.), London, New York: Routledge.

Loar, B. (1990). 'Phenomenal States', *Philosophical Perspectives*, Vol. 4, 81–108.

Locatelli, R., Wilson, K. A. (2017). 'Introduction: Perception without Representation', *Topoi*, Vol. 36, 192–212.

94 Husserl: Intentionality, Consciousness, Nature

Lycan, W. G. (2001). 'The Case for Phenomenal Externalism', *Philosophical Perspectives*, Vol. 15, 17–35.

Lycan, W. G. (2015). 'Representational Theories of Consciousness', *The Stanford Encyclopedia of Philosophy*. E. N. Zalta (ed.), URL = http://plato.stanford.edu/entries/consciousness-representational/, last visited 10–01–2014.

Marcelle, D. (2011). 'The Phenomenological Problem of Sense Data in Perception: Aron Gurwitsch and Edmund Husserl on the Doctrine of Hyletic Data', *Investigaciones Fenomenológicas: Anuario de la Sociedad Española de Fenomenología*, Vol. 8, 61–76.

Marcus, E. (2006). 'Intentionalism and the Imaginability of the Inverted Spectrum', *The Philosophical Quarterly*, Vol. 56, No. 224, 321–339.

McIntyre, R. (1986). 'Husserl and the Representational Theory of Mind', *Topoi*, Vol. 5, No. 2, 101–113.

McKenna, W. R. (1984). 'The Problem of Sense Data in Husserl's Theory of Perception', in: *Edmund Husserl: Critical Assessments of Leading Philosophers*. R. Bernet, D. Welton, G. Zavota (eds.), Oxon: Routledge.

Melle, U. (1991). 'The Development of Husserl's Ethics', *Études Phénoménologiques*, Vol. 7, 115–135.

Melle, U. (2010). 'Husserls Beweis für den Transzendentalen Idealismus', in: *Philosophy, Phenomenology, Sciences: Essays in Commemoration of Edmund Husserl*. C. Ierna, H. Jacobs, F. Mattens (eds.), Dordrecht, Heidelberg, London: Springer.

Peacocke, C. (2002). 'Sensation and the Content of Experience: A Distinction', in: *Vision and Mind*. A. Noë, E. Thompson (eds.), Cambridge, Massachusetts, London: The MIT Press.

Pokropski, M. (2015). 'Affection and Time: Towards a Phenomenology of Embodied Time-Consciousness', *Studies in Logic, Grammar, and Rhetoric*, Vol. 41, No. 54, 161–172.

Schellenberg, S. (2011). 'Perceptual Content Defended', *Noûs*, Vol. 45, No. 4, 714–750.

Schwitzgebel, E. (2008). 'The Unreliability of Naïve Introspection', *Philosophical Review*, Vol. 117, 245–273.

Searle, J. (1992). *The Rediscovery of the Mind*. Cambridge, Massachusetts: MIT Press.

Sellars, W. (1963). *Empiricism and the Philosophy of Mind*. Harvard: Harvard University Press.

Shoemaker, S. (1998). 'Two Cheers for Representationalism', *Philosophy and Phenomenological Research*, Vol. 58, No. 3, 671–678.

Shoemaker, S. (2000). 'Phenomenal Character Revisited', *Philosophy and Phenomenological Research*, Vol. 60, No. 2, 65–67.

Siewert, C. (2016). 'Consciousness and Intentionality', *The Stanford Encyclopedia of Philosophy* (Spring 2017 Edition), E. N. Zalta (ed.), URL = https://plato.stanford.edu/archives/spr2017/entries/consciousness-intentionality/.

Smith, B. (1989). 'Logic and Formal Ontology', in: *Husserl's Phenomenology: A Textbook*. J. N. Mohanty, W. McKenna (eds.), Lanham: University Press of America.

Smith, D. W. (2007). *Husserl*. New York: Routledge.

Smith, D. W. (2012). 'Perception, Context, and Direct Realism', in: *The Oxford Handbook of Contemporary Phenomenology*. D. Zahavi (ed.), Oxford: Oxford University Press.

Smith, D. W. (2013). 'Phenomenology', *The Stanford Encyclopedia of Philosophy* (Winter 2013 Edition), E. N. Zalta (ed.), URL = http://plato.stanford.edu/archives/win2013/entries/phenomenology/.

Smith, Q. (1977). 'On Husserl's Theory of Consciousness in the Fifth Logical Investigation', *Philosophy and Phenomenological Research*, Vol. 37, No. 4, 482–497.

Smith, D. W., McIntyre, R. (1982). *Husserl and Intentionality: A Study of Mind, Meaning, and Language*. Dordrecht, Boston: D. Reidel Publishing Co.

Smith, D. W., McIntyre, R. (1989). 'Theory of Intentionality', in: *Husserl's Phenomenology: A Textbook*. J. N. Mohanty, W. McKenna (eds.), Washington: University Press of America.

Sokolowski, R. (1964). *The Formation of Husserl's Concept of Constitution*. Den Haag: Martinus Nijhoff.

Solomon, R. C. (1972). *From Rationalism to Existentialism: The Existentialists and Their Nineteenth-Century Backgrounds*. New York: Rowman & Littlefield.

Stoljar, D. (2007). 'The Consequences of Intentionalism', *Erkenntnis*, Vol. 66, No. 1–2, 247–270.

Tye, M. (1995). *Ten Problems of Consciousness: A Representational Theory of the Phenomenal Mind*. Cambridge, Massachusetts: The MIT Press.

Van Mazijk, C. (2017). 'Some Reflections on Husserlian Intentionality, Intentionalism, and Non-Propositional Contents', *Canadian Journal of Philosophy*, Vol. 47, No. 4, 499–517.

Van Mazijk, C. (2019a). 'Husserl, Impure Intentionalism, and Sensory Awareness', *Phenomenology and the Cognitive Sciences*, Vol. 18, No. 2, 333–351.

Van Mazijk, C. (2019b). 'Husserl's Covert Critique of Kant in the Sixth Book of *Logical Investigations*', *Continental Philosophy Review*, Vol. 52, No. 1, 15–33.

Zahavi, D. (1998a). 'Brentano and Husserl on Self-Awareness', *Études Phénomenologiques*, Vol. 14, No. 27–28, 127–168.

Zahavi, D. (1998b). 'Self-Awareness and Affection', in: *Alterity and Facticity: New Perspectives on Husserl*. N. Depraz, D. Zahavi (eds.), Dordrecht: Kluwer Academic Publishers.

Zahavi, D. (2004). 'Husserl's Noema and the Internalism-Externalism Debate', *Inquiry: An Interdisciplinary Journal of Philosophy*, Vol. 47, No. 1, 42–66.

Zahavi, D. (2008). 'Internalism, Externalism, and Transcendental Idealism', *Synthese*, Vol. 160, No. 3, 355–374.

Zahavi, D. (2010). 'Husserl and the 'Absolute', in: *Philosophy, Phenomenology, Sciences: Essays in Commemoration of Edmund Husserl*. C. Ierna, H. Jacobs, F. Mattens (eds.), Dordrecht, Heidelberg, London: Springer.

Zahavi, D. (2017). *Husserl's Legacy: Phenomenology, Metaphysics, & Transcendental Philosophy*. Oxford: Oxford University Press.

Zocher, R. (1932). *Husserls Phänomenologie und Schuppes Logik*. München: Reinhardt.

4 Husserl
Perception, Judgment, Habit

Sensing, Perceiving, Judging

Chapter Overview

Husserl's division of spaces, as discussed in the previous chapter, opens up new ways of considering our perceptual access to reality, as well as the relation between perception and thought. In this chapter, I discuss in detail the various layers of perception Husserl distinguishes, how they can bring a world in view for the subject independently of any conceptual operations, and how they make conceptual thought possible. In the first half of this chapter, I distill from Husserl's analyses three layers of perceptual activity as well as three types of thought contents. The first perceptual accomplishment is of so-called fields of sensations. I argue that this outlines a function of consciousness capable of operating independently of conceptual and even intentional presentation, which relates to transcendent objects. These non-conceptual operations do not belong to the explanatory framework of nature, however, but bear a specific sort of motivational relation to the rational life of the subject. The second and third perceptual levels are intentional acts which make external things available to us. These can also operate, I argue, independently of functions of thought required to explicate the contents they make available, yet they bring the world in view for the subject. This means that concepts are not needed, on this account, to explain access to an external world. In the second part, I turn to Husserl's detailed work on the kinesthetic system and the role of the lived body in perception. I show that for Husserl the so-called horizonal awareness is foundational to the perception of three-dimensional objects. Moreover, I argue that such horizonal awareness in turn relies on a pre-conceptual sense of self-movement. This means that having a sense of the capacity to move oneself belongs essentially to the nexus of the perceptual accomplishment through which an external world is given, prior to the advent of any thinking capacities. The rest of the chapter elaborates on the different ways in which acquired skill (referred to by Husserl as habit) determines perception – from learning to control one's body all the way up to cultural-linguistic upbringing.

Introduction

During the last twenty years of his life, Husserl embarked on a new task of a so-called genetic phenomenology. Roughly speaking, this entails the attempt to clarify, from within the space of consciousness (see Chapter 3), the origins of intentionality, conceptuality, and ultimately of the inter-subjective, scientifically determinable world as such in which we, as adults, stand. This search for origins brings Husserl to distinguish levels of perceptual and intellectual accomplishments, which I examine in this chapter.

It is worth noting that Husserl's investigation into origins is quite uniquely accommodated within his transcendental philosophy. Kant, for instance, explicitly rejected its possibility. This is due to the fact that, as I showed in Chapter 2, Kant draws a line between pure concepts as a priori forms and the merely empirical contents of experience. This division effectively ensured that the question 'why we have precisely these and no other functions of judgment' (B146) could not be answered without rendering the pure concepts a posteriori through that very effort. As I show in the final chapter, McDowell likewise cannot explain the genesis of conceptual contents out of a more basic mental life. In his case, however, this is due how he draws a line between conceptual contents of the space of reasons and non-conceptual natural contents.

On the basis of the exposition on the space of consciousness in the previous chapter, it should be clear the situation is very different for Husserl. The task of a genetic phenomenology is to show how all accomplishments of consciousness are closely connected. Here, perceptual, intellectual, as well as more passive spheres of association and sensation all belong to a unitary space of consciousness. Moreover, as I showed in Chapter 2, Husserl's departure from a Kantian concept of a priori (based on formalization) toward one of free ideation (the imaginative variation of possible world in order to attain sine qua non conditions, as far as the imagination stretches) allows investigating the a priori structures of any level of conscious activity, whether it's 'mere' sensation or conceptual thought.

The general idea of Husserl's genetic work is easily explained on the basis of the theory of intentionality of *LI* already discussed in Chapter 3. Here I mentioned that Husserl conceives of intentional acts as being founded upon one another, an idea taken over from Brentano. Acts of feeling, valuing, wishing, or judging, for example, are construed as founded upon simpler acts of presenting (an object), such as perception. The logic behind this is simple. While we can intend an object in perception, imagination, or memory without valuing it or wishing for it, we cannot value or wish for something with no connection to such presenting acts, as they first present something to value or wish for in the first place. Founding acts (such as perceptions) are therefore more basic than valuing acts, which are always founded, as they presuppose a founding presenting act.

98 *Husserl: Perception, Judgment, Habit*

Something similar holds for the relation between sensation and perception. While it is impossible to perceive an object without sensation being involved, one can conceivably experience (in the sense of living-through, from *Erlebnis*) sensations without perceiving an object. For instance, the sensations in one's feet pressing to the ground are lived-through regardless of whether one is intentionally directed at them or not. Sensations, then, are separable from perceptual-intentional awareness, but not vice versa. Therefore the first is a more basic accomplishment.

The idea of analyzing our openness to the world in a stratified manner is thus already present in Husserl's thinking from early on. The later genetic work differs only in the attempt to arrange accomplishments in order of complexity, and by taking more time to analyze the various distinguishable levels separately (which, as Husserl notes explicitly, are actually closely entwined). By putting these analyses together in this way, Husserl hoped to generate a kind of narrative that could shed light on how conceptual thinking is conditioned by so-called prepredicative (pre-intellectual or pre-conceptual) achievements. While this narrative may mirror a story about how we grow up, its direct content matter is always and exclusively the space of consciousness as found upon immediate reflection (in the mature consciousness of the investigator).

Fields of Sensations

In my account, Husserl is best interpreted as distinguishing three levels of perceptual accomplishment. The first and most basic of these consists of contents referred to as fields of sensations (EJ 72–79). This concept is an elaboration of the idea of sensations as discussed, for instance, in *LI*. There already, Husserl suggested that sensation contents cannot be understood intentionally. That is to say, there is a mode of mere sensory consciousness that cannot be captured adequately by reference to intentional contents (that which we are directed at and which can, as he maintains like both Kant and McDowell, be propositionally articulated). Indeed, in all the earlier works, Husserl either denies that sensations can be understood intentionally or he leaves the matter open.[1] Only in later work, however, do we find an alternative theory, thereby making it clear beyond reasonable doubt that intentionality is not, for Husserl, the single mark of the mental.[2]

According to the later account, prior to our taking an interest in them, sensations are pre-structured into 'broad lived experiential fields' (APS 18). Such fields are said to form a 'more radical conception of passivity' (EJ 60) which is not intentionally brought about but instead functions as a 'background that is prior to all [intentional] comportment and is instead presupposed by all comportment' (Ideas II 291). Indeed, the suggestion that such fields are prior to intentional comportment suggests

Husserl: Perception, Judgment, Habit 99

that we cannot be properly aware *of* them. This is because if we were to direct attention to them, we would change them into intentional objects.

The concept of fields of sensations thus requires accepting that there is something it is like for us to undergo certain experiences independently of our being intentionally conscious. This idea is not altogether foreign to contemporary philosophy of mind. McGinn, for instance, writes that 'bodily sensations do not have an intentional object in the way perceptual experiences do' (McGinn 1997, 8–9). Kind, likewise, remarks that in cases of sensation 'we cannot make sense of attending to the representational content of the experience' (Kind 2007, 424). Even Dennett, albeit in a slightly different context, notes that the 'heuristic value of giving an intentional interpretation' is limited (Dennett 2010, 89).

As I discussed already, other philosophers such as Dretske, Byrne, and Peacocke seem to work with a similar idea. Dretske and Peacocke both claim that perceptual intentionality is not exhausted by what is intended. While we can say, for instance, that we intend the walls in the corner of a room as being uniformly white, there is also a sense in which our visual system represents other, slightly different shades of color. In a similar vein, Husserl, in *Ideas II,* Husserl notes that 'talk about a sounding tone [sometimes] denotes a state of sensation which [...] does indeed function as a stimulus but which does not possess the property of an object-consciousness, in which a sounding tone comes to consciousness as an object' (Ideas II 25). In other words, sometimes a tone refers to something transcendent (a tone in a melody), but occasionally it refers to the sensations that are lived-through instead.

Husserl's later concept of sensations is to be understood roughly along these lines – except that they are said to constitute fields. This means that sensations are always already grouped together; even when they are non-conceptual they don't bottom out in simple sense data for that reason. Like Kant, Husserl refers to such grouping together as synthesis. Since in this case such synthesis is entirely unconscious and indeliberate from the subject's point of view, it is called passive synthesis.

The most general and universal form of passive synthesis is what Husserl refers to as temporal synthesis.[3] According to Husserl, whatever enters into experience is, so to say, immediately glued together with the just-past. This gluing with the just-past is called retention. Husserl further believed that all experience involves empty future projections called protention. As a result of this ubiquitous conscious process of passive temporal synthesis, all mental states and contents stand in an ongoing flow, a law nothing in the space of consciousness can escape:

Importantly, the process of temporal synthesis illustrated above cannot be compared to a causal ordering of events. In the natural world, things follow up on each other causally. Consciousness, on the other hand, is said to be in a flow. The chair I see at t^1 is retained at t^2; the word spoken to me at t^1 is retained at t^2. This enables me to make sense of a spoken sentence, rather than just hearing unrelated sounds. All consciousness thus stretches over time, and without it, no world or thing could be given as causally ordered. In other words, the temporal synthesis at stake is a condition for apprehending transcendent events as causally structured.

However, since temporal synthesis works equally on all states of consciousness, it says nothing specifically about sensations. As Husserl puts it, the 'result of temporal constitution is only a universal form of [...] all immanent data' (EJ 73). In other words, it is the general form of any experience, just as Kant had suggested. Temporal synthesis therefore cannot provide a criterion for the selection of data; it cannot explain why certain data are grouped together into this background field and others into another. This is what the concept of immanent association is supposed to address (see EJ 72–76; APS 162–214).

That association is immanent is to say that it doesn't bear a relation to transcendent (intentional) objects. Instead, it is a passive (indeliberate) process that generates content independently of intentional awareness. The principle Husserl specifies for this associative process is that of similarity/contrast, or 'affinity (homogeneity) and strangeness (heterogeneity)' (EJ 74). In other words, association is said to take place on the basis of the ways in which various sensations resemble or differ from one another. For instance, a stream of color impressions – as opposed to a stream of sound data or tactile sensations – can be passively associated into one field. This is because sound data differ from color and tactile data and are therefore passively grouped into separate fields. Color impressions, in turn, also contrast from one another. A patch of red stands in contrast to a white background. Thus the red color data are associated into one field on the basis of being alike relative to the contrasting white background. As should be clear, this activity of synthesizing data has little to do with, say, seeing a red mug on a white table. Instead, I believe it must be understood as functionally distinct from intentional activity comporting toward transcendent objects. It is therefore a capacity a consciousness could principally possess independently of any intentional or conceptual functions it may have.

Although Husserl does not say much about the matter, it seems plausible, if not necessary, to speak of a concurrent plurality of fields – for example, of visual, auditory, tactile, olfactory fields etc., possibly with various subfields therein, as when pre-structuring the sound data of one's humming computer into one field and those of the jackhammer outside in another. The various sensory modalities of course differ in countless ways and so do the ways in which fields are experienced. But the general (a priori) rule of the association of data through similarity and contrast should be everywhere the same.[4]

Importantly, the law of the association of sensations based on similarity and contrast is closely tied to what may be called their qualitative, felt, or affective structure. Tactile sensations, pain sensations, or noises in the background are all immediately affective contents. For Husserl, affections are the subjective feelings (the phenomenal or qualitative content if you will) that accompany sensory stimulation which serve to motivate the agent to act (to 'awaken the ego', as he calls it). Husserl maintained that all fields harbor degrees of affections, which can grow stronger or weaker, to the extent that they either force us to become attentive or become unnoticeable.

An example can help illustrate this further. Consider hearing an ambulance pass by, which at first completely escapes your attention. At first, in this account, the sound data received are passively associated into one field, because they differ from other (e.g., visual and tactile) data. Given that the sounds do not trigger your interest, there need be no intentional act which relates to the sound as an object. At this point, then, you don't really experience an ambulance; there's only an associated field that you live through, which harbors affections too weak to entice you to act upon it. But let's say that the sounds gets louder and louder, and as a result the field as a whole comes to stand in stark contrast with other competing fields and experiences. Now the affections of the field also start to 'stand out', thus forcing you to pay attention to it – a process Husserl described as the 'turning toward' or 'penetration of' the ego.

To close this exposition on the lowest level of receptive awareness, two things can be pointed out. First, given the independence of association and intentionality – the latter being founded upon the former and requiring the ego's penetration – it is clear that Husserl allows for the possibility of sensation consciousness independently of any rational or even perceptual-intentional accomplishments. The affective contents of sensation are therefore not some kind of epiphenomenal side-effect of intentionality, as certain recent theories have it, but rather stand at the birthplace of intentional directedness.

Second, it is worth observing that these immanent fields of sensations, although quite different from the intentionality which alone relates to an external world, are not for that matter cut loose form the intentional life of the subject. Fields of sensations can entice the ego, thereby forcing it to turn toward and execute intentional acts. This ensures a crucial conceptual bridge between the merely affective, sensory life and the intentional life of the subject. I return to this in more detail in the next section, which discusses two higher levels of perception.

102 *Husserl: Perception, Judgment, Habit*

Simple Apprehension and Perceptual Explication

Because intentionality in the pregnant sense is not involved in immanent association, sensation fields aren't open to reason in any usual sense. This is different with the other two strata of our openness to the world, namely simple apprehension and perceptual explication.[5] Apprehension and explication are both intentional acts – and all intentional contents are, in Husserl's view, open to rational scrutiny, even if they are not themselves the result of rational acts.

One important way in which apprehension and explication differ from the association of sensations is that they, like all intentional acts, require the participation of the ego. That is to say, whereas sensation fields were unconsciously and involuntarily associated, perceptual acts require the subject's attention. This condition should not be over-intellectualized either, however. Attention does not need to involve reflective self-awareness or the sort of 'will to cognition' (EJ 198) characteristic of the intentionality of judgment. To the contrary, just as Kant had said, the presence of the ego (there called apperception, see Chapter 2) may often only be very weak.

By way of example, consider again being absorbed in work while an ambulance passes by outside. The sound of the ambulance is weak at first, but quickly grows stronger and more disturbing, until it eventually fades away. On Husserl's account, before giving in to the nuisance, the sound sensations are already associated into a field on account of being similar to each other (in contrast to, say, the tactile sensations of holding the pen, etc.). But as the ambulance draws nearer, the sound grows louder. At some point, the affective allure harbored in the field will grow so strong that the ego gives in to it. This yields what Husserl calls the turning-toward of the ego; the subject gives in to the stimulus. This turning-toward need not be a spontaneous performance; it can happen as a habitual or automatic response to the sound.

The ego has now been awakened and is perceptually turned-toward the source of the affection. Peculiarly, this does not yield intentional awareness of the field. Intentionality rather directs *through* it, 'toward the sound as a unity which by its essence presents itself in this change, in this flux of appearances' (EJ 107). Somehow, then, through the sound field, which was merely lived-through as a passively associated bundle of affective sensations, the ego now apprehends a thing that presents itself in this change. This intentional apprehension of a thing is only possible as correlate of the ego-subject; it cannot obtain just in sensation fields. This is essentially the same view Kant defended by saying that all (transcendent) appearances given in intuition involve transcendental apperception as a correlate.

The capacity to be perceptually presented with particular things does not, then, rest on conceptual capacities: 'objects as identical unities are

Husserl: Perception, Judgment, Habit 103

already constituted in this receptivity' (EJ 197). While the thing intended has an identity, insofar as it remains 'itself', as I look at it, this identity does not presuppose any functions which, in Kant's terms, have a seat in the understanding. Things are given first in perception, and all judgments and categories of judgment ultimately refer back to this receptive consciousness (see EJ 25–27).

Starting from a simple apprehension of a thing, Husserl points further to a third level of perceptual awareness. This is somewhat cryptically characterized as an activity of 'entering into the internal horizon' of the object (EJ 112). By this is meant the turning of attention to different parts and moments of what is given in simple apprehension. For instance, whereas a simple apprehension presented me with, say, a white coffee mug, I now slide my eyes to the black coffee stain on the mug, as it somehow draws attention by standing in contrast (through a prior association) to the white mug. This process can continue: attention might further shift to darker spots within the stain itself, and so on, until sufficient satisfaction is gained and interest is lost.

It is worth drawing out this process of perceptual explication in a bit more detail. In order to successfully explicate the stain as a moment of the mug, rather than as an object of its own, it is said that the ego must passively retain-in-grasp the mug as substrate theme while it turns attention to the stain (see EJ 112–119). Without retaining the original theme this way, the stain could not come to consciousness as a determination of the mug; it would simply be a new object of its own. This means a split of attention is required. While the ego shifts its attentive gaze toward the coffee stain, and now, so to speak, dwells in that stain, it simultaneously holds fast (passively) to the mug which was previously the focal point. This way, a passive synthetic coincidence takes place between the previous intention now retained-in-grasp and the current intention explicating the stain. The result, Husserl maintains, is perceptual awareness of 'a stain on the mug', still completely without any reference to functions of thought.

This perceptually achieved relation between a substrate (mug) and a predicate (stain) was important to Husserl, as he thought it shed some light on the origins of Aristotelean logic. It is thereby part of Husserl's attempt to clarify logic through an investigation of the space of consciousness, in other words, his transcendental logic. However, many other sorts of relations can be explicated in perception, for instance if/then relations, or relations of size or weight between different things. I can, for instance, lift two cups of coffee and realize, without forming an explicit judgment, that one is heavier than the other. In the same way, I can see two pens on the desk and attain perceptual awareness that one is larger than the other, without thinking it.

This discussion reminds somewhat of Kant's definition of perception, which could likewise involve categorial relations, such as cause and

104 *Husserl: Perception, Judgment, Habit*

effect, prior to the activity of judgment formation. On the one hand, Kant thereby separated the activity of propositional articulation from the contents of perception, insofar as only the former involves active judgment. On the other, Kant brought perception and judgment into each other's close proximity, by viewing the perceptual configuration as resulting from the synthetic involvement of concepts.

A closer consideration reveals that Husserl follows Kant only on the first point. To perceive, Husserl maintains, is never to consciously attain categorial relations. In seeing the stain on the mug, I don't apprehend the relation of substrate-predicate as such; I rather perceive a situation *with* those structures. The relations themselves can only become visible through intellectual acts, as I discuss in the following section. Depending on how one reads Kant, Husserl's denial of the second point could constitute one of the central differences between their respective theories of perception. For Husserl, perceptual intentionality pre-constitutes categorial relations autonomously; it is not in any way the result of understanding. As I will show later in Chapters 5 and 6, this view likewise diverges from McDowell's, who believes that the contents of our perceptions constitutively involve concepts.

Types of Conceptuality and Objects of Thought

It is one thing to perceive a stain on the mug, and another to form a judgment about it. It is thinkable, Husserl maintains, that a consciousness would possess the capacity to perceptually explicate relations between things perceived, yet lack the ability to attain the propositionally articulated content. A non-rational animal may have a sense of causal relations between events, see objects with their separable parts, or have awareness that one thing is heavier than another. None of these capacities are strictly natural; they belong to the space of consciousness, even though they are not conceptual.

Still, as Husserl notes, the non-rational animal lacks objectivity; it doesn't have one reality, one 'world with the sense of knowledge and sense of purpose of humans' (C 210). This doesn't mean, however, that it thereby lacks a world altogether. Intentional perception involves transcendence. A dog passively perceives things external to its own mind; its world is not somehow given as immanent to its own experiences. Still, qua intended sense, or qua object for the ego, the objects of perception are here in a specific way bound to the actually intending consciousness. This is because to perceive is to stand in a direct relation to the object that appears. In Husserl's view, this tie, characteristic of perception, can only be severed by an exercise of spontaneity. Only objects of thought are, in their very sense, not related to one's own or to any other particular intending consciousness. Insofar as they are thus apprehended as being beyond one's own temporally streaming consciousness, and as

Husserl thus obeys by a strict divide between perceptual and conceptual contents after all. As he notes explicitly, conceptual (ideal) objects 'can never be originally apprehended in a mere act of reception' (EJ 251); there is 'nothing analogous [to judgmental sense] at the lower level[s]' (EJ 239). The objects of judgment alone are 'our possession, which henceforth we have at our disposal, which we can come up with again at any time' (EJ 197). All objects of thought are 'permanently identifiable anew' (EJ 200), regardless of whether they are (still) perceptually available.

At the same time, all conceptual contents are rooted in strata of perceptual activity. Therefore the question to consider is how we get from one to the other, that is, from passive receptivity to active, spontaneous thought. To this end, Husserl introduces an intentional act referred to as the 'extraction' of the state of affairs from perception.[6] This is a case of forming a predicative judgment directly onto a perceptual explication, by as it were drawing out the conceptual content directly from the perception. This mirrors what is today called a demonstrative reference, which McDowell also discusses elaborately in *Mind and World*. Since the ideal content is here extracted directly from the perceptual content, the act of extraction still partially relies on the perception as its starting point. For this reason, Husserl considers it the most basic intellectual act.

As I showed in the previous section, perceptual explication already allows for an intentional relation to complex situations, as in seeing the stain on the mug. The question to consider is how to get from a perceptual situation to a propositional state of affairs: 'what is the new achievement which occurs when [...] we come to the predicative determination S is *p*?' (EJ 206). In short, Husserl argues that if the ego seeks to know that 'S is *p*' on the basis of the perceptually given situation 'S is *p*', it must actively and voluntarily turn back toward the synthesis 'S is *p*' as passively carried out (EJ 208). That is to say, the ego must repeat the passive process, but this time in a changed, active attitude. The extraction of the state of affairs is therefore, it seems, a kind of doing over; it is an active repetition of what was, in a way, already accomplished in perception.[7]

This may sound paradoxical. On the one hand, it is Husserl's view that the new object (the state of affairs) differs from anything found in perception. It is something articulable in language, therefore communicable, and accessible to all. Qua sense, it isn't tied to the experiencer in the way a perceptual content is. At the same time, Husserl maintains that the new, propositionally structured object can be drawn from the perception precisely because it was already pre-figured there; it only needed to be consciously attained by willfully repeating the synthesis already accomplished.

The case of extraction reminds of a phrase by McDowell in *Mind and World*: '*that things are thus and so* is the content of an experience, and

106　*Husserl: Perception, Judgment, Habit*

it can also be the content of a judgment' (MW 26). In other words, the contents of a perception and a judgment can be one and the same. But there are at least two important differences here. First, McDowell believes this is so because concepts already determine the initial perceptual experience (strong conceptualism). Husserl argues instead that the relevant match is possible because the propositional structure is pre-figured in the perception. It is thus the perception which conditions the thought, rather than the other way around.

The second kind of conceptual content Husserl distinguishes is what he calls bound essences. An essence (or universal) is basically that which general concepts refer to, such as 'dog' or 'coffee mug'. The talk of essences must not be over-Platonized; Husserl meant it simply as a description of something we do all the time. Grasping an essence demands, Husserl notes, shifting interest from a concrete intended object, which is usually the starting point, to the 'one' that can be apprehended through it (see EJ 321–327, EIP 221). To give an example, one might perceive a white coffee mug in a cafeteria, and then notice that the place is full of white coffee mugs, thus leading one to think that 'any coffee mug in this cafeteria is white'. This is a universal judgment (about any mug whatsoever) with a regional validity (the cafeteria). What one intends in this intellectual act is not this perceptually given coffee mug or that one. Instead, one intends quite simply the 'one' mug, as idea or essence, of which all particular mugs in the cafeteria are now understood to be an instance.

Finally, the third concept of ideality is the a priori essence. As discussed in Chapter 3, Husserl thinks a priori cognition is not an exclusive matter of mathematics, but has everything to do with our capacity to imaginatively vary possible worlds, through which we grasp that something could not possibly be otherwise without ceasing to be what it is. This capacity for imaginative variation is 'everywhere the same' (EJ 354). The act of intending an essence a priori, Husserl notes, requires imaginatively putting actuality 'out of play' (EJ 351, see also EIP 209–215). For instance, instead of focusing on what the actual mugs in this cafeteria look like, I start with an imagined mug (a pure possibility) and vary all its features in free imagination until I grasp the sine qua non constitutive conditions of the mug. This way, I intentionally relate not to this or that mug, within or outside of any actual confinement, but rather to the a priori essence of mug with its a priori constitutive moments.[8]

Before closing this section, it should be observed that in the case of bound and a priori essences, there can principally be no one-on-one matching of a thought onto a perception. In Husserl's account, one can perceive mugs with the senses, but one can never perceive 'any mug in general'. The universal is not something that can be sensibly seen, nor can there be any single perceptual content that adequately corresponds to it. To be sure, the proposition 'any mug in this cafeteria is white' expresses a general rule, and the validity of this rule depends on a collection of possible perceptions (of all the mugs in the cafeteria). Nevertheless, the correlate of the act of judgment isn't instantiated in perception. Therefore, contents of thought and of experience are not 'of the same kind' (HWV 264) here – as McDowell's conceptualist theory could be taken to suggest.

Horizons, Habits, and Concepts in Perception

Revision: What is Perception? On the Kinesthetic System

Husserl's genetic narrative, when broken down into something more presentable, yields a picture with three basic forms of sensible presentation and three forms of conceptuality. The idea that acts range in complexity – that certain accomplishments are conceivable without others, but not vice versa – allowed Husserl to study the origins of intentionality and conceptuality from within the space of consciousness. This yields, as the previous part illustrated, a bottom-up view on the perception-thought relation that is unknown to conceptualist approaches.

Husserl, however, also studied the effects of upbringing, learning, development, and skill acquisition on consciousness. This happens on all levels of experience. Moreover, effects can work their way back into lower levels – as in learning to play an instrument, or to read traffic signs effortlessly. Simply seeing things, then, can still be informed by rationality (through skill acquisition), even if the former are principally independent of the latter. All such effects, including top-down determinations of perception through conceptual habit, are discussed in this second part.

But before getting to that, some corrections are in place. While the previous section yielded a nicely schematic picture of distinct strata of experience, it also simplified matters. Certain key components of the perceptual accomplishment were left out, in particular (i) horizonal awareness, (ii) motivation, and (iii) bodily action. In this section I argue that, for Husserl, these elements in fact constitute a single 'kinesthetic system' (NZR 29), and that this system constitutes the heart of his theory of perception. The result of this is that Husserl's theory of perception cannot really be separated from bodily action. This further means that the idea of perception as a simple intentional relation to an object, as is still a common starting point in contemporary intentionalist and representationalist debates, is at least from Husserl's viewpoint an abstraction. Indeed, as other recent trends emphasize, the body needs to be taken into account.

In the passive synthesis lectures, Husserl famously remarks that perceptual experience involves a 'constant pretension to accomplish [something] it is not in a position to accomplish' (APS 39). With this so-called pretension, Husserl refers to the horizonal structure of perception.

Consider, by way of example, a perception of a table. In any such act, Husserl claims, there is only one side of the object actually given at any point in time. Invariantly, the table is given in what is called adumbrations, literally 'shadings' of the object. Because perception is thus adumbrated, there is a sense in which the presented contents continuously change. At least with respect to *how* the table is given, it must be said to be 'a new sense in every phase' (APS 40). This is because my perceptual taking differs constantly as I move around the table. Yet, in spite of this, consciousness does not intend just the one side, or something two-dimensional. Instead, it is intentionally related to one and the same table.

There must, then, be a sense in which sides not currently seen are nonetheless co-presented to consciousness. Husserl refers to this peculiar givenness as the object's inner horizon. The inner horizon consists of those parts of the thing intended that are not actually given, yet implicitly co-given. It is always possible to bring what's contained in the inner horizon to immediate givenness in the future, for instance by walking around the object (even if this is not actually possible due to some physical obstruction, future givenness of unseen sides would still belong to the 'essence' of a real object in general as an ideal possibility).

Besides an inner horizon, perception is also said to involve an outer horizon. According to Husserl, one never perceives just a table; it is tacitly grasped as standing in some vaguely specified context, for instance a room with other things. As with the inner horizon, the external horizon is not actually seen; it is not represented in any mundane sense. That is to say, the horizon doesn't specify objects in the way intentional directedness does. Instead, it merely provides a 'vague indeterminateness' (Ideas I 94, also CM 82), by being 'obscurely intended' (Ideas I 52). The outer horizon might be stronger or clearer near to the focal object, and then run off at its borders into an endlessly open world-horizon (see for instance LW 116–129, Crisis 31, 35).

This may sound vague. As I understand it, the main point of the concept of the outer horizon is that, just as each perceptual thing is tacitly given as having many unperceived sides to it, so too is each thing implicitly apprehended as belonging to a larger context, a world; 'every real thing is from the start apperceived as a real thing in the universal spatio-temporal world' (LW 116). While without the inner horizon there could be no objects (only 'shadings'), without the outer horizon there would be coherent world-experience into which objects are always tacitly perceived to have their place.

Because horizons don't represent objects in any clear, mundane way, they are also characterized by Husserl as empty. Yet, Husserl notes, horizons are never entirely empty. This is because some pre-figuring of future paths of perception takes place in them. For instance, in perceiving the coffee mug, the coffee stain need not be directly intended. At first glance, it may belong to the inner horizon of the mug. In spite of this, the stain, like so many things in the outer horizon, entices the ego to turn attention toward it. In other words, things pre-figured in the vagueness of the horizon battle over attention. Affective tendencies continuously emanate out of the horizons, thus enticing the ego to act, to discover further. This basically captures phenomenologically what eye tracking devices now show us empirically.

The horizon, then, is not just empty, but it 'is a prefiguring that prescribes a rule for the transition to new actualizing experiences' (APS 42). The idea of a rule should be taken lightly in this context. Rule-following here means following the strongest affection in the horizon. The horizon of the object invites further action, and it tells the body where to go: 'there is still more to see here, turn me so you can see all my sides [...], you will get to know me like this, all that I am, all my surface qualities, all my inner sensible qualities, etc.' (APS 41). The rules thus provided are only pre-delineated paths for kinetic activity – for eye movements, turns of the body, etc. They are therefore separable from all levels of conceptuality and conceptual rule-following.

Importantly, horizons cannot be conceived of without the capacity to be affected and to move oneself in response to that. Horizons and movement are therefore closely entwined: the function of horizons in co-presenting unseen (sides of) objects is at the same time a function for pre-delineating future courses of action. The two cannot be separated. As Husserl notes, the perceptual horizon is a 'horizon of doing' (LW 363). In everyday life, 'perceiving is a doing' (LW 365); each 'I am directed at something' is always an 'I am doingly directed' (LW 366). Perception is never just the representation of objects; it is a doing and a being-concerned-with (see LW 380). To see an object means to co-intend unseen sides, which continuously entice to go on, to turn the eyes and the body – a process out of which alone an object can first become given.

Through affection and action, the lived body is thus included in the nexus of the perceptual accomplishment. The body here must not be understood objectively, as a thing given to consciousness, but instead as the organ through which experience unfolds. Perceptual experiences are said to go 'hand in hand with the orchestrating movements of the lived-body' (APS 50). Movement and appearance even form a 'constitutive duet' (APS 52). The body, then, is what allows one to act, and to act involves the capacity to be affected and thereby motivated.

This idea of a constitutive duet must be taken seriously. Elsewhere, Husserl speaks of the unity of perception and action in terms of 'the kinesthetic system' (NZR 29). In this text, the body is analyzed as the ultimate reference point for the locations and movements of things (see NZR 24; also ZPI 556), thus implicating the tacit co-givenness of one's own body in each perceptual apprehension. But perception not only implies a tacit understanding of the body. As Husserl notes, 'by viewing an object I am conscious of the position of my eyes, and at the same

110   *Husserl: Perception, Judgment, Habit*

time – in the form of a novel systematic empty horizon – I am conscious of the *entire system of possible eye positions* that rest at my disposal' (APS 51, my italics). Perception, then, does not just represent an object: every 'aspect of the [perceived] object in itself points to a *continuity*, to multifarious continua of *possible new perceptions*' (APS 41, my italics). A thing 'is what it is in its mode of appearance [only as] *a system of referential implications*' (APS 41, my italics).

These fragments convey that the object intended is really only an abstract moment in the broader horizon of possible action and perception (the kinesthetic process). Far from being a simple relation to an object, perception involves awareness of the kinesthetic process itself: it means tacitly understanding the prevailing correlations between my movement and the world, such that what each movement means within the larger nexus of possible movements and correlated world-givenness, is always already tacitly understood. I don't just see an object; I grasp what it means within the larger nexus of possible perceptions and movements. This is why perceiving and doing cannot be separated. Even my *possible* movements are 'understood' in perceiving, insofar as to execute a movement (of the eye, the body) involves a skillful understanding of what that very act means within the larger nexus (the horizon) of possible movements and perceptions.

This reveals how incredibly close the ties are between perception, motivation, horizon, and action on Husserl's later views on perception. To perceive is to be concerned with what one sees, to be affected and thereby motivated to act, and to have tacit awareness at each point not only of the relation between action and perception thus actualized, but likewise of the entire space of possibilities that prevails for this unfolding process.

As a final remark it can be noted that, for us, the rule-structure of the horizon is further governed by practical aims. Husserl speaks not only of inner and outer horizons, but also of a practical horizon. That is to say, what stands out from the horizon partially depends on one's interests. The same object, say a chessboard, can yield very different actualized paths of perceptual explication dependent on the interests of the intender – for instance on whether one is playing chess or looking at the pieces for aesthetic appreciation. Husserl repeatedly emphasizes that perception is an ongoing process driven toward the satisfaction that results from explicating the empty horizons, a process that is relative to the practical aims set. This in turn means that the whole kinesthetic process is informed not only by praxis, but likewise by one's knowledge of (in the example) chess and/or aesthetics through previous experiences. Such effects of learning, skill acquisition, and development, can be gathered under the concept of habit – a central but under-emphasized concept in Husserl's theory of perception, which I now turn to.

On Habit

Husserl's key thought is that consciousness is a unitary phenomenon. This allows him, as I showed already, to understand the most basic, qualitative contents that we live through as bearing a meaningful relation to that space of understanding ourselves as free agents in an objective world. As sensing and moving creatures, we are affected by our simplest contact with the world in ways that don't reduce to concepts, propositions, or even intentionality. These structures are all equally embedded within the larger space of consciousness. Being conscious does not just mean being directed at an object; it also involves a tacit understanding of the whole pre-delineated space of possibilities within the kinesthetic system.

So far, Husserl's genetic phenomenology focused on presenting a bottom-up narrative, where basic contents condition more complex ones. But the fact that the space of consciousness is here considered in its unity also allowed Husserl to study a reverse effect, namely how consciousness learns from past experiences and how – top-down rather than bottom-up – conceptuality can enrich perception. All such effects – of how we learn, develop, and acquires skill – were studied by Husserl under the header of habit. In what follows, I overview these analyses by dividing them into three categories: habits that originate (i) in complete passivity, (ii) in perceptual-intentional acts, and (iii) in conceptuality.[9]

To start with the third: Husserl acknowledges that (iii) conceptual activity leaves a trace within consciousness: 'the world is always a world in which cognition in the most diverse ways has already done its work' (EJ 31). Knowledge, then, can work its way back into passive consciousness – as in having learned to drive a car, to taste wine, to discriminate Bach from Beethoven, or to recognize fashion styles from the 1980s. The whole perceived world, in fact, is pervaded with a manifold of styles that consciousness has grown familiar with, whether through explicit judgment or cultural-linguistic upbringing.

Second, not just knowledge, but 'each act institutes a lasting (habitual) validity which reaches beyond the fleetingness of the act, a continuing opinion taken in its broadest meaning' (LW 47). In other words, (ii) perceptual intentionality, which is not a knowledge act, also leaves imprints on the mind on its own accord. Under this kind of skill acquisition I gather what Husserl calls types or typified perception. This refers mainly to a 'character of familiarity' (EJ 105) with which things are presented in the perceptual field. Such types function as acquired norms that govern the simple apprehension of things, in part independently of our capacity to specify them conceptually. For instance, a dog may be observed as recognizing people, as having typified perception of things with which it is familiar, even though conceptual capacities aren't involved, given that it lacks the ability to spontaneously relate to these things in their perceptual absence.

Third and final, Husserl's analyses on kinesthetics indicate (i) a level of bodily habituality operative at the most passive level. Of particular interest here is the idea that the correlations between bodily action and the object perceptually given are subject to (passive) habitualization. On this topic, Husserl's work clearly mirrors, to my best estimation, what has more recently been popularized as sensori-motor correlations (O'Regan and Noë 2001; Noë 2004, 2006). For Husserl, as I argue next, the very spatiality and three-dimensionality of the perceived world is indebted to this sort of skill or habit.

This should suffice to introduce the following discussion, which considers these three classes of habit formation in greater detail.

Kinesthetic Habit and the Constitution of Spatiality

As illustrated already, whenever we see something, we inevitably have only one side given to us, even though we intend the whole thing. Put differently, there is a sense in which we really only see two-dimensional 'shadings', while nonetheless intending three-dimensional objects. Husserl addressed this problem by bringing an implicit horizonal awareness into the perceptual accomplishment. This, however, still leaves the question of the genesis of horizonal consciousness itself open. In other words, why do we have horizonal consciousness? How come we have objects given through horizons, rather than simply having nothing but 'shadings'?

As discussed in the previous section, Husserl's analyses reveal that the horizonal structure – thereby the object's three-dimensionality – can be referred to one's own capacity for movement. Not only are the unseen sides of the object horizontally given; through them, at the same time, possible future tracks of perceptual explication through new movements of the body are pre-delineated. This is no coincidence; they are two sides of the same coin. There can be no hidden sides without there being (ideally) possible tracks of movement. Put differently, on this suggestion, the object is always three-dimensional because I *could* walk around it.

A more exact consideration can help bringing out that it's not just the *capacity* for movement, but more specifically a *sense* for a capacity for movement that is required for horizonal consciousness. Admittedly, the abstract example that I use next to illustrate this goes beyond anything found in Husserl's writings, but I believe it nonetheless sufficiently reflects the spirit of his thought, and may help clarifying what Husserl was after:

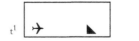 

I loosely based the above figure on a popular Android game called The Helicopter Game, designed by McCandless in 2004.[10] The game involved a helicopter (airplane in the above figure) to be navigated up and down, and blocks approaching the helicopter, which are to be avoided through appropriate navigation (by touching the screen). The figure illustrates an instance of one block approaching (presumably because the airplane is moving) at t^1, and an attempted maneuver at t^2.

This may be challenging but, for the sake of my argument, we can try to imagine that this airplane is conscious. Let's further imagine that this airplane has existed like this for an indefinitely long time, and knows nothing else. Let's assume further that it has visual perception, but lacks all other senses. As the airplane gets steered upward, it doesn't feel the wind press on its upper body. It cannot hear the blocks as they draw nearer. It cannot turn its head to the side or move its eyes to gain a different viewpoint on matters.

What, given these restricted conditions, would the airplane's experiences present? The answer is: nothing but changing patches of sensations in its visual field. Not only would it lack perspective on the triangular backsides of the approaching blocks, as it is unable to freely move itself around them. It would further lack a sense of the blocks as approaching; it indeed lacks the blocks altogether. 'Blocks' do not even 'enter' its visual field. It only has growing and shrinking patches. These patches either pop up at once, starting small, in the middle of its visual field and expanding from there (in case the block appears in its current lane at the end of the horizon), or they grow from the sides of its visual field (as the plane moves into the lane where the block is). All patches (but the last one) shrink either on the right or left side of its peripheral field.

The point of the thought experiment is, of course, to filter something out as a result of which horizonal constitution would be hindered. It can be noted first that what got filtered out is not so much the capacity for movement. The airplane does, after all, move (the controller moves it). What was filtered out is rather its tacit apprehension of its own capacity for movement. In other words, the airplane doesn't *sense* that it moves. The example, then, should convince that if a consciousness lacks the apprehension of its own capacity to move, then it also lacks the horizons necessary for an object to appear. It can still have fields of sensations constituted through association, but there will be no blocks given through them, regardless of whether it has, in abstraction potentiality, a capacity for intentionality (which brings about a transcendent world). In other words, it isn't able to bring about a transition from immanent association to simple apprehension.

If this convinces, then the second step would be to show that a consciousness which does have a passive apprehension of its own capacity for movement could develop a corresponding intentional apprehension

114 *Husserl: Perception, Judgment, Habit*

of blocks. This requires modifying the thought experiment. Let's assume first that the airplane is given the additional capacity to move forward and backward, besides going up and down. On its own, this would bring nothing new to the table. As long as the airplane lacks a sense of self-movement, moving forward or backward will only yield more changes in the visual field. Even adding a third dimension wouldn't help. Extra movement merely yields new dimensions to the growth and decline patterns of patches, without resulting in the apprehension of blocks.

If, by contrast, the airplane were to sense that it went forward, backward, up, or down, things change. For it would then be able to correlate changes in its visual field to such changes in its own position and orientation. It would acquire a frame of reference. Such correlations would then have to be habitualized; the airplane would have to learn to passively predict how the patch changes upon its own movement, and on the basis of that establish a norm for the organization of patch patterns in its visual field. That is to say, on the basis of its own actions and correlated changes in its perceptual field, it would need to develop a new sense, namely: '*this* is the patch as it "really" is, in distinction to how it *appears* to me, as a result of how it is positioned relative to my body'.

Consciousness, or so the example purports to show, can drive a wedge between 'shading' and 'thing', appearance and reality, by extracting the sense of 'thing' from the 'shading', by habitualizing correlations between self-movement and the sensed. In a mature consciousness, or even that of a young child, such correlations have been fully habitualized, thereby overcoming the need for actual movement for the perceptual constitution of things out of changing profiles. Horizons are, or so says my thesis here, the permanent habitual possession that results from one's own past movements.

While the example obviously isn't Husserl's, it captures at least the spirit of his writings on the matter, which, it must be admitted, are usually far more cryptical. Husserl at least indicates that without horizons there could be no object: 'only an uncovering of the horizon of experience ultimately clarifies the 'actuality' and the "transcendency" of the world' (CM 62). He is further clear on the links between horizon, motivation, and action, explaining frequently that awareness of objects implies awareness of one's own position, while also pointing to the importance of habit, noting that there's an 'habitual familiarity of every free change of the I move which co-motivates a range of changes in the appearance' (NZR). Perhaps, then, the idea that horizons are habitual possessions resulting from the habitualized correlations of self-movement and the sensed is more mine than Husserl's – and so is the idea that this specifically lies at the origin of the difference between appearance and reality. Nevertheless, his work indubitably contains explorations of these themes, and clearly moves in similar directions.

Pre-Conceptual Norms and Habits in the
Contents of Perception

On the interpretation just offered, the constituted object-pole – the thing given as it 'really' is through the fields of sensations – can already be considered a kind of norm.[11] If correlations between self-movement and presented contents are appropriately estimated, this constitutes a norm which subsequently guides the organization of patch patterns in the visual field. Once this process is fully habitualized, it will result in perceptual intentionality, which immediately yields external objects.

There are, however, further normative dimensions in play in the contents of perception, or so Husserl maintains. Color perception, for instance, is said to depend on a tacit apprehension of 'normal' light conditions (see Ideas II 60–95). Such a norm is not a matter of natural fact, but itself something that experience must accomplish. For instance, on a winter's eve, the white color of my coffee mug might no longer be perceptually present to me. There is a sense in which it now appears to me as having a color ranging from dark gray to black. Nevertheless, I perceptually intend a white coffee mug, with no thinking capacities required. This is because the perception involves a tacit apprehension of what would be the 'normal' light conditions, which sets a norm of which I am passively aware. This is why, when I switch on the light, I take myself to perceive the mug as it 'really' is, namely white, instead of believing it has just changed color.[12]

Such normality principles not only apply to the mug's color; they also hold for the perceiving consciousness itself. As Husserl illustrates, upon taking a drug called santonin, now fallen out of use, one's color perception of objects can change (Ideas II 67–68). The mug may now appear, for instance, yellowish. Yet, again, one's sense of its real color can remain unaltered, because one's ordinary perceptual consciousness (which one knows would present the mug as white) functions as a norm from which the current perception can be said to be a deviation. As a result, one remains, in a sense, perceptually presented with a white mug, even though it appears yellow.

As briefly touched upon earlier, a further way in which norms structure intentional perception is through so-called types (EJ 36, 124, 320, 334).[13] Husserl remarks at several places that encountered objects are never completely new to us; every perception is accompanied by a sense of familiarity (Ideas II 278, also LW 65). This is once again due to operations of habit. As Husserl notes, 'nothing in consciousness which has once been given [...] is lost, [...] everything remains efficacious in that it creates and develops a horizon of familiarities and known qualities, [even though] it has not yet become our possession, which henceforth we have at our disposal' (EJ 197). Husserl here suggests that, independently of a capacity for concept possession, perceptual intentionality is enriched by the habitual imprint left by previous experiences. Indeed, the suggestion that nothing is lost indicates that to perceive is always to learn: the objects we see inevitably leave an imprint upon the mind, no matter how weak it may be.

Husserl seems to have thought of such perceptual learning in terms of an associative synthesis between the intended and the imprinted (see EJ 72–76; Ideas II 231–238; APS 162–214). That, so to speak, in perceiving an object right now, an association would be (passively) triggered to the imprints of previously experienced, similar objects, thereby associatively re-awakening the imprint. As a result, parts of what belonged to the horizon of those previous experiences gets transferred to the ongoing act, thus providing the latter with a certain 'character of familiarity' (EJ 105). Types thus allow a 'horizon of familiarities and known qualities' (EJ 197) to be transferred into the actual perception, thereby accounting for the incredible richness of perceptual intentionality without recourse to conceptual operations (it is not unlikely that Kant meant something similar in discussing the so-called synthesis of reproduction; see Chapter 2).

Types can also help in making the observable behavior of non-rational animals intelligible. We tend to say, for instance, that a newborn 'recognizes' the mother by scent; that the cat 'knows' that the internet router is warm and therefore good for sitting on, etc. But talk of recognition and knowledge fall short of capturing these accomplishments. Cats don't (re)cognize anything. They don't *possess* types, as if they were concepts freely at their disposal. Yet we cannot conclude from this that it has no rich intentional experiences. Presumably, for a cat, seeing a router triggers a network of horizonal expectations; the router's warmth is co-presented in the perceptual act through an associative awakening of previous experiences, and from out of the new horizon there subsequently emanates an affection and incentive to move-toward, to take pleasure in that warmth. The fact that the cat doesn't possess any concepts does not take away the fact that it has a rich intentional life.

The main theoretical contribution of the concept of type, then, or so I would argue, is that it allows great depth to the perceptual field without having to refer to intellectual capacities. All that is needed are pre-conceptual perceptual skills, derived from habit acquisition through the imprints of previous experiences that are associatively awakened. This way, type habit aids the production of horizonal awareness, patterns of expectations, and helps delineate a space for appropriate future action.

Admittedly, the concept of type is somewhat poorly delineated in Husserl's work; it may sometimes seem that Husserl thought types regulate nearly all aspects of the world's intuitive appearance. In this respect, Husserl even speaks of the world's universal causal style; its typical 'behavior' of showing regularity in the order of unfolding events. All things have 'the habitual character to appear under typical circumstances in corresponding typical ways. [...] [T]he perceived world [...] also has as a whole its habitual character, namely the character to continue in the

Husserl: Perception, Judgment, Habit 117

usual way it has so far' (Crisis 31). Type habit, then, while relatively under-developed in his works, certainly constitutes a central tenet of Husserl's theory of perception.

Conceptual Capacities in Perception

If each act leaves an imprint on consciousness, then certainly intellectual acts do so too. Husserl oftentimes notes that perception is invested with operations of thought: we always see 'a world in which cognition in the most diverse ways has already done its work' (EJ 31); what we see 'is known [...] not merely as an object [...] but as a thing – as a man, a human artifact, and so on' (EJ 38); 'objects of perception appear to us as 'possible substrates of cognitive activities' (EJ 37); they are thoroughly 'impregnated by the precipitate of logical operations' (EJ 42).

Moreover, Husserl notes that objects refer in their horizonal structure to the broader community, to the practical activities of other humans and social life generally (see LW 58, 319). Not only are things seen as 'constituent[s] of existence accessible to everyone' (KI 20); what perception makes available is sometimes even due to a specific cultural world one was raised in (see LW 160–170). For a rational consciousness, experience takes place in a cultural world-horizon; things appear within the life unity of a people, a cultural group, or even a nation (see LW 58–59). There is a tacit sense of a home world, of seeing things from within the shared world-horizon of one's people, which can clash with other worlds, for instance when traveling. While, as rational creatures, we take all things to exist in a single spatiotemporal world, 'each of us [nonetheless] only understands this in the form of one's own generative [cultural] home world' (LW 163).

Husserl, unfortunately, did not write as extensively on matters of cultural consciousness as he did on many other things. It is safe, I think, to group these accomplishments together under a general header of conceptual habit, that is, of perceptual and practical skills derived from intellectual acts, cultural upbringing, and the acquisition of knowledge generally. Although remarks on these matters are scarce, they leave a definitive mark on his theory of perception. For they show that Husserl believed that perception cannot be understood without recourse to the past; that perceptual consciousness carries its own personal – kinesthetic and typical, but also inter-subjective, cultural, and intellectual – experiential history within itself.

Concluding Remarks

Husserl's master thought was that the space of consciousness can be analyzed as a unitary whole. The late genetic analyses of perception pay homage to this. They suggest that there is no need to understand perception through concepts, or to tie all intentionality into a conceptual

118 *Husserl: Perception, Judgment, Habit*

space of reasons. Even the lowest conscious activities of movement and sensation can accomplish rich contents independently of operations of thinking, and they indeed make the latter possible.

At the same time, Husserl's work on habit complicates this anti-conceptualist narrative. Social life and rationality also pervade the perceptual accomplishments which give us an external world. For us, then, perception is saddled with concepts after all. Still, or so I would contend, this only matches the conceptualist thesis in a superficial way. For Husserl, intellectual acts are not a condition of possibility for a rich perceptual intentionality. The fact that (some) perceptual contents are fit to figure in judgments does not derive from a capacity to judge; it is due to perception itself.

Notes

1 This is still a controversial point. See Sokolowski (1964) or Marcelle (2011) for two alternative readings on Husserl's development on this issue.
2 I am referring to T. Crane's 'Intentionality as the mark of the mental' (1998), also elaborated in his more recent work on impure intentionalism (2003, 2009). See also Van Mazijk (2019) for an analysis of Husserl's non-intentional account of sensory awareness in relation to Crane's intentionalist views, or Van Mazijk (2017) for a discussion of Husserl's relation to contemporary intentionalism theory.
3 For more on the concept of living presence and Husserl's phenomenology of time in general, see De Warren (2009) or Kelly (2016).
4 Note that, by pointing toward similarity and contrast, Husserl has not fully addressed the problem of finding a rule for the immanent association of data. The question remains what factors determine what counts as similarity or contrast in each case. Husserl does not indicate a basic mechanism for this, and I think it is unlikely that there could be one. Ultimately, or so it seems to me, there must be norms involved even in the processes of immanent association which are either just 'there' (because they are biological, for instance) or which derive from complex habit formation. I return to the phenomenology of habit later on. See also Doyon (2011, 2015) and Wehrle (2010) on normativity in lower levels of perception in Husserl's writing.
5 I have renamed explicative contemplation to perceptual explication. Also, Husserl discusses a third form of relational contemplation (EJ 149–194); I take this to be a form of perceptual explication.
6 The English translation of *Erfahrung und Urteil* speaks of 'eduction' here instead.
7 See also Smith (1989), whose reading, when held next to mine, could suggest a continuity between the early and later Husserl on this topic.
8 It shouldn't follow from this that imaginatively varying empirical objects such as mugs to attain their essence is a worthwhile activity. Also, it must be noted that the process isn't infallible; one can make mistakes in free variation. The limits of imagination might also change over time (we might discover new essential properties of mugs). The example, then, only serves to illustrate the general intentional act-structure of a priori judgment, which Husserl argued is the same wherever we use it.
9 I leave out a fourth possible concept of habit, namely in relation to the self. Husserl notes in *Ideas II* that any conscious position-taking may leave an

imprint on the ego itself (see Ideas II 118–127, also Moran 2011, 60–61). Once acquired, an opinion may become a part of one's sense of self-identity. The opinion no longer needs to be actively taken up by the ego-subject, but becomes a habitual part of the self. Every person is a 'subject of habits' (PP 286). As Jacobs (2010) puts it, 'position-takings endure as features of the ego or self that is the agent responsible for all its position-takings' (Jacobs 2010, 346). See also Moran (2011, 2012, 2014) and Lohmar (1998, 2003, 2008, 2014) for their work on Husserl's phenomenology of habit.

10 The game was made for Android devices. It can to this date still be played online. McCandless claims to be the designer on his home webpage, http://davidmccandless.com/.

11 See also Crowell (2013) and Doyon (2018) for more discussion of norms in Husserl.

12 McDowell, in fact, makes a similar point, see MacDonald and MacDonald (2006, xiii).

13 The concept of type is used in a variety of ways by Husserl, and it's not always obvious whether it has a technical meaning or not. It is certainly an under-developed concept. See also Schuetz (1959) for an early discussion of types, or Lohmar (2003) for a discussion of types in Husserl in relation to the Kantian schemata. Schuetz's reading, to my understanding, under-appreciates the difference between type and essence. On the interpretation I propose here, types are exclusively passive-perceptual accomplishments, whereas eidetic objects can be correlates of intellectual acts only. I also discuss this in Van Mazijk (2016).

References

Crane, T. (1998). 'Intentionality as the Mark of the Mental', *Royal Institute of Philosophy Supplement*, Vol. 43, 229–251.

Crane, T. (2003). 'The Intentional Structure of Consciousness', in: *Consciousness: New Philosophical Perspectives*. A. Jokic, Q. Smith (eds.), Oxford, New York: Oxford University Press.

Crane, T. (2009). 'Intentionalism', in: *Oxford Handbook to the Philosophy of Mind*. A. Beckermann, B. McLaughlin (eds.), Oxford: Oxford University Press.

Crowell, S. (2013). *Normativity and Phenomenology in Husserl and Heidegger*. Cambridge: Cambridge University Press.

Dennett, D. C. (2010). *Content and Consciousness*. London, New York: Routledge.

De Warren, N. F. (2009). *Husserl and the Promise of Time*. Cambridge: Cambridge University Press.

Doyon, M. (2011). 'Husserl and McDowell on the Role of Concepts in Perception', *New Yearbook for Phenomenology and Phenomenological Philosophy*, Vol. 11, 43–75.

Doyon, M. (2015). 'Perception and Normative Self-Consciousness', in: *Normativity in Perception*. M. Doyon, T. Breyer (eds.), Basingstoke: Palgrave.

Doyon, M. (2018). 'Husserl on Perceptual Optimality', *Husserl Studies*, Vol. 34, No. 2, 171–189.

Jacobs, H. (2010). 'Toward a Phenomenological Account of Personal Identity', in: *Philosophy, Phenomenology, Sciences*. C. Ierna, H. Jacobs, F. Mattens (eds.), Dordrecht: Springer, 333–361.

120 Husserl: Perception, Judgment, Habit

Kelly, M. R. (2016). *Phenomenology and the Problem of Time*. London: Palgrave Macmillan.

Kind, A. (2007). 'Restrictions on representationalism', *Philosophical Studies*, Vol. 134, 405–427.

Lohmar, D. (1998). *Erfahrung und Kategoriales Denken: Hume, Kant, und Husserl über Vorprädikative Erfahrung und Prädikative Erkenntnis*. Dordrecht: Springer Science + Business Media, B. V.

Lohmar, D. (2003). 'Husserl's Type and Kant's Schemata', in: *The New Husserl: A Critical Reader*. D. Welton (ed.), Bloomington, Indianapolis: Indiana University Press.

Lohmar, D. (2008). *Phänomenologie der Schwachen Phantasie: Untersuchungen der Psychologie, Cognitive Science, Neurologie und Phänomenologie zur Funktion der Phantasie in der Wahrnehmung*. Dordrecht: Springer.

Lohmar, D. (2014). 'Types and Habits: Habits and Their Cognitive Background in Hume and Husserl', *Phenomenology and Mind*, Vol. 6, 48–63.

Marcelle, D. (2011). 'The Phenomenological Problem of Sense Data in Perception: Aron Gurwitsch and Edmund Husserl on the Doctrine of Hyletic Data', *Investigaciones Fenomenológicas: Anuario de la Sociedad Española de Fenomenología*, Vol. 8, 61–76.

McGinn, C. (1997). *The Character of Mind*. Oxford: Oxford University Press.

MacDonald, C., MacDonald, G. (2006). 'Introduction', in: *McDowell and his Critics*, C. MacDonald, G. MacDonald (eds.), Oxford: Blackwell Publishing.

Moran, D. (2011). 'Edmund Husserl's Phenomenology of Habituality and Habitus', *Journal of the British Society of Phenomenology*, Vol. 42, No. 1, 43–77.

Moran, D. (2012). *Husserl's Crisis of the European Sciences and Transcendental Phenomenology: An Introduction*. Cambridge: Cambridge University Press.

Moran, D. (2014). 'The Ego as Substrate of Habitualities: Edmund Husserl's Phenomenology of the Habitual Self', *Phenomenology and Mind*, Vol. 6, 26–47.

Noë, A. (2004). *Action in Perception*. Cambridge: MIT Press.

Noë, A. (2006). 'Experience without the Head', in: *Perceptual Experience*. T. S. Gendler, J. Hawthorne (eds.), Oxford: Oxford University Press.

O'Regan, J. K., Noë, A. (2001). 'What It Is Like to See: A Sensorimotor Theory of Perceptual Experience'. *Synthese*, Vol. 129, No. 5, 79–103.

Schuetz, A. (1959). 'Type and Eidos in Husserl's Late Philosophy', *Philosophy and Phenomenological Research*, Vol. 20, No. 2, 147–165.

Smith, B. (1989). 'Logic and Formal Ontology', in: *Husserl's Phenomenology: A Textbook*. J. N. Mohanty, W. McKenna (eds.), Lanham, Maryland: University Press of America.

Sokolowski, R. (1964). *The Formation of Husserl's Concept of Constitution*. Den Haag: Martinus Nijhoff.

Van Mazijk, C. (2016). 'Kant and Husserl on Bringing Perception to Judgment', *Meta: Research in Hermeneutics, Phenomenology, and Practical Philosophy*, Vol. 8, No. 2, 419–441.

Van Mazijk, C. (2017). 'Some Reflections on Husserlian Intentionality, Intentionalism, and Non-propositional Contents', *Canadian Journal of Philosophy*, Vol. 47, No. 4, 499–517.

Van Mazijk, C. (2019). 'Husserl, Impure Intentionalism, and Sensory Awareness', *Phenomenology and the Cognitive Sciences*, Vol. 18, No. 2, 333–351.

Wehrle, M. (2010). 'Die Normativität der Erfahrung – Überlegungen zur Beziehung von Normalität und Aufmerksamkeit bei E. Husserl', *Husserl Studies*, Vol. 26, No. 3, 167–187.

5 McDowell
Concepts, Perceptions, Debates

McDowell's Conceptualism

Chapter Overview

This chapter deals with McDowell's philosophy of perception. In the first part, I outline McDowell's conceptualism as a response to a problem regarding our responsiveness to reasons and answerability to reality. I analyze some of the different ways in which McDowell has fleshed out the idea that perception would have conceptual content. This reveals a certain development of his thought, but also, or so I argue, a lingering unclarity as to what it means for perception to have conceptual content. This unclarity mainly concerns the division between weak and strong conceptualism, which concepts would inform perceptual experience, and how the perceptions of non-rational animals could bring an external world in view for them, given that they lack concepts. After having highlighted these and certain other difficulties, I consider in a separate section whether the theories of Kant and Husserl might offer resources to avoid them. The second part provides a brief review of some relatively recent arguments for non-conceptual content, which, I show, often do not threaten McDowell's central thesis.

Introduction

The central thesis McDowell defends in *Mind and World* and in some of his other works is that the contents of experience are all conceptual. A glance at the literature on this topic reveals that this idea has often been misunderstood by critics, and I return to some of the non-conceptualist arguments against McDowell later. For the most part, however, I want to deal with conceptualism as McDowell understands it – not as a theory concerning the psychology, phenomenology, or epistemology of perception, but as one purporting to address a problem regarding our access to reality.

To be fair, the fact that McDowell's conceptualism does not neatly fit the debate on non-conceptual content has certainly not gone completely

122 *McDowell: Concepts, Perceptions, Debates*

unnoticed. Byrne for instance, suggests that McDowell offers an 'episte-mological defense' of conceptualism (Byrne 2005, 237), rather than, say, a psychological one. The same goes for Bermúdez and Cahen (2015), who take McDowell's theory to pertain to 'rational relations' rather than, say, sub-personal psychological contents.

While an epistemological interpretation is certainly preferable to a psychological one, McDowell denies that epistemology is his primary concern. Conceptualism for him is rather about how to 'ensure [our-selves] that we are not beset by a difficulty about the capacity of our mental activity to be about reality at all' (ETW 243). This 'concern with the very possibility of thought's being directed at the external world' (ETW 243) is, McDowell contends, more basic and fundamental than concerns about psychology or epistemology. Indeed, by targeting condi-tions of possibility, McDowell suggests a connection to transcendental philosophy, Kant's in particular, one which he openly embraces.

In *Mind and World*, the aim is to develop a satisfactory understanding of the relation between thought, perceptual experience, and reality, by identifying a dilemma said to originate in modern philosophy. It is useful to follow this line of thought here by way of introduction. The dilemma McDowell identifies concerns what we can be said to be rationally responsive to. Central to his analysis of this dilemma, in *Mind and World* as well as in other writings, is the idea of two spaces of explanation. This division of spaces itself is not the source of the modern dilemma; McDowell also accepts some form of it (I discuss McDowell's views on the space of reasons and the space of nature in more detail in Chapter 6).

The general idea, essentially taken from Sellars, is that there is a space of nature and a space of reasons. Sellars referred to these in terms of epistemic versus natural facts. The space of reasons is a matter of 'not giving an empirical description of that episode or state [as would be the case with the standpoint of nature, but] of justifying and being able to justify what one says' (Sellars 1963, 169, quoted in NPM 257). In McDowell's words, it is that space we find ourselves 'moving in when we take things to be related as tribunal and respondent' (ETW 245), or again: a space 'of being answerable to criticism in the light of rationally relevant considerations' (HWV 6). Put in simpler terms, the space of reasons deals with the sorts of descriptions that we use in referring to ourselves as human beings, that is, as agents responsive to reasons. The space of nature, on the one other hand, refers to the sorts of descriptions belonging to our scientific understanding of a natural, lawful world.

The modern problem, or so McDowell argues, is one of being trapped in a dilemma that is said to result from the perceived relations between these spaces. On the one hand, it makes sense to maintain that we are responsive to perceived reality, and that perceptions can function as war-rant for beliefs. At the same time, operations of sensibility at least seem to be, or so McDowell maintains, natural operations. This can lead, for instance in a thinker like Locke, to the idea that impressions could enter the mind via the sensible faculty in such a way that facts about natural reality are directly conveyed to understanding. Our sensible faculty processes, as it were, raw facts of nature into the sorts of contents appropriate to human reason-giving capacities. This way, impressions are conveniently construed as two-legged: they inform spontaneous (in the Kantian sense) thought while offering a foothold in a lawful, external reality.

On this first horn of the dilemma, impressions thus belong to two images at once: to the space of nature on the one hand (as an image ruled by natural law) and to the space of reasons on the other (as a realm of responsiveness to reasons). This ambiguity can be said to result from the wish to account for our responsiveness to the perceived world while conceiving of sensible capacities in terms that exceed the proper bounds of the space of reasons (namely into nature). McDowell follows Sellars in calling this sort of fallacy, of stretching the bounds of reason, the myth of the given.

It is good to note that there can be different forms of the so-called myth of the given. In principle, any picture which 'extend[s] justification more widely' (MW 7) than it should be, namely outside of (what McDowell takes to be the proper conceptual bounds of) the space of reasons, would have to be considered a myth. This is why, for instance, 'empiricistic foundationalism' – a theory like Locke's, which grounds perceptual knowledge in basic impressions 'atomistically conceived' (HWV 6) – is also an instance of the myth, and so are constructions involving a noumenal world, as I discussed in relation to Kant in Chapter 1. The myth of the given need not, then, necessarily involve a fallacy with regards to the space of nature (after all, Kant's noumenal world isn't the natural world). It should rather be taken to refer to any transgression of the proper boundary of the space of reasons (which for McDowell is marked by the conceptual).

On the other horn of the dilemma, the very attempt to avoid the myth of the given can result in an outright denial 'that empirical content depends on answerability to impressions' (ETW 246). Here the baby is thrown out with the bathwater. Since whatever is located in the space of nature cannot take a place in the space of reasons, sensibility (considered to be a natural operation) is taken out of the picture altogether. This position, or so McDowell believes, is reflected in 'coherentist rhetoric [as it] suggests images of confinement within the sphere of thinking, as opposed to being in touch with something outside it' (MW 15). Basically, then, coherentism, Davidson's in particular, is accused of failing to provide our rational faculties access to the perceptually experienced world. It undermines our contact with the world, thereby resulting in (at least the threat of) a 'frictionless spinning in a void' (MW 11).

The dilemma now is this: either we commit to a given, or we lose the idea of thought-exercises onto the experienced world. Whereas the first

124 *McDowell: Concepts, Perceptions, Debates*

option undesirably makes brute facts of nature epistemically efficacious, the second cannot maintain thought's bearing on the external world at all. Here, 'nothing can count as a reason for holding a belief except another belief' (Davidson 2008, 126), a view which McDowell thinks 'restricts the way beliefs can be displayed as rational to exploitations of *inferential* structures' (HWV 270).

McDowell's conceptualism comes into view here, as an alternative theory that should avoid both a naturalistic fallacy and confinement imagery. The well-known solution it offers is, simply put, to say that all experience has conceptual content, at least insofar as it has a bearing on 'our epistemic life' (HWV 271).

Unfortunately, understanding what exactly the idea of conceptual content amounts to is troubled by the many different, sometimes (to my best understanding) contradictory outlines that McDowell provides. I return to this shortly. It is easily spelled out, however, how at least generally considered the idea of conceptual content is supposed to open the desired 'path between a mythical Given and a coherentism' (HWV 185). The motivation is simply to preserve the idea of perceptual experience – therefore of being in touch with the world – with a type of content that allows its inclusion in the space of reasons. In other words: what perception provides must be such that we as rational agents can be said to be responsive to it – McDowell's so-called minimal empiricism – while at the same time retaining something of the distinctive character of perceptual intentionality, such that perception doesn't reduce to thought or belief. To say that experience has conceptual content combines the best of both worlds.

Conceptualism, as a theory about the contents of experience, is intended as the golden mean between two equally untenable extremes. Going from this basic outline, this idea can be said to raise two questions in particular, and a good deal of McDowell's writings can, to my estimation, be read as responses to them. The first question is simply: what does the idea that experience has (some) conceptual content mean exactly? The second pressing question concerns how to understand the relation between the two supposedly distinct spaces – the space of reasons and the space of nature. Part of McDowell's answer here aims at showing how sensibility – which on his understanding consists principally of natural operations – could be said to produce contents that are in some sense not natural, insofar as they stand in a sui generis space of reasons. I will only deal with the first question in this chapter and return to the details of McDowell's construction of spaces in Chapter 6.

Conceptual Content

What does it mean for perceptual experience to have conceptual content? To answer this question, we need to know what makes a content conceptual. This is what I'll be concerned with in this section. To start, we can rule out the misunderstanding that just because perception would have conceptual content, it would be indistinguishable from judging. In McDowell's account, there is no straightforward identification of thought and perception, or of the acts of seeing and judging. This is made clear, for instance, in a distinction McDowell introduces between the 'actualization and exercise' (ETW 252) of conceptual capacities. In perception, conceptual capacities are said to be actualized, as a result of which it has conceptual content. Judgment, while also having conceptual content, involves an exercise of conceptual capacities. The difference is that perceptual experiences 'just happen, outside the control of their subjects' (HWV 72). They are characterized by an 'accepting [...] by a sort of default', therefore they do not involve the 'exercise of freedom that figures in a Kantian conception of judgment' (HWV 11). McDowell, then, does not conflate thinking and perceiving just for claiming that both have conceptual content.[1]

On a different note, it is worth remarking here briefly that McDowell does not seem to make use of the Kantian distinctions between various sorts of receptive activities. As I showed in Chapter 1, intuition for Kant referred specifically to a passive sensible intake. Perception, on the other hand, referred to a conscious or attentive intuition, while experience meant knowledge (requiring both stems of knowledge, sensibility and understanding). Moreover, the faculty of sensibility on the Kantian picture included blind plays of sensations unconnected to the epistemic life of the agent. In spite of McDowell's self-ascribed Kantianism in *Mind and World,* he does not seem to have taken over these valuable Kantian distinctions. Instead, it would appear that experience for McDowell is best understood as any 'passive mental state attributable to a subject' (Gersel & Jensen 2018, 2), and in that sense it is terminologically equivalent to intuition and even perception. All such passive mental states, then, have to be considered conceptual in McDowell's view.

A different clue as to what makes a content conceptual for McDowell might be taken from today's debates. It is common to define the idea of conceptual content by reference to the agent's capacities to specify content. Bermúdez's early definition, for instance, explicates that a non-conceptual content is one that represents the world without demanding that its bearer should possess the concepts required to specify that content, even though she may in fact possess them (see Bermúdez 1994, 403). By the same rule, a conceptual content is one that does demand that it could be so specified. This idea has been reformulated by others, such as Tye, for whom a non-conceptual content is one for which 'its subject need not possess any of the concepts [needed to] state the correctness conditions for that content' (Tye 2000, 62), implying that a conceptual content is one for which those conditions do apply. The same goes for other definitions, such as the one suggested by Gendler and Hawthorne (2006).[2]

126   *McDowell: Concepts, Perceptions, Debates*

Two things are worth briefly drawing out here. First, what's striking about these definitions is that they refer to a capacity to explicate or specify a content. In other words, while they purport to define conceptual content, the conditions for a content to be conceptual are specified by reference to a capacity to explicate that content. This has not gone altogether unnoticed in the literature; Heck's (2000) early distinction between state and content conceptualism addresses this, and so does Van Cleve's (2012) more recent discussion[3] (note that I employed my own terminology of weak and strong conceptual content throughout this work instead. In my account, a weak conceptual content is open to conceptual explication, and a strong conceptual content is, in addition to this, informed by conceptual capacities, and open to conceptual explication for that reason. Weak conceptualism thus approximates best what these authors focused on).[4]

Second, it is worth observing that the condition these definitions specify for calling a content conceptual (except for my concept of strong conceptualism) seems to be surprisingly weak. One might wonder why the fact that a content can be picked out by an agent in conceptual terms would suffice to call that very content conceptual. In normal discourse, the fact that one can pick out some thing x under some aspect y doesn't seem to imply that x is identical to or deserves the same classification as y. If a dock worker uses a crane with a hook to pick up a container, nobody would bother to argue that the container thus picked up ought to be referred to as a hook (or as having 'hookish' content).[5] Obviously hooks and containers aren't the same things as concepts and contents. But there is a point to be made that the concept of conceptual content is used too liberally.[6]

At least some of McDowell's own definitions of conceptual content clearly refer to the capacity of the bearer of that state to explicate or exploit contents. They are therefore in line with what I call weak conceptualism. Consider these three fragments:

[1] The way I am exploiting the Kantian idea of spontaneity commits me to a demanding interpretation of words like 'concepts' and 'conceptual'. It is essential to conceptual capacities, in the demanding sense, that they *can be exploited* in active thinking.

(MW 47, my italics)

[2] An intuition's content is all conceptual, in this sense: it is in the intuition in a form in which one *could* make it, that very content, figure in discursive activity.

(MW 265, my italics)

[3] [This] is what it means for capacities to be conceptual in the relevant sense: they are capacities whose content is of a form that *fits it to figure* in discursive activity.

(MW 42 my italics)

[4] Every aspect of the content of an intuition is present in a form in which it is *already suitable to be* the content associated with a discursive capacity.

(HWV 264)

These three fragments all state that it is intuition's openness to conceptual explication – not its *being* a concept or a proposition, nor its being *informed* by concepts – that defines its conceptual nature. However, as I pointed out already, it is not so obvious that this condition would be very 'demanding' (MW 47), as McDowell appears to believe it is. After all, being conceptualizable is hardly a demanding use of the term conceptual. If anything, as I illustrated already, it seems an inappropriate use of the term. It is also worth pointing out that neither Kant nor Husserl spoke of contents in this way, even though both did defend the same idea expressed in the thesis of weak conceptualism, namely that all intuitions (insofar as they concern me at all) can be determined conceptually.

While fragments [1] through [4] can be read as defending weak conceptualism, McDowell in various other places suggests a different notion of conceptuality. On this second definition, the contents of experience are all conceptual in this sense: they can be taken up into judgments in the way weak conceptualism specifies, while this is so because rational capacities already figure in them. This is the thesis I have throughout called strong conceptualism. It is the view that concepts structure what we see, and that this is what first makes perceived reality available to the subject. Consider the following fragments:

[5] I urge that even unreflective bodily coping, on the part of rational animals, is informed by their rationality.

(WM 338)

[6] [T]he ability to have objects come into view for one is essentially dependent on the ability to make judgments, and that is indeed an implication of the position I am finding in Kant.

(HWV 35)

[7] We could not have intuitions, with their specific forms of unity, if we could not make judgements, with their specific form of unity.

(HWV 264)

Here and in many other works from 1994 up to 2018, McDowell suggests that perceptual experiences have conceptual content because rationality in some way figures in them. It should be clear that this is a very different thesis than weak conceptualism. Indeed, insofar as weak conceptualism would specify the necessary and sufficient conditions for a content to be conceptual – as seems to be the case in fragments [1] through [4] – strong conceptualism rejects weak conceptualism (given that it adds another

128 McDowell: Concepts, Perceptions, Debates

necessary condition, namely that a content is informed by concepts, rationality, or conditioned by the ability to make judgments).

To clarify what exactly the term 'conceptual content' is supposed to capture a bit further, it is worth focusing in more detail on *Having the World in View* from 2009, as McDowell claims to have changed his position on the contents of experience in the final essay of this book. According to McDowell's self-assessment there, his change of position concerns the following:

> [8] I used to assume that to conceive experiences as actualizations of conceptual capacities, we would need to credit experiences with propositional content, the sort of content judgments have. And I used to assume that the content of an experience would need to include everything the experience enables its subject to know non-inferentially. But both assumptions now strike me as wrong.
>
> (HWV 258)

The most natural way to interpret the second claim in [8] (in the second sentence) is as saying that McDowell no longer believes that perceptual experience provides one with all the things that one could know on the basis of it. For instance, I might see a bird, and be justified in forming the proposition that it is a cardinal, without the perceptual presentation having the content of a cardinal. As McDowell puts it later on, 'there is no need to suppose that the concept under which my recognitional capacity enables me to bring what I see figures in that content' (HW 259). To say that perception has conceptual content, then, does not amount to saying that all the things I could know on its basis figure in the perception. While this claim is indeed new (relative to the account in *Mind and World*), it is only negative, and therefore leaves open what kind of content perceptual experience would have exactly. As the first claim in [8] specifies, it is not propositional content – which presumably means it isn't propositionally articulated on its own account. On this point, at least, McDowell can agree with Travis: that in perceiving a pig, 'the pig is *before* you. That the pig is before you is not before you' (Travis 2018, 10).

However, this characterization may still seem rather basic and uncontroversial. Moreover, if this is indeed what McDowell means with propositional content, then I don't see how this differs from what was said in *Mind and World*. In *Having the World in View*, McDowell says that perceptual experience has content of 'a sort that embodies an immediate potential for exploiting that same content in knowledgeable judgments' (HWV 267). In other words, perception has a content that could be fit to figure in discursive acts, even if it is not already articulated. But this is no different in *Mind and World*. Fragments [1] through [4], for instance, expressly avoided addressing perception's conceptual content in discursive terms. Fragment [2] says explicitly that a content is conceptual because one *could* make it figure in discursive activity – which implies that it isn't already propositionally articulated.

The first claim in fragment [8] therefore doesn't shed much light on the question that needs to be answered: what kind of content does perceptual experience have? We know that the answer is: conceptual content, and in *Having the World in View* we are told that this doesn't mean that the perceptual experience would need to contain 'everything the experience enables its subject to know' (HWV 258). But, as I said already, this description is only negative; it doesn't clarify which concepts do play a role in the experience. If, for instance, my perception does not present me with a cardinal when I see one, does it at least still present me with a bird? What about the concept of 'animal in general' or 'thing in general'? If perception is informed by concepts, as McDowell tells us, then which concepts play this informative role?

I would be inclined to say that there's no real point in asking such questions, and that it would be better not to put oneself in a position where an answer to them is expected. However, McDowell's central idea is that experience has conceptual content, and this idea is, as I have illustrated, explained on several occasions in terms of concepts or rationality that would be operative in perception. It may well seem, therefore, that McDowell has put himself in just that position.

One way to resolve this issue would be quite simply to drop strong conceptualism and to say instead that perceptual experience has its *own* kind of content, one which happens to be conceptualizable. This was Husserl's view (Chapter 4): the contents of intuition can principally be explicated in intellectual acts (weak conceptualism), but this doesn't mean that we should refer to the contents of perceptual experience as being conceptual. Instead, perceptual experience has its own kinds of content, which can bring a complex world into view even before any concepts have been developed.

Perhaps one could read McDowell as developing his views into this direction. First, as I noted already, he denied that the concept of cardinal or bird would actually figure in the perceptual experience. Second, he said that perceptual experience is better understood as having content of 'a sort that embodies an immediate potential for exploiting that same content in knowledgeable judgments' (HWV 267). But at one point, he also suggests that the concept of bird in fact captures 'the distinctive kind of unity it [the intuition] has' (HWV 261). Although perhaps far-fetched, one could read this as saying that the intuition isn't unified by any concept after all, but that it is merely 'unified by a form capturable' by a concept (HWV 261). This possibly autonomous form would then be what is meant by the term 'common sensible' (HWV 261).

If this were McDowell's suggestion, it would certainly yield a different picture of his conceptualism. It would mean that perceptual experience has its own sort of content, one that is capturable by various concepts (cardinal, bird, animal), but which could be its own kind of product. Clearly, saying that experience has its own sort of content that happens

130   *McDowell: Concepts, Perceptions, Debates*

to be capturable by concepts entails only a weak form of conceptualism – one which arguably doesn't provide a convincing reason to refer to those contents in terms of concepts at all, since they could have been just the same had there been no conceptual capacities in play at all.

It is doubtful, however, that one can consistently read McDowell's later work in this way. First, it can be noted that in later work McDowell has continued to identify the contents of intuition with those of thought. In a contribution published in 2009, McDowell again asserts that 'the experience [...] itself already has content that is *just as firmly conceptual* as the content of a judgment' (ETW 250 my italics). Also later on in the same contribution that announced his change of position, we find him saying the following:

> [9] The unity of intuitional content reflects an operation of the same unifying function that is operative in the unity of judgements, in that case actively exercised. That is why it is right to say that the content unified in intuitions is *of the same kind* as the content unified in judgements: that is *conceptual* content.
>
> (HWV 264 my italics)

If we isolate the first sentence, this fragment could well be taken to fit Kant's view. Indeed, it is almost literally copied from the first *Critique*: 'the same function which gives unity to the different representations in a judgment also gives unity to [...] representations in an intuition' (A79/B104–105), Unlike Kant, however, McDowell believes that the idea of a single unifying function is sufficient to call the contents of experience conceptual, a conclusion Kant did not draw. It is further unclear why the idea that there would be some unifying function to thought and perceptual experience would make it right to say that the latter has conceptual content, unless the function is itself construed as a concept – in which case we are back at strong conceptualism. Second, it can be noted that McDowell continues to assert strong conceptualism in later works a well, also in the sentence immediately following fragment [9]:

> [10] We could not have intuitions, with their specific forms of unity, if we could not make judgements, with their specific form of unity.
>
> (HWV 264)

This points us back to the strong conceptualist thesis that concepts are required for perceptual experience to have the content it does. Once more, then, the idea is not just that perceptual experience 'embodies an immediate potential for exploiting that same content in knowledgeable judgments' (HWV 267). This is also what was defended in fragments [1] through [4], but it only amounts to the position of weak conceptualism. Instead of defending this, McDowell again asserts that unity of intuition derives from unity of perception. Moreover, in a later contribution from

2018, McDowell again asserts that what makes a content conceptual is that conceptual capacities figure in it:

[11] [W]ith us [...] conceptual capacities must be in act in [...] perceptual awareness.

(TKFG 15)

McDowell thus clearly defends strong conceptualism,[7] but this then raises the same problems discussed earlier. If the perceptual experience need not contain 'everything the experience enables its subject to know' (HWV 258), then which conceptual capacities ('cardinal', 'bird', 'thing in general') are activated in it? What are these 'common sensibles', and if they are not the familiar concepts, then how is this still conceptualism?

It seems to me that these problems are not resolved in the more recent contribution from 2018 in *In the Light of Experience*. Consider, for instance, McDowell's remarks on what distinguishes our perceptual experiences from those of non-rational animals. At first, McDowell states that the contents of these perceptions are in fact largely the same:

[12] [P]erception does *something* for perceivers that do not have conceptual capacities in the relevant sense: something generically the same as what it does for us. [...] Items in the outer world are perceptually given to such creatures no less than to us.

(TFKG 23–24)

Non-rational animals, then, or so it is alleged here, do see 'items in the outer world', and they do so 'no less than us'. Unfortunately, 'items in the outer world' is not a concept McDowell fleshes out in any detail. Later on, he also speaks of 'things' to denote what animals see. The message, however, is clear: animals see things or items in the outer world 'no less' than we do.

But it is difficult to see how this fits into the conceptualist thesis as discussed so far. For wasn't the whole idea of conceptualism to take the very givenness of things as a result of conceptual functions of an understanding only rational creatures like us enjoy? It seems that by saying that 'items in the outer world are perceptually given to such creatures no less than to us' (TFKG 2), McDowell contradicts his own conceptualism, which rests on the idea that the sensible presentation of things in the outer world relies on functions specific to rational creatures like us, namely on concepts and the capacity to judge.

A bit further on in the same contribution, McDowell appears to moves away from this suggestion again, seemingly to the opposite end of the spectrum:

[13] That intuitions have content is an implication of the claim that capacities of the sort that are exercised in judgment are in act in intuitions.

(TFKG 27)

132 *McDowell: Concepts, Perceptions, Debates*

Here, to the opposite effect of what was just claimed in [12], McDowell appears to suggest that the very possibility of intuitions having content at all does, after all, depend on capacities of judgment – just as he stated in fragments [5] to [7] among others. It therefore appears that, since certain animals lack such capacities in his view, their intuitions cannot have content. But how, then, could they have an 'outer world', 'items' or 'things' present 'no less than us', as he claimed earlier? Certainly seeing items – even when that does not amount to seeing objects in some fuller sense – still presupposes perceptual content.

Later on in the same contribution, McDowell notes the following:

> [14] [F]or non-rational animals too, perceiving things, for instance seeing them, requires more than just sense impressions, though the extra that is required cannot be, as with us, that conceptual capacities must be in act in their perceptual awareness.
>
> (TKFG 32)

This fragment supports the view that non-rational animals do indeed perceive things in an outer world, but apparently without concepts being involved. A fair question to ask here would be: but how, then, do they see things? I have not succeeded in finding a clear answer in McDowell's writings. The idea of conceptualism was, as this fragment again shows, that to have the world in view demands conceptual capacities operative in perception – that 'the idea of encountering a particular is in place [...] *only because* the experience involves a concept' (PLA 284)[8] – yet non-rational animals are now said to encounter external things as well while lacking concepts. But how non-rational animals could see things in the outer world no less than us while lacking concepts remains something of a mystery here, and the very idea that they have such experiences in the first place appears to undermine the idea that a conceptual organization of perception first makes access to things in the outer world possible.

It thus seems that certain undoubtedly crucial questions remain unanswered. What is the added value of concepts in perception for us exactly? And which concepts, given that it isn't those of cardinal, bird, animal, etc., play an important role for us? What does it mean that concepts figure in perception? How can non-rational animals see things in an external world if they lack concepts, and how is the fact that they do have such experiences even compatible with conceptualism? These are, it seems to me, some of the questions McDowell would need to answer clearly to make his conceptualist theory convincing.

Reflections on Concepts in Perception in McDowell, Kant, and Husserl

I want to use this section to reflect on some of the differences between the role of concepts in perception in the theories of McDowell, Kant,

McDowell: Concepts, Perceptions, Debates   133

and Husserl. In particular, I aim to highlight some of the ways in which Kant and Husserl may have something to offer to the contemporary debate on conceptualism. To this end, this section briefly reiterates some of the discussions of the first four chapters.

To start with Kant, I noted already that McDowell might have benefited from adopting some of the different notions of receptive activity Kant distinguishes, in particular experience, intuition, perception, and sensation. For Kant, as I outlined in Chapters 1 and 2, these are conceptually distinct notions. First of all, experience is not a capacity of sensibility alone, but an act of knowledge acquisition, and therefore involves the activation of thinking capacities as well. Second, an intuition refers to any sensory intake that has the sort of unity that makes things available to us such that they could be determined in an experience. Third, while intuitions need not be conscious in any pregnant sense (they can be sheer intuitions), a perception is by definition an intuition with consciousness. Fourth, Kant's concept of sensation includes blind plays of sensations. While we undergo such plays of sensations subjectively (in a 'qualitative' way), they are not open to conceptual exercises. This is, moreover, 'the largest [of all classes of sensible contents] in the human being' (Anth 7: 135).

Separating different types of receptive content might prove to be a good strategy for avoiding some of the ambiguities that haunt McDowell's conceptualist thesis. In an early review of *Mind and World*, Wright (1996) noted that it need not follow from the fact that the content of a perceptual experience is (i) not a bare given and (ii) conceptualizable that it is conceptual. Put differently, if we distinguish between varieties of perceptual content, then we can create an 'intermediate space' between conceptual content and bare givens, thereby avoiding the need to qualify all perceptual experience in terms that are really only adequate to capture operations of thought.

In my reading of Kant's transcendental deduction, I further suggested that Kant's central argument was not aimed at showing that concepts would figure in all sensible intake, in the way McDowell's strong conceptualism suggests. The main thesis Kant set out to defend was that intuitions are synthesized through the imagination in a way that brings them to accord with pure concepts, and that since intuitions can in principle be linked to apperception, we are capable of bringing our thoughts to bear on them (see my exposition in the first half of Chapter 2). Such a weak conceptualist view was essentially also defended by Husserl, and it should suffice to establish intuition's inclusion in the McDowellian space of reasons.

McDowell's strong conceptualism, on the other hand, denies that this is a sufficient condition for a content to be conceptual, and adds that the content must be structured by concepts, which alone would make a world available to the subject. I argued already that this view faces two problems in particular. First, it makes us expect to be told which concepts would then play a role in receptive content, something McDowell is unable to tell us. Second, it faces the difficult task of explaining the non-conceptual presentation of things in an outer world which non-rational animals enjoy, a task problematized by the fact that strong conceptualism has made this type of presentation dependent upon conceptual capacities.

Kant has a valuable tool which may help in avoiding both of these problems. As I discussed in Chapter 1, Kant referred the synthetic operations of spontaneity in intuition to a special power called imagination. In this picture, concepts don't immediately structure intuitions at all; it is the imagination which synthesizes the contents of intuition in accordance with concepts – at least in our case. This means there is space, at least in theory, to conceive of a non-conceptual relation to external objects in the absence of concepts, since the power of the imagination could be deemed capable of synthesizing receptive contents independently of the possession of concepts of understanding.

McDowell, on the other hand, works with a simplified Kantian account of understanding and spontaneity which reduces both to talk of concepts. In his view, concepts must be said to be responsible for a perceptual relation to an outer world; there is no other option on the table (other options would here amount to the myth of the given). As a result, it becomes difficult to see how a non-conceptual relation to external things could be constituted. Kant's account does not necessarily face this problem since it employs the concept of imagination as intermediary between intuitions and concepts.

A final advantage of Kant's account derives from the crucial Kantian distinction between sensibility and understanding. As I showed in Chapter 1, Kant had a good reason to keep these faculties separate, deriving from the insight that our capacity to conceptually determine the world cannot be adequately captured by reference to a conceptual apparatus only. This is Kant's argument from incongruent counterparts, which was his main motivation for a separation of two faculties as well as his central argument against rationalist epistemology (as is discussed in the Amphiboly but also in earlier works and in *Prolegomena*). The conclusion of the argument was, in short, that one needs to obtain a concrete viewpoint from which to orient oneself in order to have the kind of access to reality that we have. While this may not suffice to establish that intuition has non-conceptual content, it is still a convincing argument for an extra-conceptual element to perceptual intentionality. Therefore, even if one reads the transcendental deduction as supporting a form of strong conceptualism, Kant still offers compelling reasons to admit that there must be a non-conceptual element to perception.

Other interesting points could be drawn from Husserl. First, as I showed in Chapter 3, Husserl insisted that the warranting or fulfilling character of intuitive acts must derive from something strictly extra-conceptual. This is because, contrary to Davidson's slogan (that beliefs can only be justified by other beliefs), meaning acts for Husserl can only be justified by non-meaning acts. That is to say, only acts which make something available through some mental grasping – whether of mathematically, sensibly, or categorially intended objects – can provide warrant for empty acts. Beliefs stand in need of the fullness which intuitive acts alone can supply, and this particular feature of fullness does not reduce to empty conceptual belief.[9] This theory of fulfillment offers a good reason not to address the contents of perceptual experience exclusively in conceptual terms.

Second, Husserl, like Kant, distinguished different accomplishments within receptivity. In his view, reality is an achievement that comes in layers. This means that the contents of receptivity do not all reduce to the one category of the conceptual. As a result of this, Husserl could shed light on the transition from the non-conceptual to the space of reasons, without committing to the myth of the given for that reason. In other words, Husserl allowed for many kinds of intermediary contents between bare givens and conceptual content.

As I showed in Chapter 4, Husserl analyzed in considerable detail three levels of receptive contents. The first of these concerns a synthetic activity that is said to be prior to intentional directedness, and thus prior to what Kant calls intuition (in which, on Kant's understanding, outer things are given). This content was called 'fields of sensations'. While these fields, on Husserl's view in *Experience and Judgment*, do not give us contents capturable by concepts, there is nonetheless said to be a specific kind of relation to the ego-subject already, and thereby to the potential intellectual life – insofar as fields of sensations are said to produce affections which can yield the attention of the ego-subject. This means that fields of sensations are epistemically efficacious, even when they do not live up to the condition of weak conceptualism.

According to Husserl, simple apprehension and perceptual explication first put us in touch with external objects, which are somehow given 'through' the field of sensations, once the subject's attention has been raised. Instead of suggesting that simple apprehensions have conceptual content, Husserl argued that conceptual relations pre-figure in apprehensions, independently of any capacity to explicate those contents. He subsequently described how we are able to form judgments that make these pre-figured categorial relations explicit. In other words, instead of suggesting that perception has the sort of content thought has (conceptual content), Husserl considered which structures contained in the perception can be carried over into thought.[10]

A third point to be taken from Husserl concerns the importance of having awareness of more than what is contained in the immediate now. A relation to an external world can only be achieved by being aware of

136 *McDowell: Concepts, Perceptions, Debates*

more than what is actually seen at any particular moment – a capacity referred to as horizonal awareness, which is more or less ubiquitous in consciousness and which does not rest on conceptual capacities. The fact that our perceptions do not yield just 'shadings' (two-dimensional profiles) is due to horizonal awareness; a thing becomes a thing only within 'a system of referential implications' (APS 41). Without horizons, there could be no transcendence, hence no external world for the subject.

I further proposed understanding this crucial concept of the horizon not by reference to concepts but in relation to having a sense of self-movement. In Husserl's view, the very three-dimensionality of the world is conditioned by our having a sense of self-movement. In order to drive a wedge between mere 'shading' (two-dimensional profile) and 'thing' (understood as three-dimensional, external thing), consciousness has to extract the sense of 'thing' from the shadings, which alone are immediately given in a stricter sense. This happens, I argued, by the habitualization (a form of passive learning) of correlations between self-movement and changes in shadings. By habitually attaining a grip on such correlations, consciousness can discover patterns in the continuously changing shadings. This process culminates, as I argued in Chapter 4, in the stable object-poles that are apprehended as being distinct from one's own moving and apprehending consciousness.

For Husserl, then, the external thing is a product of our discovering and predicting patterns. Once the correlations between self-movements and changes in sensation fields have been appropriately habitualized, the need for actual movement can be dispensed with. This is how perceptual consciousness can acquire the characteristic of putting us in touch with an external world 'in a single blow' – even though, in a stricter sense, only mere 'shadings' are given.

Finally, other processes of habit were said to function within the subject-world relation. In particular, so-called types here guarantee that things always appear to us with a sense a familiarity, prior to conceptualizing them. Furthermore, every new perception enriches future perceptions: 'nothing in consciousness which has once been given […] is lost, […] everything remains efficacious in that it creates and develops a horizon of familiarities and known qualities, [even though] it has not yet become our possession [as with propositional knowledge]' (EJ 197).

As I argued in Chapter 4, Husserl thought of types in terms of a passive (indeliberate from the subject's viewpoint) association between what's currently seen and similar past experiences. For instance, in seeing my computer, associations are passively triggered to the imprints of previous experiences, thereby also re-awakening past horizons. As a result, the currently seen computer gets a certain 'character of familiarity' (EJ 105). This doesn't necessarily mean that I see the computer *as* my computer. Instead, the type's contribution is more tacit: the computer now appears within a network of horizonal implications which delineates future paths for action, and some of these derive from my previous acquaintance with this device (I might, for instance, act differently if the computer is not typified as mine; depending on the broader horizon, this could increase or decrease my interest in it, etc.).

For Husserl, none of this requires any conceptual capacities. This shows in the fact that a non-rational animal, say a cat, may still be habitually familiar with things in its surroundings. For instance, in seeing the familiar internet router, the warmth of the router (with which it is familiar through previous experiences) can be made co-present by type processes. The cat can therefore be perceptually presented with a warm router, and it might subsequently be enticed to act in various ways appropriate to this. A lack of concept possession does not, then, take away the possibility of developing a rich intentional life, with familiar things in an external world, and so on.

It seems to me that this theory of perceptual access to things could help dissolve some of the tensions exposed earlier in McDowell's account. This is primarily due to the fact that Husserl's account quite simply resists lumping all contents of receptive awareness into the one category of the conceptual. Indeed, understanding all perceptual experiences, without any further distinctions, in terms of concepts simply might not the best way to think about our perceptual access to reality.

Arguments for Non-Conceptual Content

Misinterpretations of McDowell: Psychology, Illusions, and Skillful Coping

McDowell's conceptualist theory stimulated a lot of debates in the past 25 years, particularly regarding the existence of various sorts of non-conceptual perceptual content. A complete overview of these debates does not fall within the scope of this chapter. It can, however, be useful to consider some of his (to my mind) less successful critics, insofar as they help sharpening an understanding of what McDowell is after. I here collect some accounts of non-conceptual content in three broad groups, in order to show that they don't bear on McDowell's conceptualist thesis. The first group of arguments, I argue, conflates epistemically relevant contents and sub-personal psychological contents; the second, quite similarly, confuses intentional and non-intentional content; the third group concerns the relation between conceptual content and skillful copings (note that not all of the authors discussed explicitly raised their arguments against McDowell; my primary aim is to show that these arguments for non-conceptual content don't bear on McDowell's thesis).[11]

To the first group belong instances of the argument developed on the basis of a comparison of our cognitive structure to those of non-rational animals. This is an argument by analogy. It has been advanced as an

138 *McDowell: Concepts, Perceptions, Debates*

argument for non-conceptual content by Bermúdez (1995), Peacocke (2001a, 2001b), Speaks (2005), and Hanna (2008, 2015), among others. The argument makes an intuitive appeal to our shared biological make-up with non-rational animals in order to establish the claim that we share some (parts) of our perceptual contents with lower animals. Given that some of these animals do not seem to possess concepts, their perceptual experiences, and consequently (by analogy) some parts of ours, have non-conceptual content. As Peacocke (2001b) puts it:

> While being reluctant to attribute concepts to the lower animals, many of us would also want to insist that the property of (say) representing a flat brown surface as being at a certain distance from one can be common to the perceptions of humans and of lower animals [...]. It is literally the same representational property that the two experiences possess, even if the human experience also has richer representational contents in addition. If the lower animals do not have states with conceptual content, but some of their perceptual states have content in common with human perceptions, it follows that some perceptual representational content [in us] is nonconceptual.
> (Peacocke 2001b, 613–614)

Peacocke's argument rests on the presupposition that we share some of our representational contents with the lower animals, and that our richer contents are supplementary to that. This presupposition appears to be supported by natural facts. Given that humans, gibbons, and macaques belong to the same superfamily and evolved from a common ancestor, it is not unlikely that the biological hardwiring involved in our perception is much like theirs. Assuming that these animals lack the right concepts to explicate their experiences, those experiences would have non-conceptual content.

A simple response to this, also found in Brewer (1999), Speaks (2005) and McDowell (MW 114–126), is to deny that non-rational animals enjoy the sorts of perceptual contents we have, all biological similarities notwithstanding. In McDowell's words, the analogy argument is a 'recipe for trouble', because it conflates the 'respectable theoretical role non-conceptual content has in cognitive psychology [...] [with] the notion of content that belongs with the capacities exercised in active self-conscious thinking' (MW 55). In other words, McDowell can deny the legitimacy of the inference from a shared biological make-up to concerns about the space of reasons, since the spaces of nature and reasons are in his view distinct (I elaborate on this further in Chapter 6). The argument, then, would fail simply because observations concerning biological fact don't bear on the space of reasons.

Something similar holds for arguments belonging to the second group, which includes arguments based on certain types of illusion, what Crane calls 'real content', and Dretskean systemic representation, among others. A number of philosophers and phenomenologists have appealed to cases of illusion to illustrate that perception must have non-conceptual content (for example Crane 1988, 1992; Bermúdez 1994, 1995; Foreman 2006; De Vries 2011). The core idea here is that to make sense of illusion, we need to posit two levels of representation. One of these levels presents the intentional object at which the subject is directed; the other is a sub-personal representational content. De Vries (2011) asserts that, since McDowell is reluctant to posit the non-conceptual contents of the second level, he cannot account for illusions. For instance, in the Müller-Lyer illusion, we need to distinguish between the sense in which we are consciously aware of two lines presented with certain lengths and a different sub-personal representation of those lines. Even if we know one line to be bigger than the other, there is a sense in which our visual system continues to represent them as having the same size.

Coming from a different angle, Dretske's *Naturalizing the Mind* (1995), as I also briefly touched upon in Chapter 3, separates 'systemic' from 'acquired' representations. He illustrates the difference with an example of two dogs which are conditioned differently. Whereas one dog is trained to salivate upon hearing a clarinet play any musical note whatsoever, the other does the same thing on hearing a C-note regardless of the instrument on which it is played. Now consider a C-note is being played on a clarinet, thus causing both dogs to salivate. According to Dretske, both dogs will have different 'acquired' representations: one intends a clarinet, the other a C-note. But at a non-conceptual level, they have identical representations (as they are exposed to the same sound data).

A third variation of this argument appears in Crane (2013, also 1992), where Crane draws on a distinction between 'real' and 'general' content, inspired by Husserl's *Logical Investigations*. As Husserl writes there:

> Every chance of alteration of the perceiver's relative position alters his perception, and different persons, who perceive the same object simultaneously, never have exactly the same perceptions. No such differences are relevant to the meaning of a perceptual statement.
>
> (LI 550)

Husserl here suggests that although one is typically related to a single object over the course of a perceptual act, the exact ways in which it is given changes incessantly. The side of the object directly given changes as one moves around it, but this does not change the object of perception. It seems impossible to imagine that for every slight variation in 'how' the object is given (its current 'shading') there would be a different object given intentionally. Therefore, the contents of experience at the level of object-representation must be distinguished from those constantly changing contents. Husserl used the term 'real' (*reell*) or 'hyletic'

140   *McDowell: Concepts, Perceptions, Debates*

content here; Crane, somewhat unfortunately perhaps, calls them 'phenomenological' contents (Crane 2013, 245).

While these arguments certainly seem valid, it is questionable whether the sorts of representations they refer to have the relevant epistemic bearing for McDowell to take an interest in them. Indeed, Husserl himself also noted that the hyletic or sensation contents are not possible substrates of judgment (see Chapter 3). As it stands, then, these forms of non-conceptual content are compatible with McDowell's conceptualism, as they don't threaten the idea that whatever is made available to the subject is informed by concept and open to conceptualization.

Third, in *The McDowell-Dreyfus Debate*, H. Dreyfus (2013, see also 2005) uses examples of Heidegger and Merleau-Ponty of pre-reflective, skillful action in order to challenge McDowell's conceptualism. According to Dreyfus, the idea that the understanding is 'inextricably implicated in the deliverances of sensibility' (MW 46) is fundamentally at odds with the phenomenological description of what he calls skillful or absorbed coping.

Drawing on Heidegger, Dreyfus shows that we do not have to think about the doorknob on the door in order to use it to enter or leave a room. In fact, the doorknob does not have to be apprehended at all. Absorbed copings, on this existential-phenomenological understanding, would be mindless activities, which is to say that they don't involve objectification. For Dreyfus, this means that it is inappropriate to characterize their contents (in so far as there would be any content here at all, in his view) as conceptual. He believes that to rightly acknowledge the phenomenological structure of absorbed coping is to deny the presence of operations of understanding. The conclusion Dreyfus draws from this is that McDowell's conceptualism involves an over-intellectualization of human experience.

Does this criticism pose a genuine problem for McDowell's conceptualism? The basic structure of the argument appears to be as follows:[12]

> (P1) The involvement of concepts requires an intentional structure that is founded upon a distance between a subject and an object.
> (P2) Absorbed or skillful coping does not involve an intentional structure founded upon a distance between a subject and an object.
> (C1) Absorbed or skillful coping does not involve concepts.

The argument against conceptualism rests in part on the acceptance of (P1): that the involvement of concepts demands some kind of a critical stance that is typical for judgment. That presupposition, however, is denied by a number of philosophers, among others Noë (2013), Crane (2013), and also McDowell (MMD) himself.

As I argued previously, McDowell holds that the contents of experience (i) have the appropriate structure to figure in judgment (weak conceptualism) (ii) because of the involvement of conceptual capacities in them (strong conceptualism). In the case of skillfully opening a door, (i) is supported by the fact that one can make the skillful action of using the doorknob figure in a judgment. Also, one can give reasons for having performed this action in hindsight. This particular experience is therefore not somehow beyond rational scrutiny. With regard to (ii), it seems that if one were to lack all knowledge of how doorknobs work, of the building one was in, and of the room behind the door, then the unreflective experience of opening the door might well have a different content. This indicates that some sort of rationality may in fact figure passively in this skillful action after all.

A second example Dreyfus discusses concerns a game of chess (Dreyfus 2013, 35, MMD 46–50). Dreyfus holds that a chess master may be 'directly drawn by the forces on the board' without making his move for any consciously entertained reason (Dreyfus 2013, 35). Again, the example is supposed to show that rational capacities are not necessarily involved in experience, because these are cases of absorbed, unreflective coping.

But the argument is not very convincing. McDowell's response is simply that 'cultivated rationality [...] is also operative in his [the chess master's] being drawn to make his move by the forces on the board' (MMD 48). McDowell therefore does not reject the phenomenology of skillful coping as Dreyfus argument presupposes. He simply claims that these forces, too, are permeated by rationality in the same sense in which opening doors is. McDowell's conceptualism, then, is left unchallenged by the arguments put forward by Dreyfus.[13]

Concluding Remarks

In this chapter I discussed McDowell's central idea that perceptual experiences involve concepts. On a weaker reading, McDowell only advocates the openness of all sensible intake to conceptualization, at least insofar as any such intake has an epistemic bearing on the life of the subject. However, there is sufficient textual support for the view that McDowell believes that concepts structure sensible intake, and that this is what first makes a world perceptually available to us.

This strong conceptualist position creates, or so I argued, certain difficulties, which McDowell, to my understanding, leaves unresolved. These concern in particular the sorts of world-giving experiences non-rational animals enjoy, as well as the question which concepts would inform perceptual experiences (and if no concepts do this, why we would still want to call this conceptualism). These problems follow primarily from the fact that McDowell puts all contents of receptive awareness into the one category of the conceptual without any further distinctions. In a separate section, I then returned to my earlier expositions of Kant and Husserl, in order to show that their theories manage to avoid at least some of these problems.

142 *McDowell: Concepts, Perceptions, Debates*

Notes

1 See also Gersel's (2018) useful discussion on this difference in McDowell's theory.
2 '[T]here are mental states which represent the world, even though their subject lacks the concepts that would enable her to specify that content' (Gendler and Hawthorne 2006, 14).
3 See also Toribio (2008) for a critical assessment of the distinction between state and content conceptualism.
4 For most purposes, this distinction between weak and strong conceptualism suffices. I won't discuss other notions here or elsewhere in this book, such as Speaks's (2005) absolute and relative non-conceptual content, Hanna's (2008) contingently, essentially and highly refined non-conceptual content, or Tye's (2006) robustly non-conceptual content.
5 I take Gersel and Thybo Jensen (2018) to make a similar point with their milkman example.
6 I take this worry to reflect aspects of a much earlier criticism first raised by Wright (1996), namely that it does not follow from the fact that experiential content is (i) not a bare given and (ii) conceptualizable that it is conceptual. Wright, in this context, suggests the possibility of 'intermediate space' between conceptual content and bare givens. Similar criticisms can be found among others in Heck (2000), Peacocke (2001a) and Hopp (2010), as well as in some of my earlier work (see Van Mazijk 2014, 2016, 2017).
7 This is why I don't think it's fair to consider McDowell as defending only the weak conceptualist claim pointed out in fragment [1] to [3]. Gersel, for instance, reads McDowell as simply defending the view that 'generalities are given in experience' (Gersel 2018, 17). Given the many different things McDowell says about conceptual content, this seems to me an unfair representation of his theory. Furthermore, Gersel's reading, while defending McDowell's weak conceptualism, fails to accommodate the strong conceptualist remarks that also figure in McDowell's recent contribution in the 2018 volume *In the Light of Experience*. To give one more example: McDowell opposes Travis's (2018) view to his own, saying that '[o]n Travis's account, operations of such capacities [those of rational animals] do not enter into the constitution of the relation itself' (TKFG 24), whereas for McDowell they do. This is a stronger claim than Gersel's very general (weak conceptualist) definition of McDowell's conceptualism can accommodate.
8 This fragment is taken from McDowell's discussion on Wittgenstein.
9 See also Hopp (2010, 2011, 103–148), where this point is elaborated in greater detail.
10 Husserl can thus be said to model thought after perception, whereas McDowell believes perception must 'be understood on the model of linguistic performances in which claims are literally made' (HWV 10). It is interesting to note that Kant, as I showed in Chapter 2, also in some sense modeled his theory of perception after functions of judgment (in the transcendental deduction), although for an entirely different reason. For Kant, the reverse suggestion, that conceptual activity should be modeled after perception, wasn't available, specifically because of his construal of a priori (formal) versus a posteriori (regarding content) cognition. That is to say, to model a priori cognition (thought) after a posteriori intuition would undermine the validity of synthetic a priori propositions, the defense of which motivated the entire first *Critique*. This highlights once again the importance of Husserl's

alternative notion of a priori, which enabled him to bring the origins of concepts back to perception (see Chapter 3).

11 I will not discuss the fineness of grain argument, which McDowell has responded to quite extensively in *Mind and World* (MW 46–65). I think Heck (2000) might be right that the way in which McDowell speaks of demonstrative concepts in this context makes them essentially dependent on the perceptual state, as a result of which they do not live up to the conditions for concepts set by G. Evans, which then means there may be no genuine dispute between them on this specific point (Heck 2000, 483–492).

12 I base this syllogism largely on the one Schear (2013, 294) uses in his reading of Dreyfus.

13 Note that Dreyfus has acknowledged the failure of his dispute with McDowell in later work, see: Dreyfus and Taylor (2015).

References

Bermúdez, J. L. (1994). 'Peacocke's Argument against the Autonomy of Nonconceptual Content', *Mind and Language,* Vol. 9, No. 4, 402–418.

Bermúdez, J. L. (1995). 'Nonconceptual Content: From Perceptual Experience to Subpersonal Computational States', *Mind and Language,* Vol. 10, No. 4, 333–369.

Bermúdez, J. L., Cahen, A. (2015). 'Nonconceptual Mental Content'. in E. Zalta (ed.), *Stanford Encyclopedia of Philosophy.* URL = https://plato.stanford.edu/entries/content-nonconceptual/.

Brewer, B. (1999). *Perception and Reason.* Oxford: Oxford University Press.

Byrne, A. (2005). 'Perception and Conceptual Content', in: *Contemporary Debates in Epistemology.* M. Steup, E. Sosa (eds.), Oxford: Blackwell, 231–250.

Crane, T. (1992). 'The Nonconceptual Content of Experience', in: *The Contents of Experience.* T. Crane (ed.), Cambridge: Cambridge University Press, 136–157.

Crane, T. (1998). 'Intentionality as the Mark of the Mental', *Royal Institute of Philosophy Supplement,* Vol. 43, 229–251.

Crane, T. (2013). 'The Given', in: *Mind, Reason, and Being-in-the-World: The McDowell-Dreyfus Debate.* J. K. Schear (ed.), London, New York: Routledge, 229–249.

Davidson, D. (2008). 'A Coherence Theory of Truth and Knowledge', in *Epistemology: An Anthology.* E. Sosa and J. Kim (eds.), Malden: Blackwell Publishers, 124–133.

De Vries, W. (2011). 'Sellars vs. McDowell: On the Structure of Sensory Consciousness', *Diametros,* Vol. 27, 47–63.

Dretske, F. (1995). *Naturalizing the Mind.* Cambridge, Massachusetts: The MIT Press.

Dreyfus, H. L. (2005). 'Overcoming the Myth of the Mental: How Philosophers Can Profit from the Phenomenology of Everyday Expertise', *Proceedings and Addresses of the American Philosophical Association,* Vol. 79, No. 2, 47–65.

Dreyfus, H. L., Taylor, C. (2015). *Retrieving Realism.* Cambridge, Massachusetts: Harvard University Press.

Foreman, D. (2006). 'Learning and Necessity of Non-Conceptual Content in Sellars's 'Empiricism and the Philosophy of Mind', in: *The Self-Correcting*

144 *McDowell: Concepts, Perceptions, Debates*

Enterprise: Essays on Wilfrid Sellars. M. P. Wolf, M. N. Lance (eds.) *(Poznan Studies in the Philosophy of the Sciences and the Humanities,* vol. 92), Amsterdam, New York: Rodopi, 115–145.

Gendler, T., Hawthorne, J. (2006). *Perceptual Experience*. Oxford: Clarendon Press.

Gersel, J. (2018). 'What Is the Myth of the Given?', in: *In the Light of Experience: New Essays on Perception and Reasons*. J. Gersel, R. T. Jensen, M. S. Thaning, S. Overgaard (eds.), Oxford: Oxford University Press, 77–100.

Gersel, J., Jensen, R. T. (2018). 'Introduction', in: *In the Light of Experience: New Essays on Perception and Reasons*. Gersel, J., Jensen, R. T., Thaning, M. S., Overgaard, S. (eds.), Oxford: Oxford University Press, 1–14.

Hanna, R. (2008). 'Kantian Non-Conceptualism', *Philosophical Studies*, Vol. 137, No. 1, 41–64.

Hanna, R. (2015). *Cognition, Content, and the A Priori: A Study in the Philosophy of Mind and Knowledge*. Oxford: Oxford University Press.

Heck, R. J. (2000). 'Non-Conceptual Content and the 'Space of Reasons'', *Philosophical Review*, Vol. 109, No. 4, 483–523.

Hopp, W. (2010). 'How To Think About Nonconceptual Content', *The New Yearbook for Phenomenology and Phenomenological Philosophy*, Vol 10, No. 1, 1–24.

Hopp, W. (2011). *Perception and Knowledge: A Phenomenological Account*. Cambridge: Cambridge University Press.

Noë, A. (2013). 'On Overintellectualizing the Intellect', in: *Mind, Reason, and Being-in-the-World: The McDowell-Dreyfus Debate*. J. K. Schear (ed.), London, New York: Routledge, 178–193.

Peacocke, C. (2001a). 'Does Perception Have a Nonconceptual Content?', *Journal of Philosophy*, Vol. 98, No. 5, 239–264.

Peacocke, C. (2001b). 'Phenomenology and Nonconceptual Content', *Philosophy and Phenomenological Research*, Vol. 62, No. 3, 609–615.

Schear, J. K. (2013). 'Are We Essentially Rational Animals?' in: *Mind, Reason, and Being-in-the-World: The McDowell-Dreyfus Debate*. J. K. Schear (ed.), London, New York: Routledge, 285–302.

Sellars, W. (1963). 'Empiricism and the Philosophy of Mind', in: *Science, Perception and Reality*, London: Routledge & Kegan Paul, 127–169.

Speaks, J. (2005). 'Is There a Problem about Non-conceptual Content?', *Philosophical Review*, Vol. 114, No. 3, 359–398.

Toribio, J. (2008). 'State versus Content: The Unfair Trial of Perceptual Nonconceptualism', *Erkenntis,* Vol. 69, No. 3, 351–361.

Travis, C. (2018). 'The Move, the Divide, the Myth, and the Dogma', in: *In the Light of Experience: New Essays on Perception and Reasons*. J. Gersel, R. T. Jensen, M. S. Thaning, S. Overgaard (eds.), Oxford: Oxford University Press.

Tye, M. (2000). *Color, Consciousness, and Content*. Massachusetts: MIT Press.

Tye, M. (2006). 'Nonconceptual Content, Richness, and Fineness of Grain', in *Perceptual Experience*. T. Gendler, G. Hawthorne (ed.), Oxford: Oxford University Press, doi:10.1093/acprof:oso/9780199289769.003.0016.

Van Cleve, J. (2012). 'Defining and defending nonconceptual contents and states', *Philosophical Perspectives*, Vol. 26, 411–430.

Van Mazijk, C. (2014). 'Kant, Husserl, McDowell: The Non-Conceptual in Experience', *Diametros*, Vol. 41, 99–114.

Van Mazijk, C. (2016). 'Kant and Husserl on the Contents of Perception', *Southern Journal of Philosophy*, Vol. 54, No. 2, 276–287.

Van Mazijk, C. (2017). 'Phenomenological Approaches to Non-conceptual Content', *Horizon: Studies in Phenomenology*, Vol. 6, No. 1, 58–78.

Wright, C. (1996). 'Human Nature?', Review Article of McDowell, J. H. (1994), *Mind and World*. Cambridge, London: Harvard University Press, *European Journal of Philosophy*, Vol. 4, No. 2, 235–254.

6 McDowell
Reasons, Nature, Reality

Reasons and Nature

Chapter Overview

This chapter deals with McDowell's views on the space of reasons and the space of nature, which forms the background to his conceptualist theory. I argue that McDowell draws the line between these spaces in such a way that only that part of our mental lives relevant to responsiveness to reasons – the conceptual part that is allegedly unique to humans – allows taking in a viewpoint from which it is considered outside of the realm of natural law. Non-conceptual mental contents, by contrast, would fit unproblematically within the explanatory framework of the space of nature. I subsequently argue that this picture faces certain difficulties. In short, I argue for the following points: that (i) McDowell's conceptualism seems attractive only if his division of spaces is accepted; that (ii) his division of spaces might not be very attractive, at least not insofar as it allocates non-conceptual mental contents to the realm of nature; that (iii) the idea that the space of reasons itself ultimately consists of natural phenomena as well is not really made intelligible; that (iv) this naturalism fits uneasily with McDowell's transcendental ambitions; and that (v) the transition from the non-conceptual to the space of reasons (*Bildung*) cannot be clarified on the basis of this division of spaces. In a separate section, I illustrate how these points are dealt with differently in the Kantian and Husserlian frameworks, and discuss whether they might avoid some of these problems. In the second half, I turn to McDowell's realist intentions, in particular his interpretation of the Cartesian threat of idealism and his own response to this based on a disjunctive theory of perception. I argue that both the diagnosis of the problem as well as the solution to it are virtually identical to what was suggested by Kant in the fourth paralogism, who speaks of a 'dualism' (instead of a disjunct) in the same context.

The Space of Reasons and the Space of Nature

The previous chapter discussed McDowell's conceptualism, broadly speaking the view that the contents of experience are conceptual. I argued that McDowell introduces this theory not to discuss human psychology or phenomenology, but to address a prior – transcendental if you will – concern about our access to reality. I showed that his theory pertains exclusively to our epistemic lives as responsible agents and not to, for instance, sub-personal psychological contents. I concluded my exposition suggesting that McDowell is not clear about what the thesis that the 'content unified in intuitions is of *the same kind* as [...] in judgements [...] that is, conceptual content' (HWV 264) amounts to exactly. I argued that this is due partially to the fact that McDowell's remarks concerning what makes a content conceptual vary between weak and strong conceptualism. Also, it wasn't clear which concepts would figure in perceptual experiences, if indeed any do, or how conceptualism could be compatible with the idea that non-rational animals also have perceptual experiences of things in an external world.

Since the conceptualist thesis quickly started living a life of its own, the intimate connection of this theory to McDowell's broader ideas about the space of reasons and the space of nature has sometimes been overlooked. As I briefly discussed in the previous chapter, one of the main motivations for McDowell's conceptualist theory is to avoid the so-called myth of the given. This idea, in turn, rests on a conceptual distinction of two spaces, a distinction McDowell takes over from Sellars. It is the nature of this division that is the central concern of this chapter.

In *Mind and World,* among other places, McDowell identifies a dilemma which is said to result from a certain conception of how these two spaces would be related. It should be noted that McDowell considers these spaces primarily as 'logical spaces' (MW 73), or as 'two ways of finding things intelligible' (ETW 246). Sellars, in this respect, maintained that the space of reasons (or of epistemic facts) is one 'not [of] giving an empirical description of that episode or state [but] of justifying and being able to justify what one says' (Sellars 1963, 169, quoted in NPM 257). McDowell accepts this idea; for him the space of reasons is one 'of being answerable to criticism in the light of rationally relevant considerations' (HWV 6). To put it simply, to take a stance in the space of reasons means to consider human actions not as causal processes in nature, but rather as resulting from the motivated choices of free agents responsive to reasons.

The myth of the given is then said to result from a certain way of conceiving of the relation between both spaces. First, McDowell suggests that many of us are prone to regard ourselves as being responsive to the perceived world. At the same time, however, the operations of our receptive faculty are natural operations: 'the notion of the world's making an impression [...] is on the face of it [...] a mere natural happening' (ETW 244–245). These convictions together could lead one to believe that our sensible faculty processes impressions in such a way that facts about external nature are immediately made available to our understanding.

148   *McDowell: Reasons, Nature, Reality*

This would grant exercises of sensibility a foothold in the space of reasons as well as in external reality as a realm of natural fact.

This ambiguous status of sensible operations or experiences generally – namely as processing impressions that belong both to the realm of nature and to that of reason-giving exercises – McDowell understands as a case of the myth of the given. This is because it 'extend[s] justification more widely' (MW 7) than the space of reasons, namely into the space of nature. On the other hand, however, attempts to avoid the myth may yield a straightforward denial 'that empirical content depends on answerability to impressions' (ETW 246). This alternative approach 'suggests images of confinement within the sphere of thinking, as opposed to being in touch with something outside it' (MW 15). In other words, on the other extreme end, the myth is avoided by rejecting any role of experience in providing warrant for beliefs. This is the sort of view McDowell takes to be reflected, for instance, in Davidson's idea that 'nothing can count as a reason for holding a belief except another belief' (Davidson 2008, 126).

It would thus seem that we either commit to a given, or we accept a 'frictionless spinning in a void' (MW 11), both of which McDowell deems undesirable. McDowell's conceptualist thesis comes in here – not as a psychological theory, but as a way of addressing a concern about our access to external reality. While it purports to maintain a sense of being in touch with reality through perceptual experiences, the myth of the given is to be avoided by granting such experiences conceptual content. This way, their contents can be said to be within the (conceptual) space of reasons, which then explains why we are perceptually responsive to reasons.

So how does the space of reasons relate to the space of nature exactly? On the one hand, McDowell uses the idea of a space of reasons as a sui generis way of finding things intelligible to warrant an opposition to so-called bald naturalism. Bald naturalism, for McDowell, is the position that 'if there is any truth in talk of spontaneity, it must be capturable in terms whose fundamental role lies in displaying the position of things in nature' (MW 73). Another way to put this is to say that the bald naturalist reduces the structure of the space of reasons to lawlike descriptions of nature. Opponents of this view, including McDowell, hold instead that 'the structure of the space of reasons stubbornly resists being appropriated within a naturalism that conceives nature as the realm of law' (MW 73). Or again: 'spontaneity-related concepts cannot be duplicated in terms of concepts whose fundamental point is to place things in the realm of law' (MW 74).

This emphasis on the realm of law is important. In fact, McDowell seems inclined to admit only that the space of reasons doesn't fit the space of nature insofar as the latter is conceived of exclusively as a realm of law. In McDowell's view, however, that isn't the case. The space of nature isn't exclusively a lawful space, and therefore, in some sense at least, our (natural) faculty of sensibility can involve conceptual capacities after all. Indeed, 'a concept of spontaneity that is *sui generis* [...] can *nevertheless* enter into characterizing states and occurrences of sensibility' (MW 76, my italics). By thus widening the concept of nature beyond the realm of law, McDowell effectively maintains both that conceptual capacities are operative in sensibility as 'actualizations of *our nature*', and at the same time, in order not to regress into bald naturalism, that 'it *cannot* be as the natural phenomena they are that impressions are characterizable in terms of spontaneity' (MW 76, my italics). Somehow, then, conceptual capacities are 'actualizations of our nature' (to the extent that rampant Platonism is avoided) while, at the same time, they are not natural (to the extent that bald naturalism is avoided).

It could well seem that McDowell's position is ambivalent on the crucial point of the autonomy of the space of reasons with respect to the space of nature. While McDowell proposes that we widen the concept of nature such as to fit the space of reasons into it, we are also supposed to consider this inclusion in such a way that the idea of two autonomous spaces isn't harmed.

In *Mind and World*, McDowell acknowledges that it indeed 'looks as if we are picturing human beings as partly in nature and partly outside it' (MW 77). While he specifies that the space of reasons 'has a sort of autonomy' (MW 92) and that it 'cannot be as the natural phenomena they are that impressions are characterizable in terms of spontaneity' (MW 79), the 'naturalized Platonism' (MW 92) or 'liberal naturalism' (NPM 264) he endorses does aim to re-integrate the conceptual back into nature. In the end, then, the space of reasons turns out to be another natural phenomenon after all: natural science 'need not be conceded ownership of the very idea of natural phenomena' (ETW 247). Instead, our lives can be said to 'contain goings-on warranting characterization in terms that are special without remov[ing] those goings-on from the realm of natural phenomena' (ETW 247).

As it turns out, then, McDowell does not really believe that some mental events of the special conceptual kind would be non-natural. Instead, 'thinking and knowledge can after all be conceived of as natural phenomena' (NPM 260). This, however, does not imply their reducibility to lawlike explanation (see MTU 151). Conceptual or intentional explanation of an event 'does not [...] fill the same explanatory space as a physical explanation would' (MTU 150). While physical explanation can, at least in principle, 'completely fill that [intentional] explanatory space' (MTU 150), intentional descriptions, 'due to different explanatory pretensions', make 'no threat to the completeness of physics' (MTU 150). In other words, the kind of explanation belonging to the space of reasons 'is not in that sense scientific' – it does not compete with lawlike explanations – even though it is not '*un*scientific' either, as it does not bring along commitments to the supernatural.

150 *McDowell: Reasons, Nature, Reality*

Remarks on Drawing the Line, Bildung, and Animal Consciousness

So far we have seen that McDowell abides by a distinction between a space of reasons and a space of nature. These refer to two ways of speaking about things, of finding things intelligible. However, as it turns out, both spaces ultimately consist simply of natural phenomena. The space of reasons thus fits entirely within that of nature. While we may refer to our lives 'in terms that are special', this does not remove them 'from the realm of natural phenomena' (ETW 247).

McDowell's concept of *Bildung* might help to illustrate the relationship between both spaces further. In short, according to McDowell in *Mind and World,* human beings engage in a process of cultural development (*Bildung*) by which they attain some sort of second nature. This second nature allows one to have 'one's eyes opened to reasons' (MW 84) or, in other words, to have sensory experiences with contents, which, in McDowell's conceptualist view, are of the same kind as those of thought: namely, conceptual. *Bildung* is then characterized as an actualization of natural 'potentialities we are born with' (MW 88). It is a natural potentiality we possess for developing something that is in a sense non-natural (not fitting lawlike descriptions) or at the very least special. This makes the concept of *Bildung* a sort of conceptual bridge between the two paradigms of explanation.

Unfortunately, McDowell's theory of *Bildung* is quite abstract, and it does not generate any substantial insight as to how intellectual life would spring out of something more basic. McDowell, however, does not introduce the concept of *Bildung* to that end. In *Mind and World,* the question of a genesis of reasons out of something more basic is in fact explicitly set aside with a quietist 'shrug of the shoulders' (MW 178). Whatever kind of processes *Bildung* may refer to, the matter turns out to have been of no philosophical concern after all.

Not unimportantly, the reason that McDowell thinks this shrug is justified derives, to my understanding, from how he draws the line between the two spaces. In short, for him, the space of nature appears to include everything but the sort of intelligibility belonging to the space of reasons, while the latter includes nothing but the conceptual. In other words, the space of reasons contains only the conceptual, and everything else belongs to the space of nature. That the space of reasons includes only concepts (or the conceptual) is expressed in many places: 'if experiences are extra-conceptual, they cannot be what thoughts are rationally based on' (MW 68); the space of reasons is a 'space of concepts' (MW 7). That the space of nature includes all but what is captured in terms appropriate to the space of reasons is also clear: there are only 'some [i.e. conceptual] second-natural phenomena that [...] natural science cannot accommodate, on the ground that their intelligibility is of the special space-of-reasons kind' (RGM 236).

Interestingly, the former definition of what the space of reasons contains suffices to explain, or so it seems to me, how the characterization of contents of perception in terms of concepts becomes attractive in the first place. Conceptualism in the form McDowell defends it makes sense only if it is presupposed that 'we cannot really understand the relations in virtue of which a judgment is warranted except as relations within the space of concepts' (MW 7), in other words, that beliefs cannot be based on anything we could designate as being extra-conceptual. If that is accepted – that the space of reasons consists exclusively of concepts – then ascribing conceptual content to perception has effectively become the only way to allow a rational constraint from perceived reality. It would thus seem that McDowell's own definition of the space of reasons is what makes conceptualism attractive. Without that definition, by contrast, there doesn't seem to be any good reason to treat perception in terms that are really only appropriate to capacities of judgment (as is underlined by my earlier readings of Kant and Husserl, who both lack McDowell's incentive to speak of conceptual content in intuitions in order to make them figure as reasons; see Chapters 2 and 4).

As to McDowell's other thesis – that the space of nature includes everything but the sort of intelligibility belonging to reasons – this ensures that everything extra-conceptual must be said to fall within the space of nature intelligibility. This is McDowell's way of drawing the line between scientific intelligibility and the special space of reasons intelligibility. Furthermore, 'concepts of the mental [...] make sense only in the framework of the space of reasons' (NPM 266), in other words: we cannot use concepts of the mental to point to any achievements that lie outside of the conceptual; those belong simply to nature. All non-conceptual contents, then, are within the space of nature, and for that reason they can have no epistemic efficacy.

This illustrates that, while McDowell claims to resist reductivism ('bald naturalism'), he in fact only does so with regard to conceptual contents, which for him are the only contents capturable in mental vocabulary. All other 'mental' accomplishments – for instance those I dealt with, in discussing Husserl, in 'Fields of Sensations' in Chapter 4 – should then somehow fall unproblematically in the domain of natural explanation. Yet, arguably, these contents also have (independently of any conceptual capacities of the state's possessor) a distinctive kind of presentation that cannot be captured adequately by considering them exclusively from within the realm of nature. I return to this problem in more detail later on.

It can now be further clarified why drawing the line in the way just illustrated precludes the possibility of offering any insight into a genesis of reasons (*Bildung*). From this viewpoint, no light can be shed on the transition from the non-conceptual to the space of reasons, due to the fact that the contents of receptivity (for us) would all belong to the one

152   McDowell: Reasons, Nature, Reality

category of the conceptual, while everything outside of that in turn belongs to the space of nature. Now since there is no way of bringing natural facts into a rational relation to the space of reasons, as that would amount to a case of the myth of given, there can be no story to tell about *Bildung*. This is another point I return to later on, particularly in relation to Husserl's theory of perception, which does allow for such rational relations, and thereby also for a genesis of the McDowellian space of reasons.

The same point about *Bildung* can be used to explain why McDowell is led to adopt somewhat unattractive views regarding animal consciousness.[1] Since non-rational animals don't partake in the space of reasons, all operations of animal consciousness must be said to fall within the domain of lawful nature. This simply follows from the fact that McDowell allows only of two spaces, which he carves up in the way I just illustrated. Consequently, 'dumb animals', as McDowell notes explicitly, 'are natural being[s] and no more'; they are 'entirely contained within nature'; their 'sensory interactions with their environment are natural goings-on' (MW 70); 'they can figure [...] *only* as mere happenings' (MW 90); their actions are 'structured exclusively by immediate biological imperatives' (MW 115), and the 'merely biological [...] clearly includes the second-natural dispositions and performances of trained dogs' (RGM 236). Indeed, given McDowell's restrictions on mental vocabulary, it would seem that non-rational animals cannot be said to have minds at all.

It should be noted that McDowell does attempt to avoid a bold 'Cartesian automatism' (MW 117). Animals are said to have 'an environment' (MW 115) and some kind of 'proto-subjectivity' (MW 117). Also, he notes (as I discussed in the previous chapter as well) that 'items in the outer world are perceptually given to such creatures no less than to us' (TFKG 2).

Yet such remarks about 'proto-subjectivity' and the animal's 'environment' are not fleshed out in any detail. Moreover, given the kind of division of spaces McDowell abides by, it is unclear how we are supposed to make sense of these suggestions. First, the fact remains that such an 'environment' would have to be constructed non-conceptually for this proto-subjectivity, which prima facie contradicts McDowell's (strong) conceptualist thesis, which was supposed to make access to items in the outer world depend on concepts.[2]

Second, I don't think it is self-evident that we are capable of understanding the complex intentional achievements of non-rational animals and the sense of world that they have in terms belonging to the space of nature. That McDowell does defend this follows again from the fact that, in his view, whatever is excluded from the conceptual spaces of reasons must be explained in terms of the space of nature. I return to this point in more detail later on, in discussing the diverging views of Kant and Husserl on non-rational animal intentionality, and the possibility of bringing a world into view non-conceptually.

To conclude: the allusions to proto-subjectivities, environments, and seeing external things take us, or so I would say, in the right direction. However, they remain unsubstantiated remarks, and they do little to take away any of the more substantial worries just highlighted: that McDowell's theory of spaces arguably cannot make understandable how a relation to an external world could be brought about non-conceptually, and that the idea that animals fit unproblematically within nature – so that we don't need concepts of the mental to explain their behavior – might be an undesirable consequence of McDowell's own division of spaces.

Reflections on the Mental and the Transcendental

As I showed so far, McDowell aims to conceive of two autonomous spaces: one of reasons and one of nature. These two spaces represent ways of finding things intelligible; both consist, in the end, of natural phenomena, even when talk of reasons cannot be captured in terms of natural law. I further showed that McDowell divides both spaces in such a way that the space of reasons consists exclusively of concepts, that only the conceptual can be designated in mental terms, and that it alone falls outside of the space of nature (understood in terms of lawlike descriptions).

I already touched upon some potential difficulties regarding this division of spaces in the previous section, and I think it still remains to be seen at this point how certain aspects of this view could be made intelligible. In this section, I want to further zoom in on two of McDowell's suggestions: (i) that non-conceptual sensation contents would fit unproblematically within the space of nature and (ii) that the space of reasons itself would also, in the end, consist of natural phenomena. After discussing these points, I turn briefly to (iii) a potential problem regarding McDowell's transcendental ambitions in relation to his naturalism. These concerns, as well as those highlighted in the previous section, are then considered again in the following section in the light of the alternative theories of Kant and – in particular – Husserl.

Regarding (i), I already showed that the McDowellian picture suggests that non-conceptual sensations are not within the space of reasons, and that they therefore belong to the space of nature. To be sure, one might have the sensation of 'toothache', for example, which can be understood as a conceptual experience, and which belongs, therefore, to the space of reasons. This latter point is agreeable also from the perspective of the Kantian and Husserlian pictures. If we follow Husserl's account, then an object such as 'toothache' can be given 'through' the field of sensations by an intentional act which directs itself toward it (see Chapter 4 on simple apprehension). This content can then be called conceptual from McDowell's viewpoint.

154   *McDowell: Reasons, Nature, Reality*

However, Husserl also claimed that the organization of sensations has its own structure and even its own sort of epistemic efficacy, prior to and possibly independently of any conceptual activity. Kant likewise maintained that such non-conceptual sensations are a part of our mental lives, and even asserted that they form 'the largest [of all classes of sensible contents] in the human being' (Anth 7: 135) – even though he did not analyze them as mental contents in their own right in great detail as Husserl did (see Chapter 2).

Apart from the specifics of Husserl's analyses, with which I deal later on, I think there are good reasons to reject the idea that non-conceptual sensations would fit within the space of nature. For one, it is easily seen that non-conceptual sensations are, from a phenomenological or introspective viewpoint, present within consciousness in a manner different from the 'transcendent' manner in which natural things are manifest. Moreover, their specifically 'subjective' or 'immanent' character doesn't seem to fit the third person approach characterizing our approximations of natural, transcendent things.

These concerns are very familiar to contemporary philosophy of mind and have been discussed for decades, even centuries. One need not wholly accept Husserl's theory about sensations – that sensation fields have a special sort of epistemic efficacy, insofar as they can 'awaken' the ego and motivate (not cause) the performance of intentional acts – to accept that sensations (like all other mental contents) don't straightforwardly fit our understanding of nature. In other words, even if one doesn't grant them epistemic efficacy as I argued Husserl does, that still doesn't mean that they can be allocated straightforwardly to the space of nature.

This line of thought can be extended to the operations of animal consciousness. It is quite evident that non-rational animals experience (in the sense of living through) sensations, and that some (such as dogs and cats) also have feelings, that they have a world given in simple perceptual acts, which has a complex and consistent style which continuously evolves through complex habit formation, which is full of people and things that they are already familiar with, and so forth. It seems that for McDowell, these intentional achievements, which in many ways seem to resemble our own, somehow fit unproblematically within the space of nature, whereas our own (conceptual) mental contents evade this type of intelligibility. But simply stating that animal intentionality fits into nature doesn't take away any worries that it might not. It may well seem that we don't exhaustively capture the being of animals by treating them as we would treat rocks and stones, that is, as 'nature being[s] and no more' (MW 70), without a mental life of their own.

Indeed, it seems that this is not how we actually do understand them. That is to say, judging our own behavior, rather than those of the animals themselves, the placing of animals exclusively in the domain of nature seems misguided. As Husserl insightfully noted, in seeing an animal, we tacitly see it 'in its subjective surroundings, that of which it [the animal] is conscious, the instinctual life of the animal in its inner development [...] and its subject-intentional development in connection with the development of its subjective surroundings' (GP 98). In other words, the way we understand its behavior depends, in part, on empathy; we understand its external behavior by reference to its inner life, which we recognize insofar as it resonates with our own. We thus need reference to the inner lives of non-rational animals in accounting for our own understanding of them; we could not interpret them successfully (as we do) in terms that belong exclusively to the space of nature intelligibility.

This brings me to the second, related point. Clearly, and rightly so, McDowell wishes to avoid the impression that he is suggesting that mental concerns can be expressed adequately in terms appropriate to descriptions of natural law. In other words, while non-conceptual sensations apparently can be reduced to nature in some important sense, McDowell resists a similar reduction for the space of reasons. However, at the same time, and in order to avert rampant Platonism, he insists that even 'thinking and knowledge can after all be conceived of as natural phenomena' (NPM 260).

But it is not clear, at least not to me, how this is to be understood. One could wonder, for instance, what it means to say that thought processes are natural events, that the objects I imagine, remember, or count in my mind's eye are natural objects or events, and so forth. McDowell, as I understand him, meets these concerns halfway in accepting that an explanation in terms of natural law isn't possible at least where reasons are concerned. However, he falls short of giving any real explanation as to how any mental state or content could nonetheless be regarded as a natural phenomenon. This kind of naturalism seems simply to be accepted as default; it isn't (as far as I can tell) argued for, at least not in great detail.

Third, this naturalism that seemingly underlies even the space of reasons might generate a problem in relation to McDowell's transcendental ambitions. On the one hand, McDowell, as we have seen, invokes the context of Kantian transcendental philosophy in speaking of his own conceptualist theory. By specifying that perception has conceptual content, McDowell takes himself to address a concern prior to other theoretical concerns, namely one which deals 'with the very possibility of thought's being directed at the external world' (ETW 243). The world is not 'mediated' through concepts, as if we would only get some warped version of the real world represented through our senses. McDowell's point is rather that 'the world is conceptually structured' (HWV 144); the world itself depends, in its availability to us, upon conceptuality. It is not located outside of the realm of the conceptual (see MW 54); we must instead 'embrace relatedness to the real order within the conceptual order' (HWV 63).

156 *McDowell: Reasons, Nature, Reality*

Conceptualism, then, does not state some natural fact about our subjective constitution; it is a transcendental claim, one about the prior conditions of being directed at reality. Indeed, as McDowell puts it, 'the conception of Kantian intuitions I am urging [is] transcendental, [as it is] a matter of requirements for it to be intelligible that the picture depicts directedness at objective reality at all' (HWV 37).

Given the transcendental significance of McDowell's theory of perception, it should just as well apply to the world conceived in terms of nature. The natural world is not somehow outside of the space of reasons; that would contradict the whole point of embracing the real from within the conceptual order. Consequently, the conceptual space of reasons must be said, at least in one way or another, to include the space of nature within itself – given that we can only be directed at the natural world through the conceptual, as the transcendental claim specifies.

This suggestion, however, appears to contradict the claim that the space of reasons itself consists of natural phenomena; that 'thinking and knowledge can after all be conceived of as natural phenomena' (NPM 260), or that the space of reasons is just 'second nature' (MW 84). It now seems that while McDowell explains the space of reasons through the space of nature, he also explains the space of nature through the space of reasons. Put differently, we need the space of reasons as a condition for relating to the natural world, but we also need the natural world as a condition for the space of reasons.

It is not immediately clear to me how these claims are supposed to cohere. If, on the one hand, we take the latter claim seriously and put the natural world first, then it seems we can no longer make sense of the transcendental claim, given that it comes, by definition, before matters of fact. If, on the other hand, we follow the transcendental claim, then this could problematize the idea that the conceptual space of reasons is natural, given that that qualification itself is supposed to rest on the conceptual.

This tension can, I think, be overcome relatively simply without abandoning any transcendental ambitions, namely by exploiting the qualification of the space of reasons as natural consistently at a different order. Transcendental philosophy need not involve a commitment to there being some special 'mental' tract of reality that lies outside of nature. I turn to this issue again in the next section, where I consider how Kant and Husserl conceived of the natural in relation to the transcendental.

To close this section, let me summarize the three potential complications that were highlighted in this section: (i) McDowell's division of spaces seems to make it difficult to account for the rich intentional accomplishments of animal consciousness as well as for our own non-conceptual sensations. This is due to the fact that these conscious achievements are not within the space of reasons, and therefore, according to McDowell's theory, have to be located in the space of nature.

McDowell: Reasons, Nature, Reality 157

Also, (ii) the idea that the space of reasons would ultimately consist of natural phenomena is not really argued for in great detail and could further (iii) seem incompatible with any transcendental ambitions.

Reasons and Nature: Kant, Husserl, and McDowell

We have seen so far that McDowell draws a line between a space of reasons and a space of nature in such a way that the conceptual space of reasons alone is said to be irreducible to natural explanations. Furthermore, talk of the mental or minds is here restricted to the former space. At the same time, mental capacities are said to be natural phenomena no less than what is captured in terms appropriate to describing a thing's place in nature (they belong to second nature, rather than first nature).

There are a number of ways in which these views regarding the division of spaces differ from the previously discussed theories of Kant and Husserl, and I touched upon some of these differences already. I will use this section to draw out in more detail how their views differ. Most of my reflections here relate to the views of Husserl, which I take to provide the most interesting and viable alternative when it comes to determining reference for concepts of the mental, as well as for specifying the contents of various types of sensible operations.

To repeat briefly, as the previous sections revealed, McDowell divides spaces in such a way that only conceptual contents belong to the space of reasons. All other contents belong exclusively to the space of nature, regardless of the fact that they too are experienced by us in a distinctive way which is not *prima facie* capturable in descriptions of natural law.

Clearly, from a Husserlian viewpoint, this division of spaces must be said to fail to identify the right boundaries for that space which we cannot appropriate from a natural perspective. The basis for this claim was, as I argued in detail in Chapter 3, that on Husserl's account we have a distinctive kind of access to the totality of our own mental states, vis-à-vis our access to transcendent (external) things. In other words, Husserl maintained that there is a unique epistemic gap between the kind of access and knowledge of external (transcendent) things and of one's own consciousness. This categorical difference in access – to immanent versus transcendent being, as Husserl calls it – should then warrant differentiating a new region of inquiry, namely of (what I have throughout called) the space of consciousness. Accordingly, Husserl could be said to move from observing that there is a unique way in which one has access to the totality of one's own conscious life, to the claim that the complete space of what is thus accessible is to be analyzed in its own right.

In Chapter 3, I spent considerable time arguing that the space of consciousness thus brought into view ought not to be interpreted as consisting of some partial tract of reality. It isn't something inner as opposed to outer; it doesn't match the subject in opposition to the object.

158 *McDowell: Reasons, Nature, Reality*

Consciousness isn't cut loose from the transcendent things analyzable in terms of the space of nature, as if one sphere were 'in here' and the other 'out there'. To the contrary, I argued that the space of consciousness should only be taken to differ from the space of nature in respect of attitude. I earlier called this a double aspect theory, on account of which the whole mind-world relation can be studied either in terms of transcendent things (nature) or in terms of appearance-to-me (consciousness). Rather than pointing to some separate realm of special entities, the space of consciousness encompasses my conscious life together with the world just as I always already had it.

It can now be drawn out easily why, on this picture, non-conceptual sensations don't fit within the realm of nature. Sensations – and all other contents today generically referred to as 'qualia' – are *experienced*; they are accessible in the distinctive manner characteristic of considering things from within the space of consciousness. They therefore belong to the unitary life of consciousness, which in its totality forms the basis for all considerations belonging to a theory of knowledge in the widest sense.

As I argue in more detail a bit further on in this section, the fact that sensations fit within the space of consciousness does not mean that they could not be made intelligible – albeit in a different manner – from the perspective of natural sciences. After all, there is no division of tracts of reality, such that some things would be an exclusive concern for phenomenologists, and some other things for natural scientists.

McDowell, in fact, does seem to propose such a division. In his view, all non-conceptual contents, even when they are subjectively experienced and present in consciousness in a distinctive manner, fall exclusively within the space of nature. I would be inclined to say that, from Husserl's viewpoint, this construction must be said to obscure the motivational relations between on the one hand sensations, affections, and more broadly the passive non-conceptual life of consciousness, and rational deliberation on the other. On Husserl's alternative division of spaces, non-conceptual sensations do have a distinctive kind of epistemic efficacy, insofar as they stand within the same motivational sphere (the space of consciousness) in which we as rational subjects stand.

It therefore seems that McDowell's theory of spaces makes it needlessly difficult to see how rational capacities fit within a larger sphere of intentional achievements, and how they form a unity with the passive life of which they are a part. It does not acknowledge the fact that a new space of explanation has already entered the scene with the simplest organizational levels of consciousness, even those today commonly collected under the header of 'qualia'. Even though conceptuality, in Husserl's view, also constitutes a new intentional activity, it is not regarded as something distinct from the mental life out of which it grows. Instead, it is a part of the larger space of consciousness, and it cannot be understood in isolation from it: 'all intentional experiences [...] are interweavings of passive motivation' (EE 333). Intentionality grows within a sphere of non-conceptual passivity: 'upon the first world of recognized things given in perception there builds itself out of a new accomplishment – that of 'thinking' – the apperception of all worldly things determinable according to true reality and as distinguishable in terms of truth and appearance' (C212).

It is for the same reason, as I understand it, that Husserl's phenomenology yields a different theory regarding the way in which a world could be brought into view for non-rational animals. On the McDowellian picture, the perceptual experiences of non-rational animals ought to be explainable in terms belonging to the space of nature, for the simple fact that they don't partake in the conceptual space of reasons. As I showed already, this makes it difficult to explain how or in what sense animals would have an external world given in their perceptual experiences, especially given the fact that conceptualism specifies that concepts (which non-rational animals by definition don't possess) are a necessary condition for accessing the world.

As I argued extensively in Chapter 3, Husserl claimed to the contrary that animals have rich intentional lives even though they lack concepts. Animals are perceptually directed at transcendent (external) objects; they enjoy a 'steady perceptual field, comparable to ours, with changing perceptions in which objects [...] enter and go' (C211); they have 'one world', in some cases socially constituted, in which 'familiar and unfamiliar things' (C 213) appear, etc.

While these observations are very interesting, what really matters is the theoretical division of spaces underlying them, which makes these observations theoretically viable. Husserl approaches transcendental questions, such as those concerning the conditions for being directed at external reality, on the basis of an examination of the space of consciousness, instead of by reference to a conceptual space of reasons. This opens up numerous alternative ways of thinking about directedness at an external world that cannot be reduced to concepts; intentionality, motivation, association, and horizon are just a few examples of this. This eliminates the need to make unity within the perceptual field rely upon concepts, as McDowell's theory has it.

In this respect, it is worth noting that Kant, too, voiced the opinion that animals are not just biological machines in lawful nature. Instead, he claimed that their experiences contain representational contents 'that in spite of their differences [...] are still of the same genus as [those of] human beings' (CPJ 328). As I argued in Chapter 5, Kant's theory can even (at least in principle) facilitate a non-conceptual relation to an external world, for the operations responsible for unity in intuition are not referred to concepts, but to a separate power called the imagination, which non-rational animals might also possess.

160   *McDowell: Reasons, Nature, Reality*

Similarly, Husserl's approach is able to shed more light on the possible genesis of the space of reasons out of a broader conscious life. As I showed earlier, McDowell adopts a 'quietism' regarding this problem, as a result of which the concept of *Bildung* remains (deliberately) an empty postulation. But the real reason for this quietism is simply that McDowell allows of only two spaces, one conceptual and one natural, between which there can be no rational relations, as that would mean committing to the myth of the given.

Approaching the matter from Husserl's perspective, it is not clear why this supposed unintelligibility of *Bildung* would have to be accepted. This is easily illustrated. If we can resist the temptation to lump all contents of receptive consciousness into the one category of the conceptual – as if these contents were all of 'the same kind' (HWV 264) – then we create space to develop a more delicate theory of how beliefs find warrant, and show the relevant motivational relations between various types of content. It is only because McDowell does not make such distinctions within the contents of receptivity that his concept of *Bildung* must remain empty. Husserl's theory of perception and judgment does, by contrast, reveal a genesis of reasons out of a more basic of consciousness, the details of which I shall not repeat again here (see Chapter 4).

Lastly, as I discussed previously, McDowell's way of drawing the line between the space of nature and the space of reasons is guided by the (liberal) naturalism that underlies it. Naturalism, or so it seems to me, is here accepted beforehand as the default position – which is presumably why McDowell can consider his own liberal naturalism as 'not a label for a bit of constructive philosophy' (MW 95). It is probably for this reason that McDowell emphasizes, in *Mind and World* as well as in other places, that the space of reasons itself consists of natural phenomena.

I would say that, from a transcendental-phenomenological viewpoint at least, this type of naturalism is in fact a bit of constructive philosophy. Naturalism might seem common sense to most; it is not for that reason necessarily the best (or the most unprejudiced) ground for doing philosophy. The fact that naturalism counts as a construction here is mainly due to the fact that Husserl thought our claims about the natural world lack the kind of certainty that accompanies insights into the space of consciousness. Natural description is here secondary to the descriptions that pertain to consciousness as found upon immediate reflection. Differently put, natural facts are known a posteriori, and for that reason naturalism can never become a ground for transcendental thinking.

Relatedly, as I also discussed in Chapter 3, transcendental descriptions of the space of consciousness can, from a Husserlian perspective, never be captured in terms belonging to the space of nature. While our perceptions, for instance, can surely be considered from a naturalistic viewpoint – as I discuss in more detail a bit further on – the transcendental study of perception cannot be made comprehensible within a naturalistic framework. This is because by taking a stance in the explanatory framework of the space of consciousness, we consider things in a way that is distinct from considerations of natural being. Consciousness, then, is not *just* 'second nature' (MW 84); the very idea that it would be is incompatible with the idea of transcendental description.

While Kant did not resist naturalistic philosophy in the extreme sense that Husserl did, Kant did separate natural from transcendental concerns. On the Kantian picture, one cannot, for instance, reduce transcendental apperception to a natural phenomenon, since natural phenomena presuppose transcendental apperception. This does not mean that transcendental apperception is some sort of special, transcendental object over and above empirical apperception. Nevertheless, the explanatory work of transcendental philosophy is here regarded categorically distinct from empirical description. This holds for all transcendental concepts within the Kantian framework.

Both Kant and Husserl, then, denied that what's captured in the sorts of descriptions belonging to a transcendental study could be explicated in terms belonging to the space of nature. Thus viewed, treating the transcendental conditions for our access to reality in terms of natural phenomena is a transcendental absurdity, as it conflates distinct levels of explanation.

I am not saying that McDowell is committed to such a transcendental absurdity. But there seems to be a tension in *Mind in World* and other works, insofar as conceptualism is said to specify prior conditions of possibility for our access to natural reality, while the conceptual space of reasons is simultaneously said to be natural. At the very least, the relation between these claims could use further clarification. This is especially so since in *Mind and World* McDowell appears to end up prioritizing the natural – and this could undermine the whole idea of transcendental explanation, which is defined by being epistemically prior to natural explanation.

It might be worth considering in some detail how Husserl understands the non-naturalizability of the space of consciousness, and whether this commits him to saying that we cannot understand consciousness naturalistically at all. As I outlined already, Husserl thought that the structure of that space which cannot be made understandable in terms of the kind of intelligibility that belongs to the realm of law is not marked exclusively by conceptual activity. The very distinction between supposed natural non-conceptual contents of consciousness and higher level contents of the space of reasons kind is considered to be artificial. The problem with such a view would be that it posits 'the passivity of association and of the whole psychic life unfolding without the activity of the I at the same level with the passivity of the physical natural process' (EE 333). 'However', Husserl continues, 'passive motivation is, like all spiritual causality [...] a sphere of understandability standing under pure essential

162   *McDowell: Reasons, Nature, Reality*

laws and, therefore, having a completely different meaning than natural causality and natural lawfulness'.

Husserl's alternative view suggests that no single accomplishment of consciousness can be authentically made understandable from within the space of nature. However, this is not to deny that there is *something* to consciousness which natural science could principally make understandable from its viewpoint. Correlational studies of mind and nature are possible; this is in fact supported by phenomenological inquiry, which reveals that consciousness is essentially tied to bodies, as both always appear together.[3] Yet the type of understanding this yields, Husserl submits, will never give us the full story about consciousness. In fact, strictly speaking, it will give us no story about consciousness's own being at all. Of course, one can always choose, as for instance Daniel Dennett does, to 'maintain dead silence about the psyche, one can scornfully designate it as a façon de parler' (Ideas III 17). But such reductionism, according to Husserl, amounts to denying 'the dominant thing in the apprehension'. In other words, it contradicts the fact that we access our own mental states in a unique way, and thereby it fails to appreciate the space of consciousness as a legitimate region of inquiry.

This way, Husserl accepts that cognitive science can in principle integrate the mind into their way of understanding. It seems to me that there is in fact nothing in his philosophy that excludes the possibility that all aspects of the mind's life would one day be grounded in correlational studies. There is, in terms of the intelligibility belonging to nature, no radical line to be drawn within the contents of consciousness, such that a distinct space of intelligibility should have to be reserved for a space of concepts, while the non-rational life of consciousness would be reduced to nature. Even the space of reasons is not special in this respect, as it is for McDowell.

At the same time, on Husserl's picture, no such effort could ever yield a successful reduction of consciousness, because it doesn't address the space of consciousness in the first place. Even the simplest mental state, as in 'I move my hand, I move my foot' is a subjective process, and as such it is only directly dealt with when approached in the appropriate manner: when 'we are not concerned with this real psychophysical process' but instead with 'the subjective mode of consideration [which] excludes all recourse to brain processes, nerve processes, etc.' (Ideas II 229).

It is easily seen, then, that transcendental philosophy is not necessarily a 'profoundly non-naturalistic doctrine' (Smith and Sullivan 2011, 16), neither in Kant's form nor in Husserl's.[4] While Husserl would certainly resist an ontological reduction of consciousness, he allows for far-reaching correlational studies, which theoretically speaking even include our higher level reason-giving capacities. Consciousness is not a separate tract of reality lying 'outside' of the natural. Therefore there is certainly space for naturalism within his transcendental philosophy, to this extent

McDowell: Reasons, Nature, Reality 163

that science can study consciousness in its own way. But even so, transcendental concerns – such as those pertaining to the conditions for our perceptual access to reality – can never be assessed naturalistically without conflating distinct explanatory levels.

As I noted already, this also holds for Kant, albeit in a different way. Kant doesn't characterize a description as transcendental for the fact that it captures something essential about the space of consciousness, as Husserl does. Instead, a transcendental claim is distinguished from an empirical one for purportedly capturing something about the universal form of knowledge. Important as this difference between Kant and Husserl may be (I discussed it in greater detail in Chapter 3), it does not change the fact that both agree that the transcendental is not naturalizable.

To conclude: in this section I focused mainly on Husserl's theory of how to draw the line between two spaces of explanation, and I argued that it may provide a more fine-grained understanding of the place of reason and conceptuality within the broader life of the mind, and that it manages to avoid at least some of the theoretical difficulties mentioned above.

On Reality and Idealism

On Descartes, Idealism, and Reality: Kant, Husserl, and McDowell

The threat of idealism, as Kant spoke of it in the first *Critique*, concerns the inability to offer certain proof of our capacity to embrace reality in thought. As I discussed in Chapter 1, Kant divided idealism into the dogmatism of Berkeley, who asserted (on Kant's interpretation) that we have access only to inner ideas and never to external objects, and the skepticism of Descartes, who believed that we cannot be certain of being in touch with reality. In this section, I want to consider how McDowell diagnoses the threat of idealism, and what sort of solution he conceives for it. To this end, I focus in particular on a relatively early contribution,[5] where McDowell develops his own position through an analysis of Descartes. This should compare neatly to the earlier assessments of Kant and Husserl on the same matter.[6]

To briefly rehearse their respective constructions first: Kant agreed with Descartes's point of departure, stating that 'I am indeed conscious to myself of my representations; thus these exist and I myself, who has these representations' (A370). He deemed Descartes's subsequent inferential strategy flawed, however, since according to Descartes 'I cannot really perceive external things, but only infer their existence from my inner perception' (A368). In other words, on Kant's interpretation, Descartes locates the real, external things outside of the scope of possible experience. For this reason, he subsequently needs to resort to an inference based on the inner mental representations of these allegedly real, external things.

However, Descartes's core mistake, on Kant's assessment, was not the strategy of inference itself, but rather the supposed need for it. To circumvent that need, the idea that perceptions indicate the real world should be eliminated altogether. Kant called the position which yields this presupposition, and which both Descartes and Berkeley took as a departure point, transcendental realism. This can be roughly summarized as the tacit assumption that the external world with which we want to be in contact is radically mind-independent. In other words, it is – or at least could be – beyond the scope of possible experience, rather than as a rule accessible from within the order of experience.

Transcendental realism thereby conceives of an impossible task, namely that of proving how our supposedly 'inner' appearances relate to a world that is utterly beyond it, and which must for that reason somehow be inferred on their basis. Kant contrasts this disposition to his own transcendental idealism. Transcendental idealism is said to allow for a certain 'dualism' (A370). This dualism has nothing to do with Cartesian dualism; it specifically concerns the ability, on Kant's proposed view, to distinguish, within the sphere of appearances, 'mere' from 'real' appearance. That is to say, it allows conceiving of reality as something that is within the scope of experience, thus as principally given to us, yet without thereby reducing reality to a 'mere' empirical idea, a 'mere' appearance (in the sense of *Schein*, instead of *Erscheinung*).

Kant thereby claimed that reality must be thought of as for us principally embraceable from within experience. What we call reality is not something we have to infer on the basis of appearances; it is nothing more than the correct configuration of appearances according to universal rules of understanding. While reality is thus nothing over and above appearances, this does not make all appearance reality. In other words, there is still room to accommodate hallucinations, illusions, dreams, and other states we tend to consider as deviating from the one reality in which we all stand.

The gist of Husserl's reading of Descartes is, as Chapter 3 showed, essentially the same as Kant's. Husserl also praised Descartes for finding a correct starting point for understanding our place in the world. In his meditations, Descartes rightly kept 'only himself, qua pure ego of his *cogitationes* [...] as something that cannot be done away with' (CM 45). However, he subsequently misconstrued the ego as an axiom, a little '*tag-end of the world* [from which] the rest of the world' must be inferred 'by rightly conducted argument' (CM 63). But this way of setting up the problem neglects the fact that reality cannot be but within the grasp of consciousness, insofar as the very idea of it is to have any meaning at all. Descartes thus set an entirely unreasonable demand for the philosopher, which followed from his flawed conception of the mind-world relation, as consisting of two radically distinct parts that stand in need of bridging.

Instead of inferring an external reality on the basis of appearances, Husserl suggested that we accept that reality is constituted within experience. Reality isn't somehow 'behind' the appearances. In fact, as I argued extensively in Chapter 3, there is for Husserl no difference between the object considered as real and the object considered as subjectively intended (as appearance), save for a fundamental change of perspective.[7] To sustain this, Husserl noted first that any object at all is 'referable to a subjectivity, as experienceable and knowable by it' (PP 89). This means that a thing is essentially a possible appearance for a subject; it is by definition experienceable. Second, by contrast, 'in its sense as an object, a thing includes nothing of a subjectivity related to it'. This reveals that the real thing 'is not a second one next to mere intentional being' (EIP 276). Instead, the real thing is embraceable from within experience, even though according to its sense as an external thing this (transcendentally) necessary relation is precisely excluded.

At the same time, as with Kant's theory, Husserl's attempt to understand reality as an intentional accomplishment didn't involve the suggestion that every intentional accomplishment puts us in touch with reality. Put differently, he doesn't deny our capacity to differentiate veridical from non-veridical perception. Moreover, there is nothing that prevents us from employing all the tools at hand to assess whether the fact that at a particular moment we seem to be in touch with the external world is genuinely an instance of being in touch with the world. Other people, for instance, as well as their opinions concerning the veridicality of my perceptual takings, are also available to me through my experiences. Experience, then, isn't a private matter, and the veridicality of my perceptual acts is not determined exclusively by some solipsistic subject locked in its Cartesian theater. This ensures that the pitfalls of a naïve idealism are avoided, in a way quite similar to Kant's construction.

This should suffice as a brief reiteration of Kant's and Husserl's views on Descartes and the threat of idealism.[8] In an essay that first appeared in 1986, McDowell discusses Descartes in light of the same concern that occupied Kant and Husserl. According to McDowell, Descartes accepted a threat of skepticism unknown to the ancients, which concerned not just the possibility of certain types of knowledge of the world, but its very existence. This developed into Descartes's famous method of radical doubt, which proceeded by 'putting subjectivity's very possession of an objective world in question' (ST 237). In an attempt to safeguard at least some domain of knowledge from this skepticism, Descartes then proposed to 'retreat to [a] newly recognized inner reality, and refute the claim that we know nothing [at all]' (ST 239).

For McDowell, as for Kant and Husserl, Descartes's move to inner certainty is not so problematic in and of itself. It is rather the subsequent proposal that 'the inner life takes place in an autonomous realm' which renders proof of 'the rest of the world become [...] problematic' (ST 236). While Descartes's later retrieval of the world through inference is admittedly not very 'gripping' (ST 237), the real problem doesn't lie there. Instead, it is said to lie in the prior 'willingness to face up to losing the external world, with the inner for consolation' (ST 239). This is because, as McDowell proposes, Descartes's loss of the external world goes hand in hand with a picture that suggests that 'subjectivity is confined to a tract of reality whose layout would be exactly as it is however things stood outside it' (ST 241). In other words, the Cartesian picture 'represent[s] us as out of touch with the world altogether' (ST 242), that is, it departs from the disposition Kant referred to as transcendental realism, which allows for the possibility that we aren't in touch with reality.

As a consequence, Descartes is left with a realm of subjective appearances and a reality that appears to bear no necessary connection to such appearances. This amounts to (the threat of) idealism; it suggests a conception of the mind on account of which 'samenesses and differences are exhaustively determined by how things seem to the subject' (ST 249). That is to say, any appeal to a difference between objective reality and illusion is here problematized as a result of there being only a realm of subjective appearances. To put it in Kantian terms, Descartes lacks the relevant 'dualism' within the realm of appearances which is needed to distinguish a sense of reality from mere appearance.

McDowell's solution is to reconsider the very division of the seeming and the real on the Cartesian picture. Contrary to what Descartes suggests, we should accept that 'the notion of appearance is [itself] disjunctive' (ST 248). The Cartesian picture threatens the possibility of things seeming to one to be thus and so to be constituted by things actually being so. All appearances are thereby on a par as 'self-standing configuration[s] in the inner realm' (ST 242). McDowell, on the other hand, proposes to embrace a sense of reality from within the scope of appearances. This allows us to say that 'if one seems to be thinking about an ordinary external object in a way that depends on [...] its appearing to be perceptually present to one, the situation in one's inner world is either that one is entertaining an object-dependent proposition or that it merely appears that that is so' (ST 247). The difference between these two types of seemings is then due to how things really are, in other words, it is 'external to the layout of one's inner world' (ST 247) taken in its solipsistic Cartesian sense. McDowell concludes that he has not so much tried 'to bridge a gulf between intentionality and objects', understood as radically distinct spaces, but rather proceeded by 'undermining the picture of mind that generates the Cartesian divide' (ST 259).

It hardly needs drawing out, it seems to me, that the diagnosis as well as the solution to the Cartesian problem presented here do not just have a Kantian flavor; they are essentially reiterations of Kant's views. As I understand him, McDowell first praises Descartes's move to inner certainty, just as Kant and Husserl did. His subsequent identification of the problem – Descartes's account of the subjective realm as somehow cut off from how things stand outside – essentially repeats Kant's repudiation of Descartes's transcendental realism: the view that motivates a theory of inference on the basis of inner representations. Finally, McDowell's solution is to take the concept of appearance or seeming as itself disjunctive – a move which is virtually identical to Kant's reference to 'dualism' (A370) in the same context.

Further Remarks on Accessing Reality in Kant, Husserl, and McDowell

The previous discussion revealed that McDowell's disjunctive theory is in important respects similar to the theories proposed by Kant and Husserl. It should be clear that, insofar as the relevant disjunct is placed within the order of experience, this theory differs from what is at stake in the majority of ongoing (metaphysical) disjunctivism debates.[9] Indeed, it seems to me that if one were willing to adopt a 'sideways-on point of view on the directedness of the conceptual at the real' (HWV 63) – as metaphysical disjunctivists as well as their opponents do, but which McDowell refuses to do – then there is no good reason to regard McDowell's theory as a type of disjunctivism at all. One notable difference between Kant and McDowell, which I also emphasized in Chapter 1, is that Kant occasionally did adopt such a sideways-on viewpoint. Yet Kant only did so for the sake of clarifying his own position, which seek to address our directedness at reality from within the experiential order, and which thereby effectively denies that it makes sense to take in that sideways-on perspective.

While a failure to distinguish these different forms of disjunctivism appears to have been the cause of some confusing discussions in the past, the situation has clearly improved in recent years.[10] Sedivy, for instance, speaks of McDowell's 'conceptual direct realism' (Sedivy 2008, 349), and Soteriou seems to note correctly that for McDowell 'when a fact is made perceptually manifest to you, the obtaining of the fact is not blankly external to your subjectivity' (Soteriou 2014). Instead, as I showed previously, it is embraced from within the order of experience, as it is for Kant and Husserl.

Still, it must be noted that there are important differences between the accounts of Kant, Husserl, and McDowell regarding this matter. These can, however, only be highlighted by drawing on their broader systems of thought. McDowell's argument has been criticized, among others by

168   *McDowell: Reasons, Nature, Reality*

Glendinnig and De Gaynesford (1998), for not being able to withstand the radical skeptic. In their view, the radical skeptic is one who precisely doubts one's ground for distinguishing between cases of mere seeming and veridical perception. The same goes for Wright's criticism, which likewise denies that McDowell would refute the radical skeptic (Wright 2008, 390).[11] Virvidakis (2006) adds to this that it isn't clear why McDowell's disjunctive theory would have transcendental force, rather than just being a plausible or preferable way of framing things (see Virvidakis 2006, 40–41). Such criticisms indicate that McDowell may not have succeeded in convincingly showing how his claims are supposed to get transcendental significance. A genuinely transcendental claim should hold universally, and should therefore exclude the possibility that a more radical skeptic is meaningfully imaginable.

At first sight, it may well seem that these concerns over radical skepticism apply equally to Kant and Husserl. After all, in their views, reality boiled down to a coherent structure within the order of experience. As with McDowell's position, this did not mean that there are no external measures whatsoever by which to assess whether something successfully puts us in touch with the world or not, or, in other words, whether something constitutes a deviation from that pattern or not. However, it would seem that there is no *radically* external measure by which one could ensure oneself that the coherent pattern itself is not to be understood as a deviation. Differently put, there would be no way of discovering that we are all brains in vats, misled by an evil demon, or inside the matrix.

While I think this problem of the radical skeptic can be raised on all three accounts, their respective theories differ in how successfully they manage to exclude the meaningfulness of such thought experiments. On this point, I would submit that Husserl's account comes out the strongest. Kant's theory arguably suffers from the frequent reference to human capacities for intuition in contradistinction to a (divine) non-sensible intuition. As a result of this, it is at least possible to read Kant as undermining the transcendental force of his own 'dualism', as McDowell to some extent does in his reading of Kant (see my discussion in Chapter 1 – although I pushed against this type of reading, it cannot be altogether excluded).

Husserl, on the other hand, made a sustained effort to avoid this problem by characterizing the correlation between subject and world as a universal a priori law. This served to undermine on a priori grounds the possibility of any subject-independent, skeptical 'sideways-on' viewpoint. To be more precise, it would, according to Husserl, be formally coherent – and hence not non-sensical[12] – yet still a 'material' countersense to speak of a thing that cannot be an intentional correlate of an actual subject. For it is then altogether beyond possible experience, and this contradicts the idea of a thing in general, which Husserl claims essentially includes possible givenness to an actual consciousness (in Ideas I).

Husserl then grounds the a priority of this claim in his revised concept of a priori cognition, which does not rest on formalization as does Kant's, but on the imaginative variation of possible worlds (I won't repeat the details of Husserl's theory of a priori evidence here, but see my discussion in Chapter 3, where it is also shown how it deviates from Kant's theory).

The comparison to Husserl may provide an extra reason to side with Virvidakis (2006) that McDowell might not have succeeded in developing a robust enough theory of transcendental cognition to exclude radical skepticism. But even if this is so, it can still be concluded that at least the fundamental outline of McDowell's assessment of the Cartesian threat of idealism can be traced back to Kant. Of course, his interpretation involves certain angles which I did not highlight here, as shows, for instance, in his discussions of Russell and Frege in the same contribution. Yet such differences ultimately concern little more than the reframing of that picture that was first painted by Kant, well over two centuries ago.

Concluding Remarks

In this chapter I examined McDowell's views on the spaces of reasons and nature and considered how they relate to his conceptualist theory. I showed that McDowell's spaces are primarily ways of thinking about things (of finding things intelligible). I further illustrated that he divides both spaces in such a way that the space of reasons consists exclusively of concepts, and that, for that reason, it alone falls outside of the space of nature understood in terms of natural law.

The critical discussion that followed intended to show that the problems McDowell's conceptualism faces are not restricted to somewhat ambiguous talk of concepts in perceptual experience, but that they are rooted in a more fundamental conceptual division of spaces that is itself problematic. To summarize the main points of concern again: I argued that (i) McDowell's conceptualism is attractive only if his division of spaces is accepted; that (ii) his division of spaces is not in fact attractive, at least not insofar as it forces us to allocate non-conceptual contents the realm of nature; that (iii) the idea that the space of reasons would ultimately consist of natural phenomena is not really explained; that (iv) the naturalization of the space of reasons might fit uneasily with McDowell's transcendental ambitions; and that (v) McDowell's theory cannot shed any light on *Bildung* (understood as the transition from a non-conceptual realm to the space of reasons), as it lumps all contents of receptivity into the one category of the conceptual. In a separate section, I considered whether some of these problems can be avoided by adopting a Kantian or Husserlian framework instead, and argued they can.

170 *McDowell: Reasons, Nature, Reality*

In the second part, I claimed that McDowell's views on the Cartesian threat of idealism as well as his own solution to it strongly resemble the accounts offered by Kant and Husserl. In my interpretation at least, McDowell embraces reality from within the order of (conceptually loaded) experiences. This does not mean that no distinction can be made between veridical and non-veridical perception, between mere appearance and reality. It rather means that, for McDowell as well as for Kant and Husserl, this distinction has to be made wholly within the order of experience.

Notes

1 See also Gaskin's (2006, 131–165) extensive treatment and criticism of McDowell's views on animal consciousness. Although I certainly agree with some of Gaskin's critical assessments, I cannot follow his central argument that 'animals benefit from our presence on the scene', a benefit which is supposedly 'transcendental', because 'there is no empirical sense in which an infant or an animal needs us or any extraneous subject to effect the constitution of an object in its own consciousness' (Gaskin 2006, 143). In other words, Gaskin maintains that the consciousness of a dog has a relation to an object in virtue of the fact that we have the capacity to frame it that way. This construction seems to bypass entirely the original intentionality of a dog's consciousness in favor of a more Dennett-style intentionality ascription. At the very least, I can say that I have found nothing in either Kant or Husserl that supports such a view.

2 As I discussed in detail in the previous chapter, McDowell notes that unity of intuition derives from unity of judgment: 'We could not have intuitions, with their specific forms of unity, if we could not make judgements, with their specific form of unity' (HWV 264). Also, he notes that intuitions having content at all depends on judgment capacities: 'That intuitions have content is an implication of the claim that capacities of the sort that are exercised in judgment are in act in intuitions' (TFKG 8).

3 See Husserl (Ideas II 60–95) or Bernet (2013) for a more elaborate discussion.

4 Note that the characterization by Smith and Sullivan originally referred only to Kant.

5 "Singular Thought and the Extent of Inner Space". What I say here holds, as far as I can tell, for the later work as well, for instance the position defended in *The Disjunctive Conception of Experience* from 2006.

6 See the two sections in Chapters 1 and 3, both titled 'On Descartes, Idealism, and Reality'.

7 From the natural to the phenomenological attitude; see the more detailed discussion in Chapter 3.

8 Note that this concise rehearsal of the discussions in Chapters 1 and 3 did not include their respective views on the noumenal world, which I argued are likewise more similar than is usually acknowledged.

9 See especially Soteriou's discussion for an introduction and literature overview (Soteriou 2014).

10 See for instance the early contributions by Pritchard (2008), Fish (2009), and Haddock (2010), which correctly point out that McDowell defends an 'epistemological' disjunctivism that ought to be distinguished from the metaphysical concerns dealt with in the debate about metaphysical disjunctivism. This division has stimulated more specialized research in

McDowell's epistemological disjunctivism (see for instance Cunningham (2016) and French (2016), but has not eradicated all confusion (for instance, Burge's (2011) criticism, seems to me to rest on an attempt to undermine the reason-nature distinction. According to Burge, the 'basic deficiency in McDowell's disjunctivism is that it [...] is incompatible with well-established scientific knowledge' (2011, 43). I am tempted to side with McDowell's earlier reading of Burge in TBD. MacDonald's (2006) discussion with McDowell (in his reply to MacDonald, see RCM) offers, it seems to me, another example of a confusion about the sort of theory McDowell defends.

11 See also Pritchard (2009), who distinguishes 'McDowell's own writings on this topic and the *McDowellian* response to skepticism' (Pritchard 2009, 478). Pritchard sides with Wright's criticism of McDowell but maintains McDowell's case can be improved through 'additional argumentation', which he, however, doesn't offer.

12 For Husserl, if a proposition is not formally coherent, it is non-sensical. This applies to propositions which do not live up to grammatical rules in a way required for them to express any meaning.

References

Bernet, R. (2013). 'The Body as a "Legitimate Naturalization of Consciousness", *Royal Institute of Philosophy Supplement*, Vol. 72, 43–65.

Burge, T. (2011). 'Disjunctivism Again', *Philosophical Explorations*, Vol. 14, No. 1, 43–80.

Cunningham, J. J. (2016). 'Reflective Epistemological Disjunctivism', *Episteme*, Vol. 13, No. 1, 111–132.

Davidson, D. (2008). 'A Coherence Theory of Truth and Knowledge', in: *Epistemology: An Anthology*. E. Sosa, J. Kim (eds.), Malden, Massachusetts: Blackwell Publishers, 124–133.

Fish, W. (2009). 'Disjunctivism', *Internet Encyclopedia of Philosophy*, URL = https://www.iep.utm.edu/disjunct/#H3.

French, C. (2016). 'The Formulation of Epistemological Disjunctivism', *Philosophy and Phenomenological Research*, Vol. 92, No. 1, 86–104.

Gaskin, R. (2006). *Experience and the World's Own Language: A Critique of John McDowell's Empiricism*. Oxford: Oxford University Press.

Glendinnig S., De Gaynesford, R. M. (1998). 'John McDowell on Experience: Open to the Sceptic?' *Metaphilosophy*, Vol. 29, 20–34.

Haddock, A. (2010). 'What Is Disjunctivism?' URL = https://philosophynow. org/issues/81/What_is_Disjunctivism.

MacDonald, C. (2006). 'Self-Knowledge and Inner Space', in: *McDowell and His Critics*. C. MacDonald, G. MacDonald (eds.), Oxford: Blackwell Publishing.

Pritchard, D. (2008). 'McDowellian neo-Mooreanism', in: *Disjunctivism: Perception, Action, Knowledge*. A. Haddock, F. MacPherson (eds.), Oxford: Oxford University Press: 283–310.

Pritchard, D. (2009). 'Wright "contra" McDowell on Perceptual Knowledge and Skepticism', *Synthese*, Vol. 171, No. 3, 467–479.

Sedivy, S. (2008). 'Starting Afresh Disjunctively: Perceptual Engagement with the World', in: *Disjunctivism: Perception, Action, Knowledge*. A. Haddock, F. MacPherson (eds.), Oxford: Oxford University Press, 348–375.

Sellars, W. (1963). *Empiricism and the Philosophy of Mind*. Harvard: Harvard University Press.

Smith, J., Sullivan, P. (2011). 'Introduction: Transcendental Philosophy and Naturalism', in: *Transcendental Philosophy and Naturalism*. Oxford: Oxford University Press.

Soteriou, M. (2014). 'The Disjunctive Theory of Perception', *The Stanford Encyclopedia of Philosophy*. E. N. Zalta (ed.), URL = https://plato.stanford.edu/entries/perception-disjunctive/.

Virvidakis, S. (2006). 'On McDowell's Conception of the Transcendental', *Teorema: Revista Internacional de Filosofía*, Vol. 25, No. 1, 35–58.

Wright, C. (2008). 'Comment on John McDowell's 'The Disjunctive Conception of Experience as a Transcendental Argument', in: *Disjunctivism: Perception, Action and Knowledge*. A. Haddock, F. MacPherson (eds.), Oxford: Oxford University Press, 390–404.

Index

a priori 27, 33, 39–43, 46, 49–52, 70, 72–75, 77, 82, 87–89, 97, 101, 106, 168–169

Bildung 6, 11, 146, 150–152, 160, 169

coherentism 123–124

Descartes 5, 8–9, 12–13, 17, 22–24, 31, 33, 61, 85–86, 163–167
disjunctivism 5, 8, 11–13, 28–31, 146, 166–168

ego 48, 86, 101–105, 109, 135, 154, 164
empirical concepts 40, 49, 51
empirical foundationalism 21, 29
empirical realism 25, 88
essence 68, 102, 106, 108

fields of sensations 9, 96, 98–99, 101, 113, 115, 135, 151
fulfillment 61, 68–71, 73, 76, 135

habit 10, 96, 102, 107, 110–112, 114–118, 136–137, 154
horizon 10, 96, 99, 103, 107–117, 136–137
Hume 17, 39–40

idealism: dogmatic idealism 23–24; transcendental idealism 5, 13, 23–25, 58, 164
illusion 29, 65, 137–139, 164, 166
immanent association 100, 102, 113
incongruent counterparts 18–20, 32–33, 52, 57, 134
intentional act 10, 14, 54, 62, 64–68, 72, 96–97, 101–102, 105, 111, 153–154, 158

intentionality 9, 31, 61–69, 73–74, 79, 83–84, 88, 97–99, 101–104, 107, 111, 113, 115–118, 124, 134, 153–54, 159, 166

judgment 16–17, 20, 39, 41–42, 55–56, 63, 68, 70–71, 83, 97, 102–107, 111, 118, 125, 127–132, 135, 140–141, 151, 160

kinesthetic system 10, 96, 107, 109–111

Leibniz 8, 17–18
logical possibility 27, 33, 85, 87

myth of the given 20–24, 28–34, 56–57, 88, 123, 134–135, 147–148, 160

naturalism 10–11, 24, 81, 85, 146, 148–149, 151, 153, 155, 160, 162
noema 64, 71, 79–80, 86–87
non-rational animals 6, 9–10, 82, 104, 116, 121, 131–132, 134, 137–138, 141, 147, 152–155, 159
non-sensible intuition 26–27, 32–33, 69, 77, 87, 168
noumenon 22, 25–28, 30, 33, 87

obscure representations 8, 38, 44, 52, 54–57

passive synthesis 99, 103, 107
phenomenological reduction 66, 79–80
Platonism 149, 155
pure concepts 8, 32, 38–42, 45, 51, 53, 70, 74, 97, 133

representationalism 85–86, 107

174 *Index*

skepticism 34, 64, 163, 165, 168–169

skill: acquired skill 10, 96, 107, 110–111, 116; skillful action 140–141; skillful coping 137, 140–141

space of consciousness 6, 9, 61, 68, 71, 74–75, 77–88, 97–99, 103–104, 107, 111, 117, 157–163

space of nature 2, 6–7, 9–11, 21, 61, 68, 75, 82, 89, 122–124, 146–162, 169

space of reasons 2, 6–7, 10–11, 20–22, 56, 66–67, 82–84, 89, 97, 118, 122–124, 133, 135, 138, 146–162, 169

state and content conceptualism 58, 126

strong conceptualism 4, 10, 14, 41, 47–48, 53, 55, 57, 70, 106, 121, 126–134, 141, 147, 152

synthesis 16, 41–49, 51, 59–70, 99–100, 105, 107, 116

Transcendental Aesthetic 4, 13, 16–19, 38, 52

Transcendental Analytic 4, 17, 20

transcendental realism 24–26, 29–33, 86, 164–167

types 111, 115–17, 136–137

veridical perception 25, 28–30, 165, 168, 170

weak conceptualism 4, 8, 38, 47–49, 55, 57–58, 71–72, 126–135, 139